Journeying Through Revelation

Valerie LeBlanc

Cover photo was taken by Valerie LeBlanc

WESTBOW
PRESS®
A DIVISION OF THOMAS NELSON
& ZONDERVAN

This book is a work of non-fiction. Unless otherwise noted, the author and the publisher make no explicit guarantees as to the accuracy of the information contained in this book and in some cases, names of people and places have been altered to protect their privacy.

WestBow Press books may be ordered through booksellers or by contacting:

WestBow Press
A Division of Thomas Nelson & Zondervan
1663 Liberty Drive
Bloomington, IN 47403
www.westbowpress.com
1 (866) 928-1240

ISBN: 978-1-5127-0726-7 (sc)
ISBN: 978-1-5127-0727-4 (hc)
ISBN: 978-1-5127-0725-0 (e)

Library of Congress Control Number: 2015912854

Print information available on the last page.

WestBow Press rev. date: 08/18/2015

Contents

Dedication

On May 4, 1981 my mother passed away after several months battling cancer. As a child she gave her life to Christ and lived her life honoring Him. In the months before her death she prepared us, friends and family, for her coming transition to life everlasting. Part of that preparation included planning the songs that she wanted us to sing at her funeral. And so on May 8 as we mourned her passing, and celebrated her life, we sang songs together. Two of them have resonated with me as I have worked my way through this study thirty-four years later. They spoke to how she was able to live during some difficult times with the certain knowledge that death was approaching and how she saw what was to come. We sang "Because He Lives" written by Bill Gaither and "It is Finished", also by Bill and Gloria Gaither.

Three days later we would have celebrated her sixty-third birthday. For those who mourned my mother's passing, her life was finished far too soon. I praise God that she chose to be a follower of the Lamb— that she didn't wait to make that choice. I look forward to joining her in celebrations around the throne of God.

And so to my mother I especially wish to dedicate this book, along with special thanks to my husband, Norm and friends, Patti and Barb, who supported me with their words and with their prayers throughout this endeavor.

Before we Begin

Notes to the Reader

My Inspiration

This is not intended to be the definitive book on the meaning of Revelation. Rather it is simply a collection of thoughts, ideas and in some cases, unanswered questions. I don't claim to have all the answers to Revelation. In fact what I've had is a lot of questions. I'm not a scholar, a theologian or an historian. I am a person seeking answers.

Recently I had the opportunity to attend a seminary course on Revelation. The professor was well informed and a talented teacher[1]. His teaching focused on the biblical and historical aspects of Revelation. He was able to trigger my interest to continue studying this book long after the classes were over. From the day that class ended I have felt compelled to continue to study this fascinating book.

My Approach

I began my study by reviewing Revelation verse-by-verse, jotting down the questions, the thoughts, and the ideas that came to me as I read. Did you know that there are twenty-two chapters and 404 verses in the book? I was amazed to discover that I had two, three, sometimes even more questions for each verse! It was obvious to me that there was more to this book than just an outline of end-times, and at the same time it became clear that the message in Revelation is a very simple one.

After recording all of my questions, I started over in my review to try to find answers to them. This is the result of my efforts. As you read, you will find that I haven't found all the answers, but I have grown in my understanding of what this book has to teach me as a believer.

My Concern

My biggest concern in putting these thoughts to paper is that anyone reading them will assume that I am correct in my conclusions. My prayer is that my opinions won't mislead, but rather that they will cause you to look at Revelation in a new way. Not that you will accept my thoughts and ideas, but rather that they will cause you to question, to seek out your own answers, and in so doing, draw you into a closer relationship with our Lord and Savior, Jesus Christ.

Thoughts On Divine Inspiration

Periodically I wonder if the content of Revelation was experienced by John exactly as he has written it; if it was one great vision; or if it was a series of visions possibly experienced over time. There is a part of me that wants to believe that all he did was record what he experienced, exactly as experienced. I have always pictured a somewhat dazed looking John sitting in a cave on Patmos frantically writing down the words of Revelation as God gave them to him. I pictured John as a *recorder* of words rather than as a *writer* of the words. I know this book was divinely inspired. In 2 Timothy 3:16 we read "All Scripture is God-breathed and is useful for teaching, rebuking, correcting and training in righteousness." The challenge for me is in understanding what that means.

People tend to hold one of three slightly different perspectives when it comes to this idea of divine inspiration. The first is much as I have just described: God gave the author the words and he simply wrote them down. The second option is that God gave the author the idea or the message and inspired the author to describe it in his own words. The third option is that the author had an idea and God guided his words as he recorded it.

So it may mean that John had a series of spectacular visions or dreams and that he was divinely inspired to record them. Or, it may mean that he had some fairly straightforward visions or dreams and was divinely inspired to record and describe them in a way that would capture our attention like no other book in the Bible using the apocalyptic language that is used throughout much of Revelation. Or it may mean something else entirely. I'm keeping my mind open on this.

The process of how it happened does not sway my belief that God wanted this information recorded and available to us as believers throughout the generations. There is a message for us, for me, in this book and I don't think it's simply intended as a play-by-play of the end of the world as we know it.

A Brief Word On Dogma and Doctrine

As we walk through this look at Revelation we are going to encounter some fundamental differences in beliefs. Consequently I think it makes sense to take a quick look at the concepts of dogma and doctrine as they apply to our Christian beliefs.

Dogmas, sometimes referred to as creed, are those things that we as Christians hold sacred. They are those things that we all believe; that identify us uniquely as Christian. The Apostles' Creed states these beliefs clearly.

Doctrines, however, may vary between denominations. They are things we don't all agree on; things that we agree to disagree about but that do not impact our common creedal beliefs.

Our thoughts on end-times are an excellent example of the difference between dogma and doctrine. Christians agree that Christ is coming again. Christians agree that we will all be bodily resurrected to a life everlasting. However, we don't all agree specifically on how and when that will happen. Over the generations different views have developed on the events related to end-times. These views are commonly categorized as Premillennialism, Postmillennialism, and Amillennialism. Another concept related to end-times has to do with what is called the Rapture. Denominations differ in their take on these doctrinal beliefs and hold strongly to whichever view makes the most sense to them.

When I began my study I wanted to see if my thoughts on these specific doctrinal issues were supported by Scripture. I didn't want to bias my study which is why I started by writing down questions instead of opinions. What I discovered is that although it makes for fascinating reading and discussion I think that the question of which view is correct is a question that in the end really doesn't matter—at least not to me. I can't do anything about how the events of Christ's coming play out—only God can. The only thing I can control is what I do with my life now as I'm living it.

If it matters to you, perhaps the information provided here will help you decide for yourself.

Connections To Current Day Events

One of the things I won't be doing in this book is attempting to connect events in Revelation to current day events. Readers of Revelation have searched for current day analogies since the times in which it was first written. In first century Rome, these analogies may have made sense since that was the environment in which John was living when he wrote the book. But I don't think he knew, necessarily, that he was writing a book or letter that would last for more than two thousand years. Any way you look at it, every generation has had cause to believe that they were living in end-times just as we do today. One of the generations will be right but we are told in Matthew 24:26, "No one knows about that day or hour, not even the angels in heaven, nor the Son, but only the Father." (See also Acts 1:6–7) Seems pretty clear to me. You might not agree with me on this and that's okay. In fact you will probably not agree with me a few more times as we journey through Revelation. But with regard to knowing exactly when Christ will return and how it will happen, I've always wondered why we need to know. It's a given the end as we know it will happen. Whether it happens in our lifetime or not, we each get only one earthly life to live. There are no do-overs. And during this life we have to make a decision that will determine our fate as described in Revelation—will we be followers of the Lamb and experience eternal life or not, and end up in the lake of fire. This is a decision that cannot wait for end-times. We must decide now for each one of us has only this brief time on earth to choose.

Finding The Answers

As you read you will find that I haven't been able to answer all of my own questions. In some cases I have found it easy to put the question on the shelf because I don't feel like it makes much difference to the message of Revelation. You might not agree and if that's the case I encourage you to keep seeking answers. Other things I think, are too big for me to know the answers. A pastor I have great respect for once suggested that we exist on a need-to-know basis with God—some things we simply don't need to know. Not knowing all the answers hasn't lessened my faith. I hope that you will be able to find your way through them as well.

As I proceed you may notice that I will refer to 'the story', 'the scene' or 'the saga'. Please don't be offended by my use of these terms. They are not intended to detract from or lessen the fact that the book of Revelation is the word of God, but only that I am limited to my human frame of reference and language in describing these events.

In seeking answers to my questions I have prayed for an attitude of openness and discernment. I have drawn from what I learned in that seminary class, from sermons, and from the works of several commentators listed at the end of this book.

My primary source however, has been the Scriptures. I have used the 2011 version of the New International Version (NIV) found online through www.biblegateway.com as my primary source but have also referred to the Holman Christian Standard Bible (HCSB), the English Standard Version (ESV), the New American Standard Bible (NASB), the King James Version (KJV) and the Message when looking for greater clarity on a topic. When I make reference to the Greek word used in a passage, I have taken that information from the Holman Christian Standard Bible with Strong's Numbers for "The Bible Study App"[2].

Some Ideas On How To Read This Book

As you read this book please do so with a Bible by your side. The easiest way to follow my comments will be if you first read the related passage from Revelation. I believe that to get the most out of it, you should read the passage in Revelation, write down some questions or observations that you might have, and then look within these pages to see what I found on the passage. Take your time. Consider God's Word prayerfully, and read my words with discernment.

I hope you have as much fun as you journey through the pages of Revelation as I have had. God Bless!

About Revelation in General

Its Placement In Scripture

As I'm sure you know, Revelation is the last book in the Bible. It's not an accident that it has been placed there since the words of Revelation in many ways complete the story told in the Scriptures. This story is one of creation, of fall, of redemption, and ultimately of new creation.

When It Was Written

There is some difference in opinion with regard to when Revelation was written. Most scholars suggest it was around 95 A.D. (also written as CE 95) while others think that it was perhaps around 70 A.D. I think it is important to understand that when it was written there were many first generation Christians still around. Some of them would have likely interacted directly with Jesus and certainly with His disciples.

It was a very difficult time for Christians. Persecution was rampant. Emperor worship thrived. This was a source for much of the suffering these first-century Christians experienced. As followers of Christ they refused to worship the Emperor of the day, and they were punished as a result.

The Literary Genre Of Revelation

Revelation fits into two genres: it is a letter—actually seven short letters within a big letter—and it is an apocalypse.

Revelation is a letter. So why do we care? Well knowing it is a letter should cause us to question who was writing it, to whom, and under what circumstances. Knowing a bit about each of these things will help us to more fully understand the text. We will learn more about the letters as we proceed through this study.

Revelation is apocalyptic literature. So what does this mean, and again why do we care? Well an apocalypse is a literary genre that describes someone receiving a revelation through an angel usually about *end-times* and usually in a supernatural setting. It employs a lot of descriptive language—metaphors, similes, allegories and mythical imagery—to help describe concepts that our language can't describe in a way that our human brains can understand. For example, how can one describe the presence of God? What words would be enough? So John describes a being sitting on a throne. Does God really sit on a throne? Probably not. He doesn't strike me as the type of being that sits anywhere, but the image used clearly establishes for us a sense of majesty and authority. Understanding that this is an apocalyptic work will help us more critically, or more realistically, look at the symbols and images used in the text.

While apocalyptic literature was fairly common in first century times, it is far less common in our day. This means that the original readers of Revelation were much more likely to understand it's message than we are today.

Who Wrote Revelation

We know, because he tells us in Revelation 1:1, that this book was written by a man named John but have no specific information about which John he is. Was he the apostle John, author of the gospel of John? Was he the author of 1,2,3 John, which may or may not be the apostle John? There is nothing in the text of Revelation that tells us. Commentators don't agree on who the author is and it is in fact, one of those times when knowing for certain doesn't matter. Perhaps I'll ask around after I get to Heaven.

What we do know is that he identifies himself as a servant of God, that he is a prophet (see 1:3), and considers himself as a brother and companion to the people of the seven churches identified later in the chapter.

Based on the writing of Revelation I think it is also safe to say that he was a gifted writer and story teller and that he was intimately familiar with Old Testament and New Testament Scriptures.

The Structure Of Revelation

Experts vary on how they present the structure of Revelation. In its simplest breakdown there are three key sections to Revelation that most agree on: Introduction (1:1–3:22), Main Vision (4:1–22:7), and Conclusion (22:8–21).

There are a few things that stand out for me with regard to how it is organized. The first three chapters are written in a somewhat pleasant letter writing style, easy to read and easy to understand. Here is where we find the letters to the seven churches. As we move into chapter four, however, the language changes. This is where the apocalyptic language begins. It becomes very colorful, very dramatic, and much more difficult to clearly understand. The chapters from four through eleven seem to focus on the challenges of life in the current church age but then in chapters twelve through fourteen the perspective changes. It seems to show a higher-level view of the story of God versus Satan. And then in chapter fifteen through to mid-way in chapter twenty-two we seem to get a look at what may be considered events related to the second coming of our Lord Jesus Christ. And with the final verses of the book we resort back to the letter writing style that was used at the beginning.

I've wondered why John switches to the apocalyptic genre in chapter four. Is it because we aren't supposed to take it as literally as we might otherwise? Is it because God, through John wanted to draw us into the story, perhaps focusing more on the moral or point of the story than on its details? Or is it simply because we aren't capable of dealing with the realities if they were stated clearly and specifically? This is another one of those questions I obviously can't answer in this lifetime and will have to simply live with.

The Theme Of Revelation

Our goal in reading Scripture is, and always has been, to learn more about who God is. Although there are many stories in the Bible, they all come down to one thing— the message of Salvation in Jesus Christ.

After completing my study, this is what I believe about Revelation. Revelation is:

- a reminder of who God is,
- a review of the story of salvation,
- a message that salvation is offered freely to each one of us,
- and a reminder that we must decide if we wish to choose to accept Christ's offer and become a follower of the Lamb or refuse.

If we choose to become a follower of the Lamb then we must expect:

- to minister to others,
- to be attacked by Satan and his minions as Jesus was,
- and ultimately to participate in the marriage supper of the Lamb,
- and experience life everlasting in the New Jerusalem.

If we choose to refuse, then we are destined to become the meal at the great supper of God and experience eternity in the lake of fire.

All this will transpire according to God's timing and plan, but for each of us as individuals, our time is short—we must choose now.

Revelation Chapter 1

In this first chapter of Revelation we will be introduced to the who, what, why, and how of Revelation. We will learn who wrote it, from whom the message originated, and for whom it was intended. We will begin to learn what he wrote about and the circumstances under which it was written. We will be very briefly introduced to the seven churches but most importantly will be given very meaningful descriptions of our triune God—descriptions that will resonate throughout the remainder of Revelation.

Prologue (1:1–3)

> *¹ The revelation from Jesus Christ, which God gave him to show his servants what must soon take place. He made it known by sending his angel to his servant John,*
> *² who testifies to everything he saw—that is, the word of God and the testimony of Jesus Christ.*

"The Revelation from Jesus Christ" (v.1)

These first words of Revelation are already thought-provoking.

The original Greek term for *revelation* is *apokalypsis* which means "disclosure of truth". In fact this book is sometimes called "The Apocalypse of [Saint] John". Merriam-Webster defines revelation as "an act of revealing or communicating divine truth" or as "something that is revealed by God to humans."[3]

Although in this specific translation the opening line is "The revelation from", in most translations it is written as "The revelation of Jesus Christ." This phrase is written in the genitive case. When we see a phrase such as this we should stop and think about it a bit. Is Jesus being revealed—is He the object of the sentence? Or is Jesus doing the revealing—is He the subject of the sentence? Or is it both? Jesus appears to be acting as an intermediary here between God and the angel, but as we move through the book we will discover that not only is He revealing things to us but we have the opportunity to learn a great deal about Him as well.

So in these opening verses of the book of Revelation, we are told that through John we will have the opportunity to gain truth or knowledge both from and about Jesus Christ. God has used an angel to pass this information along to John and is using John, in turn, to pass it along to us, assuming we are His servants.

"What Must Soon Take Place" (v.1)

John tells us that we will be told about "what must soon take place". This phrase is repeated verbatim in 22:6. By the way, as we go through the opening to Revelation, you will notice several connections to the close of the book; this is the first one, and it may cause some confusion. If this is something that must soon take place, why are we still waiting more than two thousand years later? How do we make sense of it? My theory on this is very simple, and I alluded to it in my opening statements. Regardless of when these things actually take place, we each have only one lifetime on earth. It is during our time here that we must make a critical decision to become a follower of the Lamb and worship God. So on a personal level the time is soon. I might live to see the end-times, or I might not. I might live to a ripe old age, or I might not. To become a follower of the Lamb is a decision I cannot put off because I might die tomorrow. After I die, I will be judged on my actions, decisions made, and pathways taken while I was alive. I haven't seen anything in the Scriptures that suggests that at that time I will be given the opportunity to change my mind, regardless of what may be implied by movies and television shows that have proven popular over time.

It is interesting that in this first verse we are told that this revelation is intended to *show* us, rather than *tell* us what must soon take place. Showing something suggests visuals, pictures, and the use of imagery, and that is certainly true of Revelation. The apocalyptic genre used throughout this final book of the Bible is skillfully used to pull us into the action. Images are elaborately and effectively described to drive home the message of Revelation to the reader.

"Who Testifies To Everything He Saw" (v.2)

John says he testifies to everything he saw. He is telling us that what he saw is true and that this includes the word of God and the truth about Jesus Christ. In other words, we are about to learn about Jesus.

Testifying reminds me of a courtroom, and since the book of Revelation serves as a reminder that we will each be judged, it makes sense, at least to me, to see references here to testifying and to testimonies. These phrases are seen again in the final chapter of Revelation as the book comes to a close. In Revelation we will also see several echoes back to Old Testament Scripture, especially related to the story of the Israelites' exodus from Egypt. I wonder if this reference to testimonies is intended to remind the reader that the Ark of the covenant, which was placed in the Holy of Holies in the tabernacle contained the two tablets of the Testimony, which according to Exodus 31:18 were "the tablets of stone inscribed by the finger of God." Any connection intended? I'm not sure but it does cause me to wonder.

"Blessed Is the One" (v.3)

> *³ Blessed is the one who reads aloud the words of this prophecy, and blessed are those who hear it and take to heart what is written in it, because the time is near.*

This third verse introduces the first of seven beatitudes in Revelation. Before looking at the beatitude itself, this is a good time to talk about the number seven. In the NIV, the number seven is used approximately 338 times; of these forty-four uses are found in Genesis and thirty-one in Revelation. Traditionally in Scripture, it is seen as the number of perfection or of completeness. So when I learned that there were seven beatitudes in Revelation I stopped to think about them a bit more. Is it significant that there are seven and not eight beatitudes in Revelation? I'm not sure but I find myself taking a closer look at them. We will see the other beatitudes in 14:13, 16:15, 19:9, 20:6, 22:7 (22:9), and 22:14. They have been listed together in the appendix to this book.

So what does it mean to be blessed? According to the Greek word used here, *makarios*, we are told that it means to be "supremely blest: by extension, fortunate, well off"[4].

And what does this blessing actually mean? Well my take on it is that if we not only read the words—translations vary regarding the inclusion of the word *aloud*—but also hear them; that is, understand them and then take them to heart or act upon them, then we will be supremely fortunate.

And as we close this section we are reminded once again that the time is near. In verse 1 we were told this was about things that must soon take place. Just two verses later, the reminder that the time is near makes it clear this is an important point. There is a sense of urgency here, and I had better pay attention.

Greetings and Doxology (1:4–8)

As I mentioned earlier, Revelation is basically a long letter containing seven short letters addressed to seven specific churches. These seven letters are contained in chapters 2 and 3. From there the letter moves things up a notch—chapters 4–22—providing information relevant to all of the churches and in fact, to all believers. This doesn't mean that the content of the specific letters isn't relevant to all—of course it is. The difference seems to be that in the seven letters we are given encouragement and instruction in how to live our lives daily. The subsequent chapters provide insight, perhaps, into heavenly battles taking place while we go through our day-to-day routines as well as providing a higher-level perspective on the battle between good and evil both in the heavenly realm and in the day-to-day lives of those of us who live in this current church age.

This opening to the letter and letters within is similar in style to other letters included in the New Testament. We are told here to whom the letters are addressed and from whom they are being sent.

"To the Seven Churches" (v.4)

As we will learn in verse 11, the seven churches in the province of Asia include Ephesus, Smyrna, Pergamum, Thyatira, Sardis, Philadelphia, and Laodicea.

At the time, Asia Minor, modern-day Turkey, was divided into seven postal districts. These cities were at the center of the districts and as such were responsible for the dissemination of information to their districts. By writing to the main churches in each of these cities, John could be assured that the information in his letters would be passed on throughout the districts.

It is probably relevant as well that there are seven churches—again the number that represents completeness—and as such we can be assured that the messages in these letters can be applied to all Christians.

"From Him Who Is, and Who Was, and Who Is To Come" (v.4)

Here in verses 4–5a, we are basically being told that John is speaking on behalf of our triune God—Father, Son and Holy Spirit. Each entity is described in interesting and unique ways.

It begins with a three-tiered name of God: who is (currently existing), who was (always has been) and who is to come (will always be). It echoes Exodus 3:14 where God calls himself *"I AM WHO I AM"*. This phrase is another one of those concepts that is repeated here in this chapter (see verse 8) and elsewhere in Revelation (4:8), so it is obviously a point that we are intended to remember. Later in Revelation (11:17 and 16:5) we will see the name change to who is and who was. No longer will He be called the one who is to come because by then He will have already come.

These names for God serve as a reminder that He was there at creation, that He is here now as I live my life, and that He will be there eternally. God is a constant that we can always turn to, that we can always depend on.

"From the Seven Spirits Before His Throne" (v.4)

The phrase, "the seven spirits before his throne" is repeated four times in Revelation (1:4, 3:1, 4:5, 5:6). Each time it is repeated there is a little more information added, but the information remains cloaked in metaphors and analogies. Most scholars agree that the phrase refers to the fullness of the Holy Spirit. Some refer to Zechariah 4:2–6 for clarification, and some to Isaiah 11:1–2 where the seven-fold spirit is described as: Spirit of the LORD; Spirit of wisdom; Spirit of understanding; Spirit of counsel; Spirit of might (or power); Spirit of knowledge; and Spirit of the fear of the LORD. This description is a wonderful reminder of the role of the Holy Spirit in our lives.

"From Jesus Christ" (v.5)

Just as we had three names to describe God, here in verse five we see that three names are also used to describe Jesus Christ. These names remind me of the story of salvation. As the faithful witness Jesus stood before people who were in fact, false witnesses in Pilate's court. As a result of His faithful witness, He faced death on the cross and was raised from death—firstborn from the dead—to prove His lordship over the material world—ruler of the kings of the earth. So already we are beginning to learn about who Jesus is. I find it interesting that the description here moves from a faithful, humble carpenter through death to become a ruler of all!

I think it's pretty cool that in a verse and a half we are reminded of God's omnipresence, the gift of the Holy Spirit and the story of Salvation!

The Hymn Of Praise (v.5b–6)

The hymn of praise found here is an act of worship, and a narrative of salvation history. First Peter 2:5 tells us that being a member of the royal priesthood means being able to offer "spiritual sacrifices acceptable to God through Jesus Christ." In this passage, John also echoes the words of 2 Peter 1:11, where we are told that we "will receive a rich welcome into the eternal kingdom of our Lord and Savior Jesus Christ."

We will see this story of salvation, along with reminders of our responsibilities as priests of the kingdom, repeated throughout this book of Revelation. It is the key theme of the book. We are told repeatedly to worship God. In doing so we become followers of the Lamb, and we are expected to act accordingly. We will discover that the life of a follower is not easy—we will be attacked by the beast. On the other hand those who do not choose to worship God, by default follow the Beast, and will be attacked by God. If you do not know already who wins this battle, stay tuned because the outcome is pretty clear.

"Look, He Is Coming With The Clouds" (v.7)

In the opening to this letter, John has clearly indicated that these words are not his alone, but that they come from the triune God. Here in verse seven, by connecting to familiar Old Testament writings, he is making a connection with the people of the seven churches. He is using what they already know to provide insight into what he is about to tell them.

Daniel 7:13 says, "In my vision at night I looked, and there before me was one like a son of man, coming with the clouds of heaven." In Zechariah 12:10, "They will look on me, the one they have pierced, and they will mourn for him as one mourns for an only child, and grieve bitterly for him as one grieves for a firstborn son."

So here in Revelation as John draws from Old Testament prophecy, he is in fact summarizing at a high level much of what is to come and what will be described in detail as we proceed through Revelation.

"I Am the Alpha and the Omega" (v.8)

> [8] *"I am the Alpha and the Omega," says the Lord God, "who is, and who was, and who is to come, the Almighty."*

This greeting section of Revelation ends with a reminder of God's unique qualities. In verse four, we saw a reminder of God's eternal existence. Here we are told that He is the Alpha and the Omega. Alpha is the first letter of the Greek alphabet and omega is the last. I found an interesting perspective on this phrase as follows: "An alphabet is an ingenious way to store and communicate knowledge. The 26 letters in the English alphabet, arranged in almost endless combinations, can hold and convey all knowledge. Christ is the supreme, sovereign alphabet; there is nothing outside His knowledge, so as there are no unknown factors that can sabotage His second coming."[5] In 22:13 the phrase is repeated and expanded. There we will learn that God was the beginning of all things and as the end, in fact is the reason or point of it all.

And finally, God is referred to as "Almighty" nine times in Revelation. It is an indication of the importance of this aspect of His being.

So what does this all mean to me? Well as "the Alpha and the Omega" I see that He is all-knowing; as "the one who is, and who was, and who is to come" I see that He is always-present; and now as the "Almighty" I am reminded that He is all-powerful. He is a God deserving of our worship!

John's Vision Of Christ (1:9–20)

Having completed the opening to his letter, John now goes on to explain the circumstances under which he received his visions and the instructions to write these letters.

"I, John, Your Brother and Companion" (v.9)

> ⁹ *I, John, your brother and companion in the suffering and kingdom and patient endurance that are ours in Jesus, was on the island of Patmos because of the word of God and the testimony of Jesus.*

By identifying himself as a brother, John is aligning himself with the people of the churches to whom he is writing. It is interesting that he doesn't claim to be a teacher or leader in any way—he is just one of the guys, so-to-speak.

And what do we make of his references to suffering, kingdom and patient endurance? Commentators and historians tell us that first century Christians often experienced persecution socially, politically and economically. So John seems to be saying, "Just as you are, I too am patiently suffering because of my belief in Jesus Christ."

Most of these same commentators and historians believe that John had been exiled to the island of Patmos because of his actions as a Christian. This was not uncommon in those days. However, it has also been suggested that there is no real evidence that this was why he was there. Could he, in fact, have been on the island as part of his desire to share the word of God and the testimony of Jesus? Until I meet up with him in Heaven, I realize that I can't know for sure and it may not be relevant to the message John is sharing in Revelation so I'm leaving the question open in my mind. It is useful to know that he was on Patmos, an island in the Aegean sea as he experienced these things as it gives us a sense of his environment at the time of writing.

"On the Lord's Day" (v.10)

I wonder why, in a book with so many metaphors and analogies, John is so specific in telling us that this vision, or series of visions, took place on the Lord's Day? Perhaps he wants us to know that he was resting. Perhaps this day, more than others, as he honored the Sabbath he was in a quiet, receptive place both mentally and spiritually that enabled what was to follow.

And what does it mean to be "in the Spirit"? Is he praying, perhaps as part of his Sabbath ritual? Is he in a trance? Or is he having a dream? Whatever form it took, he is very clear here that he is filled with the Holy Spirit. Second Peter 1:21 says, "For prophecy never had its origin in the will of man, but men spoke from God as they were carried along by the Holy Spirit."

Just as John was in the spirit as this vision came to him, I need to pray for guidance from the Holy Spirit so that I hear—or perhaps see—the message this book has for me; that I have the ability to understand; and that I apply its teachings. In fact we are told in 1 Corinthians 2:14 "The man without the Spirit does not accept the things that come from the Spirit of God, for they are foolishness to him, and he cannot understand them, because they are spiritually discerned."

"I Heard a Loud Voice" (v.10–11)

Throughout the remainder of Revelation we will see many references to a loud voice. This phrase almost always precedes some type of announcement or instruction. Here it was a loud voice like a trumpet. I imagine it as being loud, sharp—a sound that would be difficult to ignore.

John says the voice came from behind him. I think such a voice would cause me to turn around, to pay attention to what may follow.

"I Turned Around To See" (v.12)

And apparently that is precisely what John did. When he turns he sees lampstands and someone standing—I assume he is standing—among them.

Later in this chapter we will be told that the seven lampstands represent the churches (v.20). The lampstand has held biblical significance since one was first set up as a key furnishing in the tabernacle of the Israelites as they wandered in the wilderness after fleeing Egypt. The purpose of a lampstand is to hold the lamplight. In John we are told that Jesus is the light of the world (John 8:12, 9:5) and in Matthew, Jesus tells us the we are the light of the world as well (Matthew 5:14). Churches are made up of individuals. If the church is the lampstand, then the individuals—you and I—are the lamps, the lights of, or to the world.

"Someone Like a Son of Man" (v.13)

The phrase, "like a son of man" is seen in Daniel 7:13 and appears twice in Revelation (here and later in 14:14). The shorter phrase "son of man" is used more than eighty times in the gospels to mean Jesus Christ. But here John doesn't say it was the son of man but rather that it was one like a son of man. This suggests to me that at this point in the vision he thinks that he is seeing Jesus but isn't sure; or if he knows, he doesn't want us to know for certain yet. The fact that this being is clothed in a long robe with a golden sash suggests to me that he/it is spiritually significant.

I think it is incredibly important as well to notice that we are told that this person—this one like a son of man—is among the lampstands. He is present with them. He is present with the churches. He walks with us.

The Description (v.13b–16)

John then goes on to describe this being more fully. He starts with a description of the being's head and hair. It is white like wool and has the color of snow. When I think of wool I think of texture. When I think of snow I think of cold, of purity, and of a sharpness to the color. In Daniel 7:9 the Ancient of Days is described as wearing clothing that was as white as snow and as having hair that was white like wool. However, in Daniel's vision the Ancient of Days is described in this way, and then there is a separate being called the Son of Man. I'm not sure what to make of the fact that here the one like the son of man is described in a way that is similar to the description of the Ancient of Days.

At the very least, the description John has given us should be reminding us of Daniel's visions, and that there is a connection between what Daniel saw and what John is experiencing. But I'm not sure what to do with the connection. Are the passages referring to the same thing? Is the message of Revelation a fulfillment of Daniel's vision? These are questions I cannot resolve.

Moving on with the description, John tells us that his eyes were like blazing fire. I picture them as sharp, piercing, penetrating eyes that can see right into the depths of my soul.

His feet were like bronze. The altar of burnt offering in the tabernacle of the Israelites, was made of bronze. Perhaps these feet that were like bronze are a reminder of Jesus' supreme sacrifice. The fact that they are like bronze glowing in a furnace also suggests to me that they have been refined, tested, strengthened. Commentators also suggest that this image represents divine judgment.

Notice as well that the voice that started out sounding like a trumpet in verse ten now sounds like rushing waters. Other translations refer to this as the sound of many waters, or of cascading waters. The sound has changed from one of *hear me* to *listen to me*. This is a much broader sound compared to what would have been a shrill sharp sound like a trumpet. It is a voice of authority.

The description goes on to show us that he is holding stars—seven of them—in his right hand. Later, in verse twenty we are told that the seven stars mentioned here, are the angels of the seven churches. He is holding them in his right hand, a place of honor and control. I get a sense of comfort and reassurance from this image. It suggests to me that the churches—or stars in this case—aren't randomly doing their work. God holds them, and us, in the palm of His hand—we are not alone.

And then John tells us that he has a sword coming out of his mouth—a sharp, double-edged sword. In Hebrews 4:12 we are told, "the word of God is living and active. Sharper than any double-edged sword." There is no doubt in my mind as I read this that this being is about to share God's word with us.

And the final piece of the description is that his face was shining. The face shining like the sun reminds me of Moses' return from Mt. Sinai after seeing God. In Exodus 34:29 we read, "When Moses came down from Mount Sinai with the two tablets of the covenant law in his hands, he was not aware that his face was radiant because he had spoken with the Lord." This one like a son of man must be strongly connected with, or to, God.

"I Fell At His Feet As Though Dead" (v.17)

I picture John lying flat on his face terrified and not moving. But then he is reassured when he is told that the one like a son of man is "the First and the Last." Personally I'm not sure how I'd react to that information. I think it would be somewhat intimidating but at the same time, it would be pretty cool. I think I'd still be inclined to remain at His feet.

In verse eight, we were told that God is the "Alpha and the Omega" and now we are told that He is the "First and the Last". In 22:13 these two titles are combined but for now they appear to be separate. This is a name that was used for God in the Old Testament. For example in Isaiah 44:6 it says, "This is what the Lord says - Israel's King and Redeemer, the Lord Almighty: I am the first and I am the last; apart from me there is no God." However, the remainder of the description in verse 18 tells me this is Jesus. How cool that the image John saw caused him fear but that once he knew that it was Jesus his fear was released.

"I Am the Living One" (v.18)

And now the one like a son of man confirms His identity in describing himself as the one who died and overcame death—as Jesus Christ. As I read the rest of this verse it seems to me that He is saying that as the one who holds the keys of death and Hades, that He decides who lives, who dies and when.

And what's the difference between death and Hades? Commentators suggest that death is the condition and Hades is the place of the dead.

"Write, Therefore" (v.19)

> ¹⁹ *"Write, therefore, what you have seen, what is now and what will take place later."*

And finally we are given some insight into the key components of the book of Revelation. I've been a bit confused as I've read this verse; are there three things that John is to write about or two? It refers to "what you have seen", "what is now", and "what will take place later". I've finally decided that it is two things. John is being instructed to write about what he has seen in his visions and that those things pertain to what is currently happening in the world and to what will take place when Christ returns. Commentators differ on this point but this is the perspective that seems to make most sense to me.

The Mystery Explained (v.20)

And in the final verse of chapter 1 we have the answer to the "mystery of the seven stars" and "the seven golden lampstands". As mentioned earlier, we are told that the seven stars are the angels of the churches. I wonder what it means to be an angel of the church. We are not told they are angels of God but rather of the church. The role of angels in the Bible is typically that of messengers from God, so I suspect that in this instance the angels of the church are supposed to be messengers of, from, or to the churches—perhaps like a pastor or an elder.

And as discussed with verses twelve and thirteen, we see here the confirmation that the seven lampstands are indeed, the seven churches.

The Letters to the Churches: Revelation 2

Each of the letters that follow contains some or all of a clear set of components. Each letter includes:

- an opening in which Christ is described in a unique way. This **Self Description** often corresponds to something we have already been told about Christ in chapter 1.
- a closing section which includes:
  - a **Refrain.** The Refrain is always "Whoever has ears, let them hear what the Spirit says to the churches."
  - a **Promise**. The Promise usually corresponds to something we will learn about the New Jerusalem in the final chapters of Revelation.

Between these 2 bookends, the letters typically, but not always, contain:

- a **Commendation**—a comment about something good they are doing;
- a **Complaint**—what they aren't doing well;
- an **Instruction**—how to fix what they're doing wrong; and
- a **Threat**—what might happen if they don't shape up.

An Aside: *There is a great deal of information available online about the history of each of these cities and about the messages to Christians within the letters. What is fascinating in my opinion is how different, and at the same time how similar, they are. As I've gone through my study I have not attempted to work my way through all that has been written on the topic of these seven churches as I know that I cannot do an adequate job of bringing it all together. I do encourage anyone who is looking for more information to search online, see what others who are more knowledgeable than I have to say, and learn from them.*

To the Church In Ephesus (2:1–7)

In the first century CE, Ephesus was a major port city in Asia Minor. As a port city it had a problem battling against a continuous build-up of silt. It was one of the three most influential cities in the eastern part of the Roman Empire. The temple to Artemis (also called Diana), one of the ancient wonders of the world was located there and a major industry was the manufacture of images of this goddess. Judaism was strong in Ephesus. In fact, the Jewish community experienced many special privileges. This resulted in a great deal of hostility between the Jews and the Christians in Ephesus.

The church in Ephesus was likely founded by Aquila and Priscilla who went there from Corinth with Paul (Acts 18:18). During his ministry, Paul spent two years preaching in Ephesus. Later Timothy carried on the ministry there.

> [1] *To the angel of the church in Ephesus write: These are the words of him who holds the seven stars in his right hand and walks among the seven golden lampstands.*

Christ's Self Description (v.1)

Christ describes himself to the church at Ephesus as the one who holds the seven stars from verses twelve and sixteen of the first chapter of Revelation. So why does He describe himself in this particular way for this church?

This is a society that was economically successful and powerful. Perhaps this description was a way for God to remind the Christians of Ephesus that He is even more powerful than their oppressors. At the same time, He reassures them that despite the persecution they experience, He is walks with them. He holds them in His hand.

Commendation (v.2–3)

In Acts 20:29–31a, as Paul addressed the Ephesian elders he left them with this bit of advice, "I know that after I leave, savage wolves will come in among you and will not spare the flock. Even from your own number men will arise and distort the truth in order to draw away disciples after them. So be on your guard!" Now in the commendation to this church we see that they obviously worked hard. They didn't tolerate wicked people and seemed to be able to discern false teachers. Apparently it wasn't easy for them, but they were able to hang in there.

Complaint (v.4)

In Ephesians 1:15, Paul commented on their faith and their love for all the saints. But some years later, it appears that this congregation had become busy doing things and apparently lost their focus— understanding that the things they were doing were supposed to be done to honor Christ.

Instruction and Threat (v.5–6)

And so, here in Revelation, Jesus, through John is instructing them to do those things they did at first. A quick read of the book of Ephesians provides insight into what those things are. I am reminded of how easy it is to get carried off down a path that is just slightly off course, and how important it is to stop, reevaluate and get back on the right path. As a city that always had to be on the watch, clearing the silt from the harbor so that they could continue to thrive economically, this idea of losing focus, of losing sight of what they hold dear would likely have resonated strongly on many levels.

The threat to this church is that they may have their lampstand removed. What would it mean to have a lampstand removed? Is the threat that the church here would fall into ruin?

We are told that they hated the practices of the Nicolaitans. Although there is some controversy regarding who these Nicolaitans were, they seem to be believers who compromised their faith in order to enjoy some of the sinful practices of society. They are mentioned here and again in the letter to the church at Pergamum. Here the church seems to have been able to separate from this group—the church in Pergamum was not as strong (see 2:15).

I think it's important to notice here that it doesn't say that they hated the Nicolaitans but rather that they hated the *practices* of the Nicolaitans. It's a classic lesson in hating the sin, not the sinner.

Refrain and Promise (v.7)

> *7b To the one who is victorious, I will give the right to eat from the tree of life, which is in the paradise of God.*

I'm assuming that being victorious meant getting back on the right path; following Jesus out of love instead of doing things because that is what is expected of a good Christian.

Notice that the promise to those who are victorious is the right to eat from the tree of life. There is a connection between this promise to the church at Ephesus and the seventh beatitude in Revelation 22:14. In 22:2, we will see that the tree of life stands on each side of the river that flows down the great street of the New Jerusalem. Here's a flashback to the fall of man in the Garden of Eden. Adam and Eve were denied the fruit from the tree of life and were ultimately banished from the garden because they didn't obey. What an amazing promise to the Ephesians that they would be given the right to eat from this tree.

An Aside: *The cool thing about this book of Revelation is how 'inter-twingled' within its pages are reminders that reach back to creation, to the fall of man, to the story of salvation and ultimately take us to the promise of a new creation. This biblical story is repeated many times in the chapters that follow.*

To the Church In Smyrna (2:8–11)

Smyrna (called Izmir today) was north of Ephesus. It was known for its great architectural beauty. As a port city, it was prosperous and in fact competed with Ephesus for the honor of being the most important city of Asia. This city was a great supporter of Rome and became the site of a great deal of emperor-worship. In fact, emperor-worship was mandatory in this society during the first centuries. By not participating in emperor-worship the Christians were marginalized. They had difficulty earning a living and were persecuted, not only by the Romans but also by the Jews of Smyrna. The story of Polycarp, the martyr, takes place in Smyrna. I won't go into it here but if you'd like more information there is lots available online.

There is no complaint or threat to this church. Rather it appears to be a letter of encouragement to a church that is experiencing some serious persecution often resulting in violent death.

> *⁸ To the angel of the church in Smyrna write: These are the words of him who is the First and the Last, who died and came to life again.*

Christ's Self Description (v.8)

In the description of Jesus here, John connects back to verses seventeen and eighteen of the first chapter. Perhaps because the people of this church were experiencing persecution, this description as the one "who died and came to life again", was used to remind them of Christ's victory over death—a reminder that death is not the end. In other words, "hang in there, trust in me, I'm in charge".

Commendation (v.9)

It is interesting that in this prosperous seaport, these Christians experienced poverty. Was it the result of whatever persecution they experienced? Yet we are told that this situation didn't hinder them from being rich in their faith.

As we continue here we run into a phrase that has been misused throughout history as a justification for the mistreatment and persecution of the Jews. John refers to "those who say they are Jews and are not, but are a synagogue of Satan." How can one say they are a Jew and then not be one? In Romans 2:28–29 Paul says "A man is not a Jew if he is only one outwardly, ... No, a man is a Jew if he is one inwardly." So what I get from this is that these were people who acted as they were expected to but missed the point of honoring God. Some commentators suggest that they were not Jews because they didn't recognize Jesus as the Messiah. The reference to a synagogue of Satan suggests that because these Jews weren't worshipping Jesus or honoring God as His chosen people, Judaism became as much a tool for Satan as did the emperor-worship of the time. Perhaps because they were actively persecuting the Christians their example to others was confusing and misleading and opened the door for Satan. Perhaps similar to what can happen when we, as professing Christians act in ways that do not bring honor to God.

Instruction (v.10)

They are told that they will experience persecution and that it will last for ten days. So we know that even if they hadn't already been persecuted that they would be soon. And now we have to decide what to do with this reference to ten days. Were they going to experience suffering for precisely ten days or is this time frame meant to suggest that it would last a short, definable period of time? Throughout Revelation we see many references to time periods. In order to make sense of things, I think it is necessary to decide whether to regard them as literal or metaphorical. My tendency is to take them metaphorically. Consequently, I'm inclined to think that the implication here of ten days was intended to tell the church of Smyrna that their suffering would be contained within a short period of time or that in the grand scheme of things, was temporary.

Smyrna was also famous for its athletic games so the analogy to a victor's crown given to the winner in a competition would have been very meaningful to the people of this church. Note the link between the Instruction here and the beatitude outlined in 14:13.

Refrain and Promise (v.11)

11b The one who is victorious will not be hurt at all by the second death.

Reference is made to the second death four times in Revelation (here, 20:6, 20:14, and 21:8). If the first death we experience is the earthly death of our bodies, the second death described in the final chapters of Revelation refers to eternal death and is a fate awaiting non-believers.

So, the promise that they would not be hurt by the second death is, in fact, a promise of eternal life.

And this letter to the church in Smyrna ends with a link to the beatitude in 20:6 assuring them that if they persist they will be blessed.

To the Church In Pergamum (2:12–17)

Pergamum was not a seaport. Instead it was more of a fortress situated high on a hill. It was important as a political and religious center. It was home to four different cults and had a temple dedicated "to the divine Augustus and the goddess Roma"[6]. It had a huge altar to Zeus and a temple to the goddess Athena. It was also known for its worship of Asclepius, the serpent-god of healing—we still see the serpent symbol on many things related to healing and medicine. With all the pagan worship going on here it was a very difficult environment for a Christian church.

> [12] *To the angel of the church in Pergamum write: These are the words of him who has the sharp, double-edged sword.*

Christ's Self Description (v.12)

We were introduced to this description of Jesus in 1:16. In chapter 19, verses 15 and 21, we will learn that it is with a sharp sword that Satan and his followers are destroyed. By using this description here, I think God was reminding the people of the church in Pergamum that He was stronger than all those other gods and goddesses prevalent in the society around them.

Commendation (v.13)

They are being commended for managing to continue to worship Jesus in spite of all the pagan worship going on. Although we don't know exactly who Antipas is, we do know from this verse that he was martyred for Christ and we know that even this persecution did not dissuade them as believers.

This ability to remain focused on their faith in the midst of an environment where "Satan lives" reminds me of the difficulty many Christians today have in staying focused on Christ, and not being distracted in our current society.

Complaint (v.14–15)

However, it seems that not all of the churchgoers in Pergamum remained true. There were some in their midst who followed Baalam and the teachings of the Nicolaitans. In Numbers 25:1–3, a similar problem is described. There in verse three it says, "So Israel yoked themselves to the Baal of Peor. And the Lord's anger burned against them." Some of the people of the church in Pergamum compromised their faith; they chose a middle ground that allowed them to participate in some of the less savory aspects of society while they tried to be followers of Jesus.

Wow, that hits close to home doesn't it! How often do we as Christians find ourselves compromising our beliefs simply because it's easier than taking a stand.

And here we see reference to those Nicolaitans again. The church in Ephesus was commended for standing strong against their practices. Some of the people in Pergamum had not been as strong. One might wonder why not. Perhaps, in Pergamum, because of all the pagan worship going on it was harder to resist or perhaps they didn't even notice it happening—sound familiar?

Instruction and Threat (v.16)

They are told that if they don't repent, Christ will come and fight those who follow the teachings of Balaam and of the Nicolaitans. John says Christ will fight them with the sword of his mouth. My first reaction to this statement is that he will come and speak/preach to them. However, when I read ahead in Revelation to chapter 19 as mentioned before, this is a much stronger threat. This is a threat of destruction if they don't repent.

Refrain and Promise (v.17)

> *17b To the one who is victorious, I will give some of the hidden manna. I will also give that person a white stone with a new name written on it, known only to the one who receives it.*

What do we make of this promise of hidden manna? Why is it hidden? There is an obvious echo back to the exodus where the Israelites were given manna to eat to sustain them in the desert. In Exodus 16:32b we read, "Moses said, "This is what the Lord has commanded: 'Take an omer of manna and keep it for the generations to come, so they can see the bread I gave you to eat in the wilderness when I brought you out of Egypt" And in verse 34, "As the Lord commanded Moses, Aaron put the manna with the tablets of the covenant law, so that it might be preserved." Is this reference to hidden manna connected to this omer of manna saved with the tablets of the covenant law? There is a spiritual connection between manna and the bread of life (John 6:32–33) and it seems a simple leap from there to consider the manna and the wedding supper of the Lamb (chapter 19) as promised to believers.

Part of the promise here includes a white stone with a new name on it. In first century times, the white stone had a variety of uses. One of these was that it acted as an admission ticket to a special event. So here, as I read this, I'm thinking that the stone represented the admission ticket to the wedding feast.

Why a new name? When I think of the names of people I know, I realize how over time I associate a person's name with their character. But here the promise is that they will receive new names—a new character— each will be made new in Christ.

To the Church In Thyatira (2:18–28)

Thyatira wasn't a prosperous seaport, instead it was more of a blue-collar working-man's city. It was noted for its trade guilds. In order for a citizen to participate in trade in Thyatira he would have had to belong to a trade guild. Members of the trade guilds would often gather together to enjoy a common meal. Unfortunately, this meal was usually dedicated to some pagan deity, so Christians in Thyatira who belonged to a guild had to deal with the difficult question of whether they could participate in these guild meals.

From Acts 16:14 we learn that Lydia (in Philippi) was a dealer in purple cloth from Thyatira.

> [18] *To the angel of the church in Thyatira write: These are the words of the Son of God, whose eyes are like blazing fire and whose feet are like burnished bronze.*

Christ's Self Description (v.18)

I find it interesting that this is the only place in Revelation where Jesus is called the Son of God; particularly since it is a name used many times over in the Gospels. I wonder if that's because as we move through Revelation we will see the separate identities of the Father and the Son gradually meld into one identity; which now has me wondering what happens to the Holy Spirit through end-times—will there still be a role to play or do the three persons of the Trinity merge into one being? Or will we interact with the three separate identities of God? Hmm, I guess I'll have to wait for that answer.

The remainder of this description comes from 1:14–15. I mentioned that the image of feet like burnished bronze, glowing in a furnace, implied divine judgment and that the eyes like blazing fire could see all. In this address to the church in Thyatira, this description suggests that Christ could see what had been happening there and that He was about to pass judgment.

Commendation (v.19)

On the surface it appears that this church had it together. They have been commended not only for their actions but also for their love, faith, and perseverance. So not only were they acting like Christians, they were doing so from a place of love. In fact it sounds like they were growing and maturing in their faith.

Complaint (v.20–21)

But there were problems here as well. Despite all the good things they did, they tolerated "that woman Jezebel, who calls herself a prophet." The only other time we read of a Jezebel in the Bible is in 1 and 2 Kings where we find the story of Jezebel, wife of Ahab—a very evil woman. Is it likely that there was a specific woman named Jezebel living in Thyatira at the time or is it more likely that the name has been used metaphorically to illustrate the evilness of the woman in their midst who had been misrepresenting herself as a prophet and leading others away from the teachings of Jesus? I tend to believe that this is a metaphorical reference rather than a literal one. It may be that the result was acts of literal sexual immorality, but often such references implied pagan or idol worship as well.

Regardless of what she had been encouraging them to do, we are told that she had been given an opportunity to repent but hadn't done so. Oh, how often has this happened in our own lives. We sin, are given a chance to repent, but refuse to do so!

Threat (v.22–23)

So she will be forced to suffer. Interesting that it is a "bed of suffering" considering her charge of sexual immorality. Her buddies will also suffer. However, it appears that they still have a chance to repent.

But then we are told that her children will die. Who are her children and why are they to die while those who consort with her will only suffer? Doesn't seem fair, although perhaps death is easier than long-term suffering. If we read ahead to 19:15, "Anyone whose name was not found written in the book of life was thrown into the lake of fire" we can see what intense suffering might look like.

The statement that all will know that He is the one "who searches hearts and minds" seems consistent to me with the description of Christ as the one with eyes like blazing fire.

We cannot hide from God. And the statement that each will be repaid according to their deeds reassures us that justice will prevail. We see this played out in the judgment scene later in 20:12.

Instruction (v.24–25)

It's interesting here that we started with the complaint that the church tolerated this Jezebel but there are no instructions to the church to deal with her. In fact, Christ has made it clear that He will be dealing with her. He seems to be telling us that we are not the judges or the jury—He is and He will take care of it.

How wonderful that He then reassures the people of the church at Thyatira who have been able to keep separate from Jezebel that He's not going to impose any other burden on them. Or in other words, "I'll take care of Jezebel, her cohorts and her children, the rest of you are good-to-go."

And what of the phrase "Satan's so-called deep secrets"—sounds very mysterious and at the same time sounds sarcastic. As if this Jezebel was falsely promising some deep insights to those who believed her to be a prophet.

Promise and Refrain (v.26–29)

> *26 To the one who is victorious and does my will to the end, I will give authority over the nations—*
> *27 that one 'will rule them with an iron scepter and will dash them to pieces like pottery'—just as I have received authority from my Father.*
> *28 I will also give that one the morning star.*

This promise to the victorious at Thyatira is a direct tie-back to Psalm 2:8–9, "I will make the nations your inheritance, the ends of the earth your possession. You will rule them with an iron scepter, you will dash them to pieces like pottery."

The reference to the morning star appears again in 22:16 and is also seen in 2 Peter 1:19, "We also have the prophetic message as something completely reliable, and you will do well to pay attention to it, as to a light shining in a dark place, until the day dawns and the morning star rises in your hearts." The morning star is the one that shines most brightly in the sky just before dawn when the night is often its darkest and its coldest.

The Letters to the Churches: Revelation 3

To the Church In Sardis (3:1–6)

Sardis was an aging city situated at the meeting place of several Roman roads. As such, it was an important industrial center—the home of woolen and dyed goods. It was also important for its military strength. Sardis was zealous in promoting emperor-worship. The people were known for their luxurious, loose way of life. There are no words of commendation for this church, which suggests that they were in pretty rough shape.

> [1a] *To the angel of the church in Sardis write: These are the words of him who holds the seven spirits of God and the seven stars.*

Christ's Self Description (v.1a)

This is an interesting description that Christ, through John, uses here. Earlier we said that the reference to the seven spirits suggested the completeness of the Holy Spirit. I think of the Holy Spirit as the being in the trinity that is always with me—that knows me through and through. Of course that's true for God and his son Jesus as well but when I think of God my imagination takes me to a visual of a great being out there and when I think of Jesus, I think of the man. So if you follow my imagery here, the suggestion could be that the words to Sardis come from one who understands them through and through and from someone who has authority over them as well—holds the seven stars. Another perspective on the analogy of holding the seven

stars could be one of comfort—we are held in the palm of His hand—
He cares for us.

Sardis was also a military stronghold, and so it makes sense that
Jesus would describe Himself this way to remind them that He is the
one who holds the power just as He holds the seven spirits and the
seven stars.

Complaint (v.1b)

He doesn't waste any time getting to the point with the people of the
church in Sardis. They are told that he knows what they've been up
to and that even though it may appear that they have been actively
following Jesus, they are not. In fact, they are so infested with sin that
he says they are dead!

Instruction and Threat (v.2–3)

Why the instruction to wake up? When I checked the commentaries
I discovered that the "city was an impregnable acropolis which had
never been seized by frontal attack; twice, however, in the history of
the city, the acropolis had been taken by stealth because of a lack of
vigilance on the part of its defenders."[7] So, this instruction would have
resonated strongly with the people of the church of Sardis.

It seems that they had been starting things, perhaps for the right
reasons, but not finishing them or at least not finishing them the way
God wanted them to.

This perspective resonates for me quite strongly—I'm a great starter—
not such a great finisher. For example, I began this study to satisfy my
own curiosity. When I was about two-thirds of the way through it
I started to drag. I came close to stopping. But then I felt a distinct

prompting from God to continue. The phrase "I gave you this to do—now finish it" has been bouncing around in my consciousness since then. I thought the only one I had to please was myself—apparently God had something else in mind. I needed to stay with this until it was complete in His sight.

It seems that not all was lost for this church. There must have been some who were faithful or at least remembered the teachings that they were asked to return to, to hang on to and to repent. And the threat; just as happened with the acropolis, if they don't wake up, he will come like a thief in the night.

There is a connection in these two verses with two more of the Revelation beatitudes. The first one we've already seen in 1:3 connects with the instruction to hold fast to what they have received and heard. Another beatitude in 16:15 related to staying awake seems particularly appropriate to the church in Sardis.

Promise and Refrain (v.4–6)

> *⁴ Yet you have a few people in Sardis who have not soiled their clothes. They will walk with me, dressed in white, for they are worthy.*
> *⁵ The one who is victorious will, like them, be dressed in white. I will never blot out the name of that person from the book of life, but will acknowledge that name before my Father and his angels.*

Since Sardis was the home of woolen and dyed goods, fabrics basically, it seems appropriate that the reference here was to clothing. The concept of not soiling their clothes suggests to me that there were a few people in this church who remained faithful—who weren't drawn into the loose and luxurious lifestyle common to others in Sardis.

In 7:14 we are told that those who are dressed in white robes are the ones who have washed their robes and made them white in the blood

34

of the Lamb and in 19:14 that the armies of heaven were dressed in white. So these people will be set apart—their names appear in the book of life. We will see more about this book of life in 20:15 where we are told that if your name isn't in the book of life you will be thrown into the lake of fire. The promise that "they will walk with me" links directly to 21:3 where we are told that in the New Jerusalem, God will dwell with the people.

There's one thing that I'm still struggling with here though; it's the statement "I will never blot out the name ... from the book of life." Is this telling me that my name can be erased from the book of life? Or is it just the opposite—that once my name is in the book it cannot be removed? Wow, my search to resolve this question took me to some interesting reading. I found one article[8] online that pointed out that we can definitely have our names removed from the book of life. This argument is based on Revelation 22:19. To make a connection to the book of life I had to go to the King James Version (KJV) of this verse which says, "and if anyone takes away from the words of the book of this prophecy, God shall take away his part from the Book of Life, from the holy city, and from the things which are written in this book." A second reference that could support the argument is in Exodus 32:33 which says, "The Lord replied to Moses, "Whoever has sinned against me I will blot out of my book"." The counter-argument I found on this specific passage is that the book referred to in Exodus is not the book of life but is in fact something called the *book of the living*. This book of the living was like a register of the citizens of a city. If someone died, or committed a serious crime, their name was erased from this book. "The threat, then, is not eternal damnation, but physical death."[9]

Most of the theologians and commentators that I investigated seem to agree that the point here is not the threat that your name will be removed but rather the promise that to the one who is victorious, once your name has been written in the book of life it will not be removed.

For clarification on what it means to be victorious I've turned to 1 John 5:1–5, "Everyone who believes that Jesus is the Christ is born of God, and everyone who loves the father loves his child as well. This is how we know that we love the children of God: by loving God and carrying out his commands. In fact, this is love for God: to keep his commands. And his commands are not burdensome, for everyone born of God overcomes the world. This is the victory that has overcome the world, even our faith. Who is it that overcomes the world? Only the one who believes that Jesus is the Son of God."

So I'm going to focus on the promise here resting on the fact that having believed that Jesus is the Christ, the Son of God who died for my sins and rose from the grave and is now sitting at the right hand of the Father, my name has been entered into the Book of Life and will not be removed.

To the Church In Philadelphia (3:7–13)

The main problem faced by the church at Philadelphia was from the Jews. The citizens of Pergamum founded this city. It was built in a frontier area as a gateway to the central plateau of Asia Minor. Philadelphia's residents kept barbarians out of the region and brought in Greek culture and language. An earthquake in CE 17 destroyed the city and aftershocks kept the people so worried that most of them lived outside the city limits. Since there is no complaint or threat to this church it would appear that this letter is intended to encourage them.

> *⁷ To the angel of the church in Philadelphia write: These are the words of him who is holy and true, who holds the key of David. What he opens no one can shut, and what he shuts no one can open.*

Christ's Self Description (v.7)

Here Christ refers to himself as the one who is holy and true. We haven't seen this description before in Revelation but it is repeated later in 6:10.

I find the phrase "holds the key of David" rather interesting. Earlier in 1:18 we were told that he holds the keys to death and Hades; determining who lives, who dies, and when. And now we see that he also holds the key of David. Since Jesus is of the line of David, a quick look at this phrase tells me that by holding the key of David, just as Jesus determines who lives and who dies, he also determines who will enter the kingdom of God. There is perhaps more to the story. According to one commentator "The immediate background of the phrase was the claim of the Jews in Philadelphia that they were the true people of God who held the key to the Kingdom of God. John contradicts this claim by asserting that the key to the kingdom that had belonged to Israel really belongs to Jesus as the Davidic Messiah and had been forfeited by Israel because she had rejected her Messiah. It is Christ alone and no longer Israel who can give men entrance into the messianic Kingdom."[10]

This phrase also echoes Isaiah 22:22 "I will place on his shoulder the key to the house of David; what he opens no one can shut, and what he shuts no one can open."

Commendation (v.8–10)

The problem, if there is one, with the church in Philadelphia is that they weren't very strong. In light of the persecution they experienced from the local Jewish community, the reassurance is that they were on the right path; the one who holds the key of David (to the kingdom) had opened the door for them, and no one could cut them off from God. The beatitude in 22:7 resonates with the commendation to this church in that they have kept his word.

We saw a similar reference to the synagogue of Satan in the letter to the church of Smyrna who also experienced persecution from the local Jewish community. There they were told that they would go through a time of suffering. Here in Philadelphia the promise is that there will come a time when the Jews will eventually acknowledge that the Christians were right. I wonder if that means that they will seek conversion, will become Christian as well?

It seems that this church would be saved from experiencing the "hour of trial that is going to come on the whole world." Apparently, they had suffered enough and had proven themselves worthy.

Instruction (v.11)

And just as the church of Smyrna was promised the crown of life if they held on, the church at Philadelphia is reminded that they already hold the crown and that it cannot be taken from them as long as they hold on to what they have. What wonderful words of encouragement!

Promise and Refrain (v.12–13)

> *[12] The one who is victorious I will make a pillar in the temple of my God. Never again will they leave it. I will write on them the name of my God and the name of the city of my God, the new Jerusalem, which is coming down out of heaven from my God; and I will also write on them my new name.*

The promise to this church is all encompassing and very closely tied to much of what we will read in Revelation 21. Clearly it is a promise of life eternal in the Holy City—the New Jerusalem. For a people who lived with the uncertainty and instability of regular earthquakes, this promise to be made a pillar in the temple suggests strength and endurance. It would have been particularly reassuring.

To the Church In Laodicea (3:14–22)

"Laodicea was the wealthiest of the seven cities, known for its banking industry, manufacture of wool, and a medical school that produced eye salve. But the city had always had a problem with its water supply. At one time an aqueduct was built to bring water to the city from hot springs. But by the time the water reached the city, it was neither hot nor refreshingly cool - only lukewarm."[11]

> *[14] To the angel of the church in Laodicea write: These are the words of the Amen, the faithful and true witness, the ruler of God's creation.*

Christ's Self Description (v.14)

The word *Amen* used here is of Hebrew origin and means *trustworthy* which is confirmed by the remainder of the description here as the faithful and true witness. We first saw reference to the faithful witness back in 1:5. The reminder that he is the "ruler of God's creation" would have been particularly meaningful to this church because it had experienced a devastating earthquake in the years just before John wrote this letter.

Complaint (v.15)

Just as the water that arrived in their city as neither hot nor cold, the people of this church were lukewarm. What does a lukewarm Christian look like? I imagine a person that attends church gatherings when it is convenient; that admits to being a Christian if asked but doesn't offer up the information without prompting. She knows Biblical teaching. She has heard the good news of the Gospel and has likely even professed to accept Jesus Christ as her Lord and Savior. However, she hasn't taken her faith any further. It sort of sits on the surface of her being, never having made it into her soul. James 1:22 says, " Do not merely listen to the word, and so deceive yourselves. Do what it says." A lukewarm Christian likely doesn't "Do what it says."

Threat (v.16–17)

These people were wealthy and didn't appear to be experiencing any significant persecution—sounds a lot like the church in North America today doesn't it. But they were about to be spit out, a fairly violent action. I wonder if there is significance to this phrase beyond the obvious sense of God saying 'yuck'.

The message to the Laodiceans is just as applicable to us today. Is a lukewarm Christian truly a Christian? If I have accepted Jesus Christ as my Savior, but don't act like it, am I saved? Will I gain eternal life? These questions may be too big for me to answer. The good news as we will see in the verses that follow is that they are still referred to as "those whom I love" so all is not lost.

If the concept of being lukewarm causes me to wonder about my own behavior then this passage has done its work. It has, or should have, caused me to wake up and consider how I am as a Christian; to re-evaluate, to seek forgiveness, to pray for clarity in seeking new directions, and then change a few things before it is too late.

Instruction (v.18–19)

It's interesting that the instructions to this church revolve around those things their city was noted for—just spiritual versions. They were wealthy so He speaks in terms of buying things. They were a banking center and He wants them to buy gold refined in the fire—purified. They manufactured wool and He instructs them to get white clothes to wear, and at their medical school they produced eye salve and here He suggests that they get salve to put on their eyes so they can see.

Just as it says in Hebrews 12:6a "the Lord disciplines those he loves", here Jesus, through John, tells the church in Laodicea "Those whom I love I rebuke and discipline." So in spite of their waywardness he reminds them and us that he still loves them.

Promise and Refrain (v.20–22)

> [20] *Here I am! I stand at the door and knock. If anyone hears my voice and opens the door, I will come in and eat with that person, and they with me.* [21] *To the one who is victorious, I will give the right to sit with me on my throne, just as I was victorious and sat down with my Father on his throne.*

In Matthew 7:7b and Luke 11:9b we read "knock and the door will be opened to you." In both passages, Jesus is talking to his followers—or potential followers—telling them to knock. Here, on the other hand, the image is different. Here it is Jesus standing at the door and knocking. He is not talking to unbelievers but rather to this group of lukewarm believers. He is making it clear that He is pursuing them and the result—well it's a wonderful meal. Notice how it says "I will come in and eat with that person," and then goes on to say "and they with me"—it's a two-way relationship!

The promise of sitting with Him on His throne is a promise of Christ-likeness. Interesting that this last of the letters brings us to the throne that is then described in great detail in the next chapter.

Revelation 4

As we enter into this chapter of Revelation the tone of the big letter changes. No longer is John writing in a somewhat folksy way to his companions of the churches. This content is certainly intended for that same audience, including us, but here we move into the apocalyptic genre.

With this change in genre it seems appropriate to also change one's attitude towards what we read. As I mentioned in the opening to this book, this literary style employs a very descriptive language with metaphors, similes, and so on to describe concepts. Although the style was relatively common in the time that Revelation was written it is not as common in today's world. Consequently it is difficult for us to know how to receive the words. I've chosen to take things like references to numbers and symbols metaphorically rather than literally. If you don't agree and choose to be more literal, that's okay with me. I believe that we will still get the same key message from the stories that follow.

And so, let's move on to this next segment in the book of Revelation where we seem to change planes so-to-speak moving from what has been a basically land-based vision so far to a first look at the throne in heaven.

The Throne In Heaven (4:1–11)

"Door Standing Open In Heaven" (v.1)

> *¹ After this I looked, and there before me was a door standing open in heaven. And the voice I had first heard speaking to me like a trumpet said, "Come up here, and I will show you what must take place after this."*

It is with this opening phrase "after this", that we know we are moving on to a new section of Revelation. The phrase suggests that this vision may have been a separate experience or event for John. In 1:10 John said that he was "in the Spirit" and when we read ahead to verse two here, he says that he was "once again in the Spirit." Together the two phrases seem to support the idea of a new vision. Now, I'm not sure it matters whether we think of this as a separate vision or as simply part of one big vision. For me, imagining how this would have happened for John makes him seem more relatable. I feel some empathy for the onerous task God placed on John to share these visions with us. We will see reference to being in the Spirit two more times in Revelation (17:3 and 21:10) each time John is shown something extraordinary.

In that seminary class I mentioned in my opening words to this book, the professor drew an image on the whiteboard to illustrate his image of this door in Heaven. He drew a dome-like structure covering the earth, and a stick-man version of John climbing up through a trap door to whatever lies above the dome. John is leaving earthly beings behind, safe and sound under the dome.

I find it interesting that some of the last words in the previous chapter were about how Christ is standing at the door knocking, and here we are introduced to another door. But this door is standing open. John didn't have to open it. He was freely granted access to heaven. All he had to do was walk, or in this case climb, through the door.

Just as he did at the beginning of the first vision (1:10), John again hears the voice like a trumpet—this is a voice that wants to be heard.

The voice says he will show John what must take place. As we said at the beginning, this is a very visual story. It is filled with images and I am certain that the use of the word *show* here is absolutely intentional and meaningful. It is almost impossible to read these next chapters of Revelation without creating pictures in our heads. I believe that this is why John switched his writing style to this apocalyptic genre because it is such an effective tool for drawing us into the story.

This first verse is fairly critical to our understanding of what follows. In Matthew 24:6, Jesus makes a similar statement, "You will hear of wars and rumors of wars, but see to it that you are not alarmed. Such things must happen, but the end is still to come." In Matthew, Jesus was speaking of the period between His first time on earth and His return—the current church age. I believe that here in Revelation 4:1, the voice that John hears is referring to that same time period when it refers to "what must take place after this." You might not agree with my take on this but bear with me for a bit. Let's see how this plays out and if you still don't agree, that's okay, at least I've caused you to think about it and decide for yourself.

One of the things that we will see as we move forward is that in addition to some level of confusion regarding timing and time frames, we are also going to move about in different planes of existence. For now we are in a scene taking place in heaven and that seems pretty clear but it can, and will, change frequently as we proceed.

Someone Sitting On The Throne (v.2)

> [2] *At once I was in the Spirit, and there before me was a throne in heaven with someone sitting on it.*

45

Interesting, John doesn't identify who is on the throne. He simply says "someone". It's as if he doesn't know who it is. Much like he did in 1:13 when he introduced us to "someone like a son of man." Only here he doesn't connect to the son of man piece. Most of us simply assume that it is God sitting on the throne, so why wouldn't he simply say so? Throne scenes appear often in the Old Testament. Check out I Kings 22:19, Isaiah 6:1–4, Daniel 7:9–10 and Ezekiel 1:4–28. In each of these we learn that the one on the throne is the LORD, God. So as readers somewhat familiar with Old Testament Scriptures we immediately jump to concluding that this was God—so why didn't John? Or maybe he did, and he simply wanted to pique our interest a bit more before telling us the full story.

"Had the Appearance Of Jasper and Ruby" (v.3)

In describing the one who sat there, John uses an interesting technique. He doesn't use typical terms for describing a person or being, instead he tells us he "had the appearance of jasper and ruby." These stones have fire-like colors, but if the color is all John wanted us to be aware of, he could have said it looked like fire. But he doesn't, he relates it to stones. By using stones, he gives us a sense, not only of beauty and radiance, but also of solidness. God is real. Earthly leaders decorate themselves with precious stones but God *is* them.

Further in this verse he tells us about the rainbow resembling an emerald that surrounded the throne. Again, notice we aren't told it was green, rather we are told that it is solid, emerald-like. This, of course, is a reminder of God's covenant faithfulness. It takes us back to the flood in Genesis 9:12–13, "And God said, "This is the sign of the covenant I am making between me and you and every living creature with you, a covenant for all generations to come: I have set my rainbow in the clouds, and it will be the sign of the covenant between me and the earth.""

"Twenty-four Elders" (v.4)

Around the throne were twenty-four more thrones with people sitting on them. Interesting that although John couldn't identify the being on the main throne, he does know that these twenty-four are elders. And who are these twenty-four elders? Commentators vary on who they think they are. Some suggest that they represent an angelic counsel. Others that twelve represent the tribes of Israel—Old Testament—and the other twelve, the apostles of Christ—New Testament—and that together they symbolize all who are a part of God's family.

And what do we make of their attire? The white clothing implies purity and righteousness; the crowns of gold—royalty. Perhaps there is an intended link back to 1:6 where John tells us that he made us to be a kingdom and priests.

I see these elders as our representatives around the throne of "someone."

"Flashes Of Lightning, Rumblings and Peals Of Thunder" (v.5)

As sound effects are introduced here, the vision seems to get more intense, more chaotic. Anytime I experience a summer storm with lightning and thunder I can't help but be reminded of God's might and power, so as I read this description I immediately understand that the someone on the throne is a being with great power and authority. The thunder and lightning are reminiscent of the throne scene in Ezekiel mentioned earlier. There is another aspect to this that may also be worth considering. When experiencing a thunderstorm, I remember being told as a child that angels bowling in heaven created the noise of the thunder. A thunder and lightning storm seems to connect the heavens—okay, I realize it's just the clouds, but work with me here—with earth. We will see many more such storms in the chapters that follow. It's an analogy worth watching for.

As I was considering the seven lamps mentioned here I assumed that these seven lamps were in fact, the seven lampstands mentioned in John's first vision (1:12,20). However, in looking at it more closely I see that this is not so. The Greek word for lampstand used in chapter 1 is *lychnia* and for lamps used here is *lampas*—two different words with different meanings. Besides all that, in 1:20 we were told that the lampstands represent the churches, and here we are told that the lamps are the seven spirits of God. We were first told about these seven spirits in 1:4 when we were told even then that they were before the throne of him who is, and who was, and who is to come, and that they represented the Holy Spirit.

An Aside: *Has that ever happened to you? I mean, have you ever read something through quickly and assumed that you understood it, only to discover upon second reading that you got it completely wrong? I share my confusion regarding the lamps and the lampstands because I think it illustrates a problem many of us have particularly when reading Scripture. Even when reading passages that are familiar, it is so important to take the time to think about what we're reading so we don't miss the message.*

"A Sea Of Glass" (v.6)

Just as the stones mentioned earlier, this sea is very tangible. In our modern-day society, glass is a familiar material. I can touch glass. It is usually smooth, and is typically clear. It protects us in the form of windows. It contains things when formed into dishes, cups, and glasses. When not colored we can see through it. It evokes a feeling of calmness.

However, in the first century, glass was not a common material. It would have been considered to be quite rare and certainly very special. It is mentioned again in 15:2 and we'll talk about it again there.

"Four Living Creatures" (v.6–7)

One of the first things we are told about the four living creatures around the throne is that they were covered with eyes. Without knowing anything more about how they looked, this description immediately evokes an image for me—I see a shapeless figure covered with eyes. It seems that John wants us to know that these creatures can see everything.

I wonder why they are called *living* creatures. If John had simply referred to them as creatures, would we have assumed they were dead? I think my natural inclination would have been to think of them as being alive, so is there more to it? Perhaps it is a way to reinforce the fact that this scene is actively taking place.

There are a few different explanations about who or what these living creatures are, or about who they are supposed to represent. There are connections to the visions in Daniel 7, to Isaiah 6 and to Ezekiel 10. Some commentators suggest that the lion represents wild beasts; the ox, tamed beasts; and the eagle, birds of the air; basically covering all land-based life. Other commentators have suggested that the lion represents strength and courage; the ox—or calf in some translations—represents faithfulness; the man represents intelligence; and the flying eagle represents swiftness.

Most commentators agree that they are cherubim or seraphs guarding the throne. Perhaps in its simplest form the best way to consider them is that they represent diversity.

"Each Of the Living Creatures Had Six Wings" (v.8)

Similar to living creatures in other biblical visions, not only do these have many eyes which we have already discussed, but wings as well. When I consider the wings, I think of fluttering movement, which seems to add to the sense of activity in the scene.

> *⁸ Each of the four living creatures had six wings and was covered with eyes all around, even under its wings. Day and night they never stop saying: "'Holy, holy, holy is the Lord God Almighty,' who was, and is, and is to come."*

Worshipping (v.8–10)

But here lies the most important aspect of these living creatures. We see that day and night they never stop worshipping God. We will see this scene repeated throughout Revelation and always they are worshipping God.

Notice as well that they refer to the Lord God Almighty as He "who was, and is, and is to come" just as God was described to us in 1:4, 8.

This is interesting. We are told in verse 8 that the living creatures "never stop saying" and then in verses 9 and 10 that whenever they give glory, the twenty-four elders fall down and worship as well. So basically, we are seeing a picture of non-stop worship.

As we listen closely to the words of their worship we see the message of Revelation repeated once again—God is worthy to be worshipped because He is the creator of all things!

> *¹¹ "You are worthy, our Lord and God, to receive glory and honor and power, for you created all things, and by your will they were created and have their being."*

This throne scene will continue to play a central role throughout the remainder of Revelation. We will return to it frequently.

Some Things To Think About

Before moving on, there are some things to think about from this chapter. Did you notice that nowhere in this chapter were we told that the scene around the throne was going to take place sometime in the future?

- Our triune God is on His throne—now and always will be!
- He is solid and reliable—now and always will be!
- He is being worshipped continuously—now and always will be!

And did you notice that before moving on to all the intriguing events that will be shared with us in the remainder of this book of Revelation, that these are the first things God, through John wanted to share with us?

The book of Revelation is a call to worship God.

Revelation 5

The Scroll and the Lamb (5:1–14)

Chapter 4 started with "after this", which seemed to suggest the start of something new or perhaps more specifically the end of something and a new beginning. This chapter starts with the word "then" which suggests a continuation of the previous chapter—it is all part of the same vision.

The Scroll (v.1)

> *¹ Then I saw in the right hand of him who sat on the throne a scroll with writing on both sides and sealed with seven seals.*

Immediately my curiosity was piqued. Where did this scroll come from? What is written on it? I looked to Scripture to find some clues. In Isaiah 29:11 we read "For you this whole vision is nothing but words sealed in a scroll. And if you give the scroll to someone who can read, and say to him, 'Read this please,' he will answer, 'I can't; it is sealed." Ezekiel 2:9–10, "Then I looked, and I saw a hand stretched out to me. In it was a scroll, which he unrolled before me. On both sides of it were written words of lament and mourning and woe." And in Daniel 8:26, "The vision of the evenings and mornings that has been given you is true, but seal up the vision, for it concerns the distant future." and again in 12:4 "But you, Daniel, close up and seal the words of the scroll until the time of the end." The vision in Isaiah gives us no clues regarding the content of the scroll but contributes to the understanding that no one will be able to read it. Ezekiel's vision is the only one that tells us that there was writing on both sides— very unusual for a scroll—and that it contains words of lament and mourning and woe. Many commentators seem to connect the scroll here in Revelation with the one mentioned in Ezekiel but it's hard to ignore the scrolls mentioned in Daniel as they specifically make reference to the significance of the scroll in end-times. And could they all be referring to the same scroll? It's another one of those things that I personally can't resolve.

Loud Voice and Mighty Angel (v.2)

Here's that loud voice again (see 1:10) so we know an announcement is coming. I wonder why we're told that this is a mighty angel? It makes me think that the voice would be especially loud, much louder than if it were just an ordinary angel—Is there such a thing as an ordinary angel?

It is interesting that the criterion for being able to open the scroll is one of worthiness, not strength (Who is strong enough to open the scroll?), or intelligence (Who knows how to open the scroll?). What makes one worthy to break the seals? So far we don't know.

"No One In Heaven or On Earth or Under The Earth" (v.3)

Up to this point the events of this vision seem to have been taking place in heaven since we know that John had entered through the door into heaven. Here we are told that no one in heaven or on earth or under the earth for that matter, could open the scroll. Obviously there is at least an awareness of earth in the vision as well. This is probably not a big deal except to recognize that the search for someone to open the scroll wasn't just confined to heaven.

I wonder what is meant by "under the earth"? The only other place this phrase appears in the NIV, is in Philippians 2:9–11 where it says, "Therefore God exalted him to the highest place and gave him the name that is above every name, that at the name of Jesus every knee should bow, in heaven and on earth and under the earth, and every tongue acknowledge that Jesus Christ is Lord, to the glory of God the Father." Some commentators suggest that these three realms; in heaven, on earth, and under the earth, refer to the angels, living people, and departed spirits. However, most agree that the point being made both here and in Philippians is that it is universal. Here the entire universe is searched.

As I read verse 3 I can't help but feel a sense of hopelessness—of sadness.

"I Wept" (v.4)

And as we read on we see John expressing that sadness. It provides insight into just how important the contents of the scroll are, and how important it is that the scroll be opened.

"One Of the Elders Said" (v.5)

John tells us of an elder speaking to him only two times in Revelation—here and in 7:13. Typically the angels do the talking, and the elders do the worshipping. So I wonder why, in these two passages they interact with John? In both cases, the elder is speaking directly to John, and is setting the scene for us to learn something very important. The elder tells John to see the Lion of the tribe of Judah, and that He is able to open the scroll.

The only other place in Scripture where I can find a connection between a lion and the tribe of Judah is in Genesis 49:9a where it says "You are a lion's cub, O Judah." Matthew 1:1–16 records the genealogy of Jesus. There we see that His lineage is through the tribe of Judah.

Isaiah 11:1 says, "A shoot will come up from the stump of Jesse; from his roots a Branch will bear fruit." David was the son of Jesse who also descended from the tribe of Judah. For the reader of Revelation who is familiar with Old Testament Scripture, these two unique and interesting names—the Lion of the tribe of Judah, and the Root of David—would likely confirm that the one who was found worthy, was indeed the promised Messiah. He proved His worth by dying on the cross for our sins and rising victorious over death.

See The Lion, Saw The Lamb (v.6)

> ⁶ *Then I saw a Lamb, looking as if it had been slain, standing at the center of the throne, encircled by the four living creatures and the elders. The Lamb had seven horns and seven eyes, which are the seven spirits of God sent out into all the earth.*

Now things get a bit weird again. John was told to see the Lion, but what he actually sees is a slain Lamb. It's like a hologram. Look at it one way and you see a Lion of the tribe of Judah. Look at it another and you see what appears to be a slain Lamb. He doesn't seem to be bothered by this difference. Rather it seems that even as he sees the Lamb he knows it is the Lion—cool stuff!

I find it interesting to consider the concept of a lion—which I think of as powerful—juxtaposed over the image of a lamb—which I think of as submissive. He is both at the same time. As one commentator states, "In one brilliant stroke John portrays the central theme of NT revelation - victory through sacrifice"[12].

Have you ever stopped when reading this passage and wondered about the concept of a slain lamb standing? This is an image that for years I've simply glossed over, rarely giving it a second thought. But even in this familiar image, there is great meaning. It is another reminder of his victory over death. How else could something that is slain, stand?

To this point in this second vision, I have assumed that the one on the throne was God, but here we're told that the Lamb is standing at the center of the throne. This seems different than in 4:6 where we were told that the living creatures were at the center, *around* the throne. So it would seem to me that this slain Lamb is *on* the throne. So is it God on the throne, or is it Jesus on the throne? In the letter to Laodicea (3:21) in the promise to the victorious, Christ tells us that He sits with his Father on His throne. This confirms for me that it is the Father and the Son on the throne together.

And all those horns and eyes—what do we make of them? It says they are the seven spirits of God that earlier we said represented the Holy Spirit.

Therefore, on the throne we seem to have melded God the Father, with Jesus the Son and the Holy Spirit—the Holy Trinity together as one. What a wonderful reminder of the miracle of the Trinity.

He Took the Scroll (v.7)

But here the identities are again separated as the slain Lamb, Jesus, takes the scroll from the hand of the one sitting on the throne. They are one but separate.

Four Living Creatures and Twenty-four Elders (v.8)

Once you start asking questions, seeking meaning, it seems that everything is up for grabs. I wonder why John doesn't simply refer to the living creatures and the elders. Why does he so often specify the *four* living creatures and the *twenty-four* elders? What are we to make of this? Is it a level of detail that is intended to constantly remind us of the accuracy of the vision? Or are the numbers intended to constantly remind us of who these living creatures and elders represent? Or is it simply a path down which one could wander and end up missing the fullness of the message of Revelation?

They each had a harp and a golden bowl. The harp is used to make music, a common part of worship, especially of corporate worship. The golden bowls of incense, we are told, represent the prayers of God's people. Together I see two key aspects of our relationship with God. One is an outward expression of praise and the other is more internal. Each are a key component of our relationship with Him.

"Every Tribe and Language and People and Nation" (v.9–10)

> [9] *And they sang a new song, saying:*
> *"You are worthy to take the scroll and to open its seals, because*
> *you were slain, and with your blood you purchased for God persons*
> *from every tribe and language and people and nation.*
> [10] *You have made them to be a kingdom and priests to*
> *serve our God, and they will reign on the earth."*

Why is this referred to as a new song? Is it because this situation hasn't occurred before and so the occasion calls for something new? The phrase "new song" appears six times in the Psalms (in the NIV), once in Isaiah, and then twice here in Revelation. "The content of the song is always an expression of praise for God's victory over the enemy, sometimes including thanksgiving for God's work of creation."[13] The details of this new song are a celebration that someone is worthy to open the seals. They serve as a review and reminder of the story of salvation; something that we see repeated in many ways throughout Revelation.

If there was any doubt in my mind regarding who was the slain Lamb and the Lion of Judah and the Root of David, it is made very clear here that John is showing us the many sides of Jesus.

I am struck by the significance of this reference to "every tribe and language and people and nation." When reading it casually, I understand this to mean that salvation is available to everyone. But this time in reading it, I've come to realize what that means. My image of life in heaven has always been of everyone looking like me, speaking like me, and having similar attitudes. I realize that I haven't even thought about the fact that diversity would continue to exist eternally. It seems such a silly point and I'm sure that the idea of diversity in heaven is something most people probably take for granted—but what can I say. I find the thought that we will retain those things about ourselves that make us each unique extremely comforting. Did you notice the link from verse 10 back to 1:6?

"The Voice Of Many Angels" (v.11–12)

As we move on to verse 11, notice that he heard the *voice*, not the *voices*, of many angels. There are so many that they can't be counted surrounding the throne scene. Yet they speak as one.

> ¹² *In a loud voice they were saying: "Worthy is the Lamb, who was slain, to receive power and wealth and wisdom and strength and honor and glory and praise!"*

Back in 4:11 we saw a similar song of praise directed to our Lord and God. Here it is directed to the Lamb. I wonder why these seven things are mentioned: power, wealth, wisdom, strength, honor, glory, and praise. Is it significant that there are seven attributes mentioned? Or is the significance in what each attribute represents? The list seems to cover pretty well everything we aspire to achieve in our lives—it seems to be a rather complete list.

"Every Creature" (v.13)

And then, not only the angels around the throne, but every being is involved in the act of praising. If everyone is praising the Lamb doesn't that suggest that there are no non-believers left? How does that work?

An Aside: *If we try to follow these chapters in Revelation as a sequential unveiling of events, things like this seem out of whack. Perhaps if we look at it as the view from heaven where the concept of time is very different than it is here on earth, it may become possible to see this chapter as a fifty-thousand-foot view of all that follows —a synopsis of the events of Revelation.*

"Amen" (v.14)

And once again we are pulled back to the four living creatures and the elders. I wonder if there is any significance to the fact that it doesn't say there were twenty-four elders here. It is one of those things I'm not going to worry about. The important point, I believe, is that they were all worshipping God. With the amen we are told so be it or to quote the captain of the Starship Enterprise, "make it so".

Some Things To Think About

As I look back on chapter 5 some key thoughts emerge.

- The content of the scroll suggests that God has a message for us that is important for us to hear.
- The message is sacred and only our Lord Jesus Christ, is worthy to reveal it to us.

- Our triune God—Father, Son and Holy Spirit—continues to reign on His throne.
- We are all invited to join in the praises, the worshipping, taking place around the throne both corporately (harps) and privately (prayers).

Revelation 6

The Seals (6:1–17)

Most commentators tell us that what follows is the first of three judgments in the book of Revelation; the opening of the seals, the trumpets, and the bowls. I'm not sure why they are called judgments but I'm sure there is a good reason. However, what we learn about here in the opening of the seals doesn't feel like how I'd expect a judgment to feel. In many ways it feels more like a review of life in the current church age.

There is a strong parallel between the opening of the first six seals and the passages in Matthew 24 and Luke 21 where Jesus responds to the question of "What will be the sign of your coming?" (Matthew 24:3) My understanding of this passage in Matthew, the Olivet discourse, is not that these are signs of end-times but rather are realities of life during our present church age. They are relevant to our lives today and have been relevant to all generations throughout the centuries. Because of this, I'm inclined to believe that what we read here relates to things happening around us either here on earth or in the heavenlies right now, and that the purpose of this passage is to capture the attention of Christians familiar with the message of the Olivet discourse as a way of reminding us of who God is.

First Seal and the First Living Creature (v.1)

> [1] *I watched as the Lamb opened the first of the seven seals. Then I heard one of the four living creatures say in a voice like thunder, "Come!"*

The openings of these first four seals are the only times where we see or hear the four living creatures speak about anything other than worship. Naturally, I wonder if that's significant. Earlier I wondered if the fact that they are called *living* creatures was meant to remind us that they are active today. By using the living creatures to introduce the four horses and riders are we being told that these are current day events—that they are happening now?

As I am writing these words, there is a storm brewing outside my home. With that as my background, it's not hard to understand that a voice like thunder would be hard to ignore. It would be very loud and perhaps somewhat sudden.

When the living creature says "come", to whom is he speaking? Is it John? Or is it someone or something else? We are about to meet what is often referred to as the 'Four Horsemen of the Apocalypse'.

As we move through the openings of these first four seals, we will be introduced to four different horses and riders. Each horse is a different color. Oddly we are told about the color of each horse before we learn anything about its rider, so I'm certain that the color, and what it symbolizes is important to the message.

First Seal—White Horse (v.2)

This first horse is white. The color white symbolizes victory, purity and resurrection[14]. As we read further into the description and combine the color white with the fact that the rider is wearing a crown, it makes sense that here the color symbolizes victory.

There is another white horse and rider in Revelation in chapter 19:11. Is this the same horse and rider? That rider is armed with a sword out of his mouth—this one carries a bow. While most experts suggest that they are not the same, I'm not sure and will leave the question unanswered.

This rider has a crown and carries a bow, but we don't see reference to arrows so is he expected to actually do anything with the bow or is it simply symbolic? In the Old Testament the bow was a symbol of military prowess. Is the crown a victor's wreath?

Other translations of this verse tell us that "he came out conquering, and to conquer" (ESV) rather than "he rode out as a conqueror bent on conquest" as it does in the NIV. I think there is a subtle difference possible in the interpretation of these two phrases. I can imagine a rider on a white horse, proudly riding out as a conqueror bent on conquest but never actually doing anything. Whereas, if I'm told that same rider on the white horse went out conquering, I'm left with the impression that he is actually doing something. As I proceed here I'm going to assume that the horse and rider are actually doing something rather than just posing as a conqueror.

Antichrist? (v.2)

There are some interesting differences among commentators on the meaning of the white horse and the bow. Some see the rider on the white horse as the antichrist or as a false Christ bringing a false peace tying this text to Mathew 24:5, "For many will come in my name, claiming, 'I am the Messiah,' and will deceive many." Makes sense to me but I've had some other thoughts on this first horse and rider that take things in a different direction.

An Aside: *As you read my thoughts that follow please don't take my word for it just because I've written down my opinion. Think it through for yourself. Discuss it with others. Prayerfully consider the text and form your own opinion.*

Could this horse and its rider represent the spread of the gospel? Could the conquering be an active, present-day, on-going activity of kingdom advancement—see Matthew 24:14? Is it a reminder that through Christ we can have victory over sin?

By being introduced first, are we to see him as the most important of the four horses and riders? What if this is the same horse and rider that we see in 19:11? And if it is, then this is the only one with true power and authority, and in fact, is the only one that actually wins the victory.

So many questions—so few answers.

Second Seal—Red Horse (v.3–4)

> [3] When the Lamb opened the second seal, I heard the second living creature say, "Come!"
> [4] Then another horse came out, a fiery red one.

And now a different living creature is doing the talking.

In this case the horse is not just red, but fiery red. Red represents slaughter, war, and violence[15]. The fact that it was fiery red makes it seem intense.

And as we read on in the verse we will learn that the power given to the horse's rider, and the fact that he is carrying a sword is consistent with the concept of slaughter, war and violence. Here we are told that the rider was given the power to do some things but we aren't actually told that he did it. I find this a bit disconcerting, but perhaps I'm getting a bit too nitpicky.

The connection here seems to be with Matthew 24:6–7a, "You will hear of wars and rumors of wars, but see to it that you are not alarmed. Such things must happen, but the end is still to come. Nation will rise against nation, and kingdom against kingdom." The message is that another of the realities of our lives is the reality of war, of international strife.

And is war a fact of our everyday lives? Of course it is, and has been since the beginning of time. Every generation that has lived since these words were written has experienced war in some form.

Third Seal—Black Horse (v.5–6)

> [5] *When the Lamb opened the third seal, I heard the third living creature say, "Come!" I looked, and there before me was a black horse! Its rider was holding a pair of scales in his hand.*

Black represents disaster, or famine[16]. In our modern-day society, the pair of scales typically represent justice. Historically scales were used for the purpose of measuring out grain. So, in this case, I think the scales represent the act of buying and selling.

And in verse 6 we learn that grains used for food—wheat and barley—have become scarce. In fact even the luxuries of oil and wine are scarce. Matthew 24:7 talks of famine and indeed, famine is another reality of our lives in many parts of the world.

I can't help being intrigued by the phrase "what sounded like a voice" in verse 6. Because this thing that sounded like a voice actually speaks I wonder why he didn't just say 'voice'. Perhaps it was because he didn't actually see who, or what was speaking—or perhaps he simply didn't want to tell us at this point in the story.

An Aside: *As I continue to investigate the opening of the seals, I am having trouble rationalizing the things that I think I'm learning with some of the perspectives on these passages. Some people interpret them as events of the second coming, but the concepts of world wars, of famine and disasters aren't future-based. They are and have been realities of life for every generation. I'm becoming more and more committed to the connections to Matthew 24, particularly as it relates to the four horsemen described here.*

Fourth Seal—Pale Horse (v.7–8)

> *⁷ When the Lamb opened the fourth seal, I heard the voice of the fourth living creature say, "Come!"*
> *⁸ I looked, and there before me was a pale horse!*

The pale coloring of this horse is a reflection of the pallor of death, and we see that the rider is indeed Death. It's not clear whether Hades— the place of the dead—is on another horse, sitting on the same horse, or just floating through, so I'm inclined to think that it doesn't matter.

Here again we are told that the rider was given a power to do something, but we have no evidence that a fourth of the earth was actually killed—only that Death and Hades were limited in the size of their target area so-to-speak.

This is the first time in this passage that we are told that the power given wasn't over all the earth, but only over a portion of it. I'm not certain what the significance of this is, or of the fact that we're told it was over one-fourth of the earth. In the message of the trumpets that follows we will see that destruction there is over one-third of the earth. Perhaps there is a pattern of increasing destruction. Or it may be that what we are to take from this is a sense of increasing urgency.

Once again, if we look back at Matthew 24 we can see that death through wars, natural disasters and persecution are to be expected during our lifetimes.

A quick look back in Revelation (1:18) reminds me that Jesus was described as the one who holds the keys to death and Hades. For me, this acts as a reminder that whatever we may make of the where and when of these events, it is still God that remains in control.

Another interesting correlation here is with Ezekiel 14:21, "For this is what the Sovereign LORD says: How much worse will it be when I send against Jerusalem my four dreadful judgments—sword and famine and wild beasts and plague—to kill its men and their animals!" I'm not sure what to do with this connection other than to note that it connects the word 'judgment' to all these thing, so am leaving it for now.

Fifth Seal and the Altar (v.9–11)

> *⁹ When he opened the fifth seal, I saw under the altar the souls of those who had been slain because of the word of God and the testimony they had maintained.*

This is the first time an altar is mentioned in Revelation. I wonder if this altar is an echo to the altar of burnt offering, or the altar of incense in the tabernacle—see Exodus 27 and 30? On one altar, sacrifices were made. From the other, the prayers of the saints were offered. I found opposing opinions expressed by different commentators on this topic. I'm inclined to see this altar as a reminder of the altar of burnt offering—of sacrifice—because we are told that these are ones who had been slain because of the word of God. But it isn't hard to accept the concept that they would be offering up prayers—the prayers of the saints. Maybe it represents a blending of the two altars.

I wonder if there is any significance to the fact that they are under the altar. The first thought that comes to mind is that this would mean that they are under God's protection as they wait. I like that idea.

Later in chapter 7 we will be told about the 144,000 who are sealed, and I wonder if these are the same—more on this later.

Just as in 5:12, where we heard many angels cry out in one loud voice, here we hear many martyrs calling out in one loud voice. They are united in their question. They are wondering how much longer they must wait for justice to prevail. I have no trouble relating to their cry. It reminds me of the many times I've wondered about what appears to be an unfairness in society. About how those who do evil often seem to go unpunished, and of how those who do good often suffer. My question tends to be "Why?" but sometimes it changes to "When will they get their proper punishment?"

And the answer to their question is to wait. To wait until the full number of their fellow servants are killed. That's a hard answer to swallow and leads to so many more questions. What is the 'full number'? Why must more die? More questions with no clear answers.

Times of waiting can be used as teachable space, when God wants to reveal things to us about ourselves or about Him. Are the martyrs told to wait so that we, the rest of mankind, can learn more about Him?

But there is also the matter of the white robes that they were given. Without looking too closely, the feeling that I get from the fact that they were each given a white robe, is one of significance—that they are special. The robe must signify something important. One commentator says the "white robe is a symbol of blessedness and rest"[17]. In the letter to the church of Sardis, the promise there was that those who are victorious will be dressed in white.

Matthew 24:9 says, "Then you will be handed over to be persecuted and put to death, and you will be hated by all nations because of me." The persecution of Christians—of martyrdom—is another one of those realities of the current church age. Although it is not all that visible in our typical North American society, as I write this, the media is filled with news stories of the killing and persecution of Christians in many parts of the world. So do these first five seals point to things to come or are they a reflection of life in the here and now? It feels pretty much like an on-going reality of life.

"The Sixth Seal" (v.12–17)

> [12] I watched as he opened the sixth seal. There was a great earthquake. The sun turned black like sackcloth made of goat hair, the whole moon turned blood red,
> [13] and the stars in the sky fell to earth, as figs drop from a fig tree when shaken by a strong wind.

To this point, the seals have revealed events or actions that have a man-made quality to them. Although we have been told of the wars, famine, and disasters that we should expect, the results of these things have been described in a fairly low-key manner.

Now things start to get really interesting! With this sixth seal, it feels like God is taking charge. The events described here are not of man. Following on the theme of looking back at the Olivet discourse in Matthew 24, we continue to see a parallel with verse 29 where it says "Immediately after the distress of those days the sun will be darkened, and the moon will not give its light; the stars will fall from the sky, and the heavenly bodies will be shaken." Although we are reminded in Matthew 24:36 that "no one knows about that day or hour", this type of cataclysmic event does seem to portend the beginning of end-times. There are several passages in the Old Testament that provide similar warnings. Check out Joel 2:31 and 3:15; Haggai 2:6, Isaiah 13:10 and 34:4 or Jeremiah 4:23–28.

All of this is so terrifying that everyone hides! Looking back to Isaiah 2:19, we read "Men will flee to caves in the rocks and to holes in the ground from dread of the LORD and the splendor of his majesty, when he rises to shake the earth." In John's description here, it is very clear that everyone will be equally afraid. God's might is so great that it will instill fear, not only in the hearts and minds of the ordinary person on earth, but on those who in theory hold great power and authority. God's might trumps everyone else's.

And in these final verses of chapter 6, there is once again a subtle reminder of the triune God. Notice that the people are calling out to be hidden from "him who sits on the throne and from the wrath of the Lamb". It sounds like two separate entities and yet they share their wrath as a single emotion—who can withstand it.

Some Things To Think About

As I review this chapter with the opening of the six seals, and its parallels to the Olivet Discourse, I wonder about the significance of the relationship between these passages in Scripture. First century Christians would have been familiar with the words of Matthew and Luke—the authors who recorded the Olivet Discourse. For them, hearing similar words from John would have been a reminder that God understands the challenges faced in their lives as Christians and that they are not forgotten. That same reminder holds true today, just as it has through the generations between.

With the opening of the sixth seal we are also reminded that God's patience will run out—the "great day of their wrath" will come. When it does, justice will prevail.

Revelation 7

This chapter is seen as an interlude in Revelation. Some believe that the purpose of the interlude is to provide more information about the martyrs seen under the altar when the fifth seal was opened. The change in pace certainly feels like an interlude, or stop-action, from what was becoming pretty intense in chapter 6. It's interesting that the last words in that chapter were "who can withstand it", and here in chapter 7 we learn about the sealing of the servants of our God, and then further in Revelation learn that those who have been sealed will indeed withstand the day of their wrath. So perhaps it's an aside more than an interlude whose purpose is simply to address the question of chapter 6.

As we proceed through this chapter I believe we are given the answer to the question from two different perspectives. The first part of the chapter talks about the process of sealing, and the second part is a scene showing us the reward for those who have been sealed.

144,000 Sealed (7:1–8)

> [1] After this I saw four angels standing at the four corners of the earth, holding back the four winds of the earth to prevent any wind from blowing on the land or on the sea or on any tree.
> [2] Then I saw another angel coming up from the east, having the seal of the living God. He called out in a loud voice to the four angels who had been given power to harm the land and the sea:
> [3] "Do not harm the land or the sea or the trees until we put a seal on the foreheads of the servants of our God."

Four Angels, Four Corners Of the Earth, Four Winds (v.1)

We saw the phrase "after this" used at the beginning of chapter 4 where John transitions from the letters to the seven churches to this more all-encompassing portion of Revelation. Used again here, I believe this may be a new vision to John rather than a continuation of the vision he has been describing thus far. As I imagine John's experience in my human terms, as chapter 6 ends it would be like waking up from an intense dream—one that leaves you feeling quite shaken. Then you gradually fall back asleep—or into a spirit-filled vision state—and the vision takes on a gentler tone, at least for a short while.

The imagery of the four angels standing at the four corners of the earth holding back the four winds is cool. Referring to the four corners of the earth is often used to mean the entire earth. The reference to the four winds seems to imply pending judgment or destruction.

The part that strikes me most strongly in this visual however, is the sense of calm that comes to me as I imagine this event. Imagine no wind blowing anywhere. Things would be still. It would be like standing in what could be the eye of a storm or perhaps the calm before the storm. It could make one feel almost hyper-aware; very sensitive to what happens next.

Angel From the East (v.2)

I wonder if it is significant that the angel came up from the east? This causes me to think about the story of the birth of Jesus, and the fact that the wise men came up from the east to worship at the baby's side. Another thought is that the sun rises in the east; an indication, perhaps, of a new day dawning. One commentator says "some see in it a reminiscence of Ezek 43:4"[18] which says "The glory of the LORD entered the temple through the gate facing east." I find that I favor the idea of the dawning of a new day here. For those who are about to receive the seal it is the beginning of a new day, as we know that this seal will protect them from many of the things that follow.

Four Angels Given Power (v.2–3)

I'm having trouble understanding who the four angels in verse 2 are. I've assumed that they are the four angels mentioned in verse 1, but here we are told that they had been given power to harm the land and the sea. Are they connected to the four horsemen discussed in chapter 6? What if they are the four horsemen? Earlier I suggested that they represented the realities of life in the church age (based on text in Matthew 24). At the end of chapter 6 we saw what could be identified as the beginning of the end, and here, in this pause, we see that the horsemen—or angels—are told to stop what they're doing until the servants of God have been sealed.

My mind just took off on a path that may or may not make sense here but I was thinking about the Israelites on the night of Passover when they were told to go into their homes, put the seal of lamb's blood on their doors and wait while God did his work. So here in these early verses of chapter 7, we have four angels holding back the winds, and another set of four angels who have been told to stop what they're doing. Everything has come to a standstill so that the sealing process can take place.

The Seal (v.3)

Most commentators seem to agree that historically the seal would have been thought of as something like a signet ring used to press an image into wax. "The resulting imprint implied authenticity and ownership and protection."[19]

In Ephesians 4:30 it says "And do not grieve the Holy Spirit of God, with whom you were sealed for the day of redemption." And in 2 Timothy 2:19, "Nevertheless, God's solid foundation stands firm, sealed with this inscription: 'The Lord knows those who are his," and, "Everyone who confesses the name of the Lord must turn away from wickedness."" It is very difficult to ignore the significance of these passages to the concept of the servants of God being sealed as described here in Revelation.

This is a special seal; it is the seal of the living God! We are His and He will protect us.

One of the best passages in my mind that gives us an insight to what the phrase "Living God" means is in Jeremiah 10:10 which says, "But the LORD is the true God; he is the living God, the eternal King. When he is angry, the earth trembles; the nations cannot endure his wrath." So this angel that has come from the east has the seal of the most powerful being.

Why put the seal on their foreheads? I wonder if the link to the forehead goes back to Exodus 13:9, "This observance will be for you like a sign on your hand a reminder on your forehead" as part of the instructions for the Feast of the Unleavened Bread. Or looking at it in simpler terms, perhaps the forehead is one of the most visible parts of a person's body, and hence the message here is that the seal of the living God should be visible in our lives.

And finally, we need to consider who are the servants of our God. Frequently we see Moses referenced as the servant of God—see 1

Chronicles 6:49, 2 Chronicles 24:9, Nehemiah 10:29 and Daniel 9:11. In the New Testament Paul identifies himself as a servant of God in Titus 1:1, and James does so as well in James 1:1. In his second letter to the Corinthians, Paul refers to them all as servants of God (2 Corinthians 6:4) and in 1 Peter 2:16 we are instructed to "live as servants of God."

So the servants of God mentioned here are all who are followers of Christ.

Heard the Number 144,000 (v.4–8)

Now it gets a bit confusing. Who gets sealed here? Is it all servants of God, or is it simply 144,000 people from all the tribes of Israel?

144,000 is 12 x 12 x 1000. The number twelve signifies completeness and in this case, I believe that the number 144,000 is meant to confirm that all the servants of God will be sealed. In fact, if we look at Ephesians 1:13–14, "And you also were included in Christ when you heard the word of truth, the gospel of your salvation. Having believed, you were marked in him with a seal, the promised Holy Spirit, who is a deposit guaranteeing our inheritance until the redemption of those who are God's possession - to the praise of his glory."

But why then are we given such a specific list of tribes? And why, by the way, is this list of tribes different from the one in Genesis 49 and another one in Ezekiel 48? This question is too big for me.

My simplest thought here is that John specifically mentions the tribes of Israel because his audience here is not only the Gentiles of the first century but also the Jews. The Jews knew they were God's chosen people, but were often openly opposing the Christians in their beliefs. But God, through John, wanted to reassure them that they were not forgotten. But perhaps He was also making a point that they can't get in, so-to-speak, simply because of their Jewish heritage. They must first acknowledge Jesus as the promised Messiah, and accept His promise of salvation. Perhaps that's why there are numbers attached to each tribe rather than saying "all those of the tribes of Israel." He's making a statement that a subset of the tribes will be sealed. I don't know, this is a tough one to get a grip on. It's one of those questions that will remain unanswered for me, a Gentile. However, if I were of Jewish descent, I would probably take more time to consider it—would my Jewish heritage guarantee entry to Heaven, or do I need to consider Christ's offer of salvation, and accept, and acknowledge, that He is indeed the promised Messiah?

The Great Multitude in White Robes (7:9–17)

The previous verses describe the sealing process. The verses that follow describe their heavenly reward.

Saw the Multitude (v.9)

> ⁹ *After this I looked, and there before me was a great multitude that no one could count, from every nation, tribe, people and language, standing before the throne and before the Lamb. They were wearing white robes and were holding palm branches in their hands.*

Remember in chapter 5 when John was told to see the Lion, but when he turned he saw a Lamb? Here John *heard* the number of those who were sealed—144,000—and now when he looks he *sees* a great multitude. The multitude represents more than those listed from the tribes of Israel, which reassures me that the heavenly reward is available, and will be given, to many more. And we know that the multitude expands beyond the limits of those who belong to the tribes of Israel because we are told that they are from every nation, tribe, people, and language.

We are back viewing the throne with the great multitude worshiping God. In 5:9 the crowd around the throne was celebrating the fact that they had found the one who was worthy to open the seals. They were singing: "You are worthy to take the scroll and to open its seals, because you were slain, and with your blood you purchased for God persons from every tribe and language and people and nation." And here we see the persons from every nation, tribe, people, and language standing before the throne and the Lamb.

If there is a connection to the previous verses of this chapter it is to tell all of us that salvation and sealing is available not only to God's chosen people, the tribes of Israel, but to all of us. God is confirming the original covenant with the Jews, and then also confirming the inclusion of all believers regardless of birth.

Just as the martyrs under the altar in 6:11 were given white robes, the multitude before the throne are also wearing white robes. We are assured of their special relationship with God because of the white robes that have been washed in the blood of the Lamb. These robes represent blessedness, holiness and purity.

The reference to the palm branches they were holding reminds me of John 12:13, "They took palm branches and went out to meet him, shouting, "Hosanna!"" In the Old Testament, in Leviticus 23:40 we are also told, "On the first day you are to take choice fruit from the trees, and palm fronds, leafy branches and poplars, and rejoice before the LORD your God for seven days." So the palm branches represented celebration.

Team Chant (v.10–12)

They are all celebrating and worshipping together—like a team chant. This scene of worship in verse 10, is similar to the ones in chapters

4 and 5. It feels like this jump back to the throne scene is intended to remind us that regardless of what else may be happening, God is on His throne and we should be worshipping Him.

The Elder Asks (v.13–14)

Then we get in verse 13, what seems like an odd question. One of the elders asks John who the ones in white robes are. The only other time we have heard an elder speak to John was in 5:5 where he told John not to weep. It seems strange to me that the elder wouldn't know who the ones in the white robes are, so I have to assume he is testing John to see if he has figured it out, or perhaps this exchange has been included in the text simply as a way to bring the information out.

And based on how verse 14 begins, it seems that John agrees with me; the elder knows who these people are. We are told that they have come out of the great tribulation.

"The Great Tribulation" (v.14)

In the NIV, this is the only place that the word *tribulation* appears although it is used frequently in many of the other translations. The Greek word here is *thlipsis* which is the same word used in Matthew 24:21 during the Olivet Discourse I mentioned earlier. In the NIV it has been translated as *distress*—"For then there will be great distress, unequaled from the beginning of the world until now—and never to be equaled again."

So is this great tribulation mentioned here referring to the persecution that is a reality in the current church age, or to a coming period yet to be experienced? I know that on this point there are differences of opinion, and I have come to realize that I don't have an answer to the question. Do I need to know? I think, as I've said before, that I need to know that I have made a decision to follow Christ; to accept the salvation He has made available to me. If I am living in the age of the great tribulation right now or if it is yet to come and I am still alive for it, my decision, and my subsequent actions do not change.

They Serve Him and He Will Shelter Them (v.15)

As we are shown the redeemed in Christ around the throne serving and worshipping Him—are those two different things?—we are reminded that this is a two-way relationship. We serve and worship Him and He shelters us.

"Never Again" (v.16–17)

And here in this confusion of present and future, is a link to the final chapters of Revelation where we are told in the wonderful description of the New Jerusalem, that God will live with us (21:3); he will wipe every tear from our eyes (21:4); we will drink from the spring of the water of life (21:6) and there will be no sun or moon (21:23).

Some Things To Think About

Our God is an awesome God. He made a covenant with Israel and continues to honor that covenant. Similarly, He has made a new covenant with all of us as we see in Hebrews 9:15, "For this reason Christ is the mediator of a new covenant, that those who are called may receive the promised eternal inheritance."

And here in this chapter, we have seen that covenant honored when we were given a glimpse of the multitude from every nation, tribe, people, and language standing before the throne.

Our God keeps His word.

Revelation 8

The Seventh Seal and the Golden Censer (8:1–5)

> *¹ When he opened the seventh seal, there was silence in heaven for about half an hour.*

And now we return to the action. When we left the opening of the sixth seal we read about the great earthquake that had everyone hiding. They were questioning who could withstand the wrath of the Lamb. With that question answered in chapter 7, we can move forward with the opening of the seventh seal.

"Silence In Heaven" (v.1)

I have been curious about the silence mentioned here. Is there a biblical significance to the concept of silence, and if there is, how does it fit here? In Zephaniah 1:7 it says, "Be silent before the Sovereign LORD, for the day of the LORD is near." This concept of silence appears to have a sense of reverence combined with pending judgment. Psalm 101:5, "Whoever slanders his neighbor in secret, him will I put to silence" is just one of many passages where we are given the sense of punishment or judgment associated with silence. As we progress through the message of Revelation we will certainly see the judgment side of things. But why the silence here with the opening of this seventh seal?

Chapter 7 started with a sense of silence, and what followed seemed to be an aside from the action of chapter 6. Could the silence here be intended for the same purpose? I'm not sure how to explain the thoughts that are spinning in my head here, so forgive me if I wander about a bit in trying to make sense of it. With the opening of the sixth seal (6:12) we saw that God's patience had come to an end. He knows life in this current church age isn't easy. He knows what we've had to deal with, and He's let it go on as long as He can. But now it is time to bring it to an end as indicated by the cataclysmic events of 6:12–14. John took a time-out to assure us that as the sealed in Christ we have been promised a place around the throne of God, and now he takes us back to the opening of the seals. This is the seventh, and final seal. Its opening is almost anticlimactic, at least for now. Instead of some final event taking place, we are instead introduced to the seven trumpets. It's like opening one box, and finding inside it another box, and so on, and so on. Is the silence a way of holding open the first box while we look into the next one? Is it God's way, through John, of giving us another chance; of stating things another way in case we don't understand? Is it possible that ultimately with the boxes all open, the judgments will come to an end all at the same time, and finally we will see what has been written on the scroll that has been sealed thus far? I wonder.

"About Half an Hour" (v.1)

This is the only place in Scripture where I can find a reference to half an hour. It seems to be suggesting a very short period of time.

This is also the only time in Revelation that a time period is approximated. He doesn't say "for half an hour," he says "for *about* half an hour." Why the *about*? Elsewhere in Scripture when the word about is used in conjunction with numbers or time periods, the numbers are generally quite large, except in Luke 22:59 where we see reference to "About an hour." This is one of those things that I'm not going to lose any sleep over, but it does cause me to wonder just a bit.

"The Seven Angels" (v.2)

John says he saw seven angels. These aren't just any seven angels, they are *the* seven angels who stand before God. We haven't seen them referenced this way before, but will in the chapters that follow. I wonder if there is a connection between these angels and the angels of the seven churches (see 1:20). If there is, how is that connection significant?

It's also important, I think, to be reminded that they were standing before God. As I delve into the details about these judgments, I find it very easy to get caught up in the drama of it all. It comes as no surprise, therefore, that John has taken the opportunity to remind us that God is in control. These events aren't a freak of nature like the summer snow storm brewing outside my window right now. God is orchestrating this for a reason!

The seven angels were each given a trumpet. Why trumpets? Why not harps? What makes the trumpet particularly significant here? Trumpets remind me of sharp, clear sounds. They are usually quite loud. Trumpets are often sounded before announcements of great significance. I'm sure that their purpose here is to get, and to hold, our attention. And to top it all off, in Matthew 24:31 we are told, "And he will send his angels with a loud trumpet call" So, is this intended as a transition from the realities of life in the church age, to the time of Christ's return? Or is it a call to attention while we are given a final word of warning? I'm still not sure—can we ever be completely certain?

"A Golden Censer" (v.3–5)

So we have seven angels standing before God, and they are each holding a trumpet. Now, along comes another angel with a golden censer standing at an altar. Later in verse 3, we will learn of a golden altar, and that it stands in front of the throne.

The Golden Altar of Incense stood before the entrance to the Holy of Holies in the tabernacle that Moses and the Israelites were instructed to build while wandering in the desert after fleeing Egypt. It is from this altar that prayers of intercession were offered to God through the burning of incense. But there are two altars mentioned in this sequence of verses. Are they the same? Or, is the first altar the same one mentioned when opening the fifth seal where the martyrs were under the altar?

If I follow the logic of two altars, then the action would appear to be that the angel started at the altar where the martyrs were waiting and asking for judgment. Here he (does an angel have gender?) is given much incense representing the prayers of these martyrs and of all God's people. From there he moves to the golden altar to offer up the prayers to God. This is consistent with the use of the altars in the tabernacle. During the days of the Exodus, the priest picked up coals from the altar of burnt offering, carried them in his censer to the altar of incense where he threw incense on the coals and the smoke rose up to God. See Exodus 30:1–10 and Leviticus 16:12–13 for more background.

My take on this scene is that we, or rather the martyrs waiting under the altar, are being told that our prayers are about to be answered.

As the censer is hurled on the earth, it feels like the gunshot at the starting line of a race. A scene of thunder, lightning, and earthquake is kicked off that will be repeated in the following chapters of Revelation. The question that continues to revolve in my mind is whether they all refer to the same event, or are they different events?

Something else has just struck me about this chapter. The opening of the seals started in chapter 6 with the role of the Lamb front and center. The message would immediately capture the attention of New Testament believers—both Jew and Gentile. Here, however, we begin with a throwback to the Old Testament story of the Exodus—a story that would speak to the people of the tribes of Israel, including those who may never have chosen to acknowledge Jesus Christ as the promised Messiah.

The Trumpets (8:6–13)

Joel 2:1 says, "Blow the trumpet in Zion; sound the alarm on my holy hill. Let all who live in the land tremble, for the day of the LORD is coming. It is close at hand." First century Christians would understand immediately what John's words could mean.

One commentary attaches the following title to verses 6–12 of this chapter: "The First Four Trumpets: God Deprives the Ungodly of Earthly Security Because of Their Persecution and Idolatry in Order to Indicate Their Separation from Him"[20]. It's an interesting perspective and although I agree fundamentally with what the title suggests, it raises for me the bigger question of whether these judgments were intended to describe real events that people alive at the time of Christ's second coming will experience. I keep thinking that as John wrote these words he would be thinking about his target audience— the Christians of the seven churches—and consequently all of us. He would be trying to capture their attention. He would be trying to tell

85

them something that was important for them, and also for us, as they lived their lives. So what I'm struggling with here, and will continue to struggle with I'm sure, is that fundamental question: Has God given John a detailed description of actual events that will take place; or, is He trying to make a point about how we should be living our lives right now?

An Aside: *I'm willing to consider that I am completely wrong in my approach here—perhaps John wrote this Scripture in a trance-like state given the words directly from God. Don't get me wrong. I'm not suggesting that this Scripture isn't inspired by God. But even if John simply recorded words and visions, after the writing there was something about Revelation that allowed it to stand the test of time. Something that caused readers, when considering what should be included in the canon of Scripture, to agree that the message contained in Revelation should be preserved for all to read. Keep in mind that this decision would have been made generations after the text was written. Wouldn't it be cool to be a fly on the wall in a first century home church listening to the conversation of believers as they listened to the words of Revelation spoken?*

"The First Angel Sounded His Trumpet" (v.7)

> *⁷ The first angel sounded his trumpet, and there came hail and fire mixed with blood, and it was hurled down on the earth. A third of the earth was burned up, a third of the trees were burned up, and all the green grass was burned up.*

In Exodus 9:23–25, we are given a description of the plague of hail that fell on Egypt as part of God's demonstration of His power preceding Israel's exodus. "When Moses stretched out his staff toward the sky, the Lord sent thunder and hail, and lightning flashed down to the ground. So the Lord rained hail on the land of Egypt; hail fell and lightning flashed back and forth. It was the worst storm in all the land of Egypt since it had become a nation. Throughout Egypt hail struck everything in the fields—both people and animals; it beat down everything growing in the fields and stripped every tree." The similarities between this description of the plague of hail and the first trumpet judgment are striking.

It's interesting that only a third of things—earth, trees, and green grass—are affected. But then, when I reread the Exodus story I am reminded that the plague there was selective as well. The hail didn't fall on everything as we read in Exodus 9:26, "The only place it did not hail was the land of Goshen, where the Israelites were." So just as God controlled the amount of devastation then, here with the sound of the first trumpet, He continues to show His control.

Where the seal judgments would have been familiar to first century Christians regardless of whether they were of Jewish or Gentile birth, this one would hit at the minds, and hopefully the hearts, of those who were familiar with the story of the Exodus, but weren't necessarily Christ-followers. It will be interesting to see if any of the other trumpet judgments echo back to the Exodus as well.

It's interesting that the destruction here is directed only on things of this earth—the earth, the trees, the green grass. There is no mention of people being injured. However, if these events were taking place around me, I'm certain my sense of security would be challenged—or put another way—I'd be quite frightened. I wonder if this judgment would result in food shortages? And that takes me once again to the story of the Exodus. The Israelites, after leaving Egypt, soon ran out of food. They had to depend completely on God to provide manna for them to eat as they wandered in the desert. Would the words of this judgment cause a first century Jew to recall the stories he or she were told about the days of the Exodus? Would it remind them that God provided?

"The Second Angel Sounded His Trumpet" (v.8–9)

> ⁸ *The second angel sounded his trumpet, and something like a huge mountain, all ablaze, was thrown into the sea...*

There is a strong connection between this second trumpet judgment— and the third as well—with the plague of blood cast against Egypt in Exodus 7:20–25.

But what of the huge mountain being thrown into the sea? There appear to be three different types of references to mountains in Scripture. The first, refers to mountains simply as a location. For example, in Matthew 17:1, "After six days Jesus took with him Peter, James and John the brother of James, and led them up a high mountain by themselves." The second refers to the "mountain of the LORD's temple" as it does in Isaiah 2:2 (we will discuss this more in chapter 21). And finally in Jeremiah chapter 51:25, we read ""I am against you, O destroying mountain, you who destroy the whole earth," declares the LORD. "I will stretch out my hand against you, roll you off the cliffs, and make you a burned-out mountain."" In this case, Jeremiah is referring to the city of Babylon comparing it to a mountain because of its greatness and power during that time. Later in Revelation we will see several references to the destruction of Babylon, so it isn't difficult to assume that here in 8:8, the reference to the mountain is intended to connect there as well. This confirmation of God's great power, able to destroy even the great city of Babylon as foretold in Jeremiah should cause all of us to sit up and listen.

Notice that the destruction that follows this trumpet is another natural phenomenon. Where with the first trumpet it was things of the land that were being destroyed, here it is the things of, and on, the sea. For the first time as well we see living creatures being destroyed, and although we can surmise that human beings on the ships would also be destroyed, interestingly there is no mention yet of the loss of human life.

The idea of a shortage of food continues here. With this judgment, access to fish of the sea would also be restricted.

"The Third Angel Sounded His Trumpet" (v.10–11)

> *¹⁰ The third angel sounded his trumpet, and a great star, blazing like a torch, fell from the sky on a third of the rivers and on the springs of water—*

With the second trumpet, "something like a huge mountain, all ablaze" was thrown into the sea. Here John sees a "great star, blazing like a torch" fall from the sky affecting the rivers and springs. I'm not sure what the special significance of the great star is, but as I read this the thought that keeps resonating is that these actions are not the acts of man—they are much bigger than we are—they continue to act as a reminder of how great and powerful our God is.

We are told that the name of the star is Wormwood. What is this thing called Wormwood? It appears that wormwood is a plant or root of a plant, that would cause waters to become bitter. In other translations such as the NASB verse 11 reads as follows, "The name of the star is Wormwood. A third of the waters became wormwood." This word 'wormwood' appears a few other places in Scripture in these other translations. One place is Jeremiah 9:15 (NASB), "therefore thus says the LORD of hosts, the God of Israel, "behold, I will feed them, this people with wormwood and give them poisoned water to drink"."

Hebrews 12:15 (NIV) says, "See to it that no one misses the grace of God and that no bitter root grows up to cause trouble and defile many." This passage, with its reference to bitter root has me wondering about the implication that the star called wormwood, a bitter root, falls on the earth. Is God saying that the bitter root that has grown to cause trouble is being destroyed? I think I may be going too far with this analogy but then again, I wonder.

Notice as well that with this third trumpet, we are now told that people are dying—not because someone directly killed them, but indirectly because of the poisoning of the water. And now access to all water becomes an issue. Again as the Israelites wandered in the desert they ran into problems with bitter water (see Exodus 15:23) and once again, God provided for them.

"The Fourth Angel Sounded His Trumpet" (v.12)

> ¹² *The fourth angel sounded his trumpet, and a third of the sun was struck, a third of the moon, and a third of the stars, so that a third of them turned dark. A third of the day was without light, and also a third of the night.*

The land has been affected, then the waters, and now the heavens are affected as well. This trumpet judgment correlates directly to the plague of darkness described in Exodus 10:21–23, "Then the Lord said to Moses, "Stretch out your hand toward the sky so that darkness spreads over Egypt—darkness that can be felt." So Moses stretched out his hand toward the sky, and total darkness covered all Egypt for three days. No one could see anyone else or move about for three days. Yet all the Israelites had light in the places where they lived." That plague was selective as well—it did not affect the Israelites. Here with this fourth trumpet once again it affects not everyone, rather it affects a third of the heavens and a third of the day and night. So the natural order of day and night is also affected.

The Eagle Flying In Midair (v.13)

> [13] *As I watched, I heard an eagle that was flying in midair call out in a loud voice: "Woe! Woe! Woe to the inhabitants of the earth, because of the trumpet blasts about to be sounded by the other three angels!"*

In the final verse of this chapter John sees an eagle flying in midair calling out. Why an eagle? The King James Version says "heard an angel"—interesting. I'm not sure what to make of that. Whether it's an eagle or an angel, as it flies overhead I'm certain the sound would be difficult to ignore. The idea of it, fills me with a sense of foreboding.

And what about the fact that this eagle is flying in midair? I imagine that this action is taking place somewhere between Heaven and earth. In our current culture we often use the phrase when referring to midair collisions referring to any air space. One commentator describes midair as "the meridian or zenith of the sky where the sun stands at midday where it can be seen by all"[21]. I like this concept of midair. I like the idea that this eagle is in a position where everyone can hear what he is saying. We will see references to similar midair announcements later in 14:6 and 19:17.

This verse seems to indicate a transition point. We've heard about four trumpet judgments thus far, three more remain and the tone here would suggest that they will be much more intense then what we've seen so far.

Some Things To Think About

I keep returning to these questions:

- Are these real events that will, or that have perhaps already occurred?

- Or, are these judgments, as described, meant to capture our attention and remind us of God's power?
- Which perspective is most meaningful for me, for you, for each of us as we read these Scriptures?
- Is it more important for us to see them as events that will happen sometime in the future, or, should we be reading them as a way to learn something more about ourselves, about God and about our relationship(s) with Him?

Revelation 9

One of the first things I've noticed as I move on to chapter 9 is how much time is allotted to each of the final trumpet judgments compared to the first four. The first trumpet judgment was described in one short verse, the second in two verses, and the third in two, and the fourth in a single verse. Looking ahead, the description of the fifth trumpet judgment takes eleven verses, and the sixth takes nine verses. We won't read about the seventh trumpet until midway through chapter 11 where there are at least five verses devoted to it. This, along with the eagle's cry of "Woe, woe, woe" in the last verse of chapter 8 leaves me quite certain that what follows is going to be a biggie.

"The Fifth Angel Sounded His Trumpet" (v.1–11)

> [1] *The fifth angel sounded his trumpet, and I saw a star that had fallen from the sky to the earth. The star was given the key to the shaft of the Abyss.*

With the third trumpet we saw a star fall from the sky onto the rivers and springs of water. Now with this fifth trumpet, John doesn't actually see the star fall, but rather he sees a star that had *already* fallen to the earth. Isn't it interesting that the angel isn't given the key, but rather it is given to the star. Why give human characteristics to an inanimate object? The answer that makes the most sense to me here, is that in describing things in this way, John is once again reminding us that the activity is not of man, rather it is of God.

As I tried to learn more about this star I ran into some interesting conflicting commentaries. Some say that this star is most likely a good angel because it holds the key to the Abyss, which is normally held by Christ. Other commentaries suggest that the star must be either Satan or his angels because it has fallen from heaven.

An Aside: *This difference of interpretation confirms for me how important it is to read other people's opinions with discernment. Because someone has written a commentary doesn't make him or her correct in their interpretation. Similarly just because I've recorded my opinions in this way doesn't make me right either. We need to discuss what we read with others. We need to pray for insight and listen for God's direction. That's why my primary reason for publishing my thoughts in this book was not to tell you what to think, but rather to stimulate discussion—to encourage further study.*

Let me get back to the verse at hand. The star was given the key to the shaft of the Abyss. Some translations refer to it as the "bottomless pit." The NIV uses the term *Abyss* eight times in total. Seven references are in Revelation (here, 9:2, 9:11, 11:7, 17:8, 20:1, and 20:3). The only other reference is in Luke 8:31. The story there is about Jesus casting the demons out of the demon-possessed man. There the demons "begged him repeatedly not to order them to go into the Abyss." The Abyss must be a pretty bad place if even the demons didn't want to go there—and now the star has been given the key. What follows certainly can't be good.

"Smoke Rose From It" (v.2)

What is the significance of the smoke? There is obviously a great deal of it because we are told it is like it is from a gigantic furnace. This is a visual that also stimulates my sense of smell—the smell of smoke would be overwhelming. Beyond that we are told that there is so much smoke that the sun and sky were darkened.

Because I've read ahead and know that this smoke precedes a swarm of locusts. I've gone to the book of Joel for some insight here. Joel 2:10 says, "Before them the earth shakes, the sky trembles, the sun and moon are darkened, and the stars no longer shine." The "them" referenced in this verse, are locusts.

I continue to be amazed at how the words of Revelation echo the words of Old Testament prophets such as Joel. For readers throughout the generations who are familiar with the writings of Joel, the description of this trumpet judgment would be chilling. Add to that the strong link here with the plague of locusts cast upon the Egyptians described in Exodus chapter 10. Surely there can be no doubt that this is the hand of God at work.

"Locusts Came Down" (v.3–4)

Swarming locusts had the power to completely destroy the harvest within days. If you want to get a better sense of this, take the time to read the book of Joel. And for those of us who have never experienced locusts, a favorite pastor of mine suggests that we think of the locusts as a metaphor representing forces we come against, and that the message of Joel and the locusts, is that a devastating situation has come.[22] How do you respond? I believe that the message is the same here with the trumpet judgments.

I find it interesting that they were given power like that of scorpions. Why? Aren't locusts sufficiently destructive with their own powers?

We think of locusts as naturally eating grass, grain, plants and such, but God has them abandon their natural diet to instead attack people— hence the power like that of scorpions.

And this is where having that seal of God described in chapter 7 comes in handy. This is the first place in Revelation where we can see the seal of God protecting us from harm.

It is also the first time in the judgments thus far, that people are specifically targeted. In all of the previous judgments when harm has come to people it is more as a by-product of the judgment itself. Here there is no doubt who is the target.

"They Were Not Allowed To Kill Them" (v.5)

Isn't it interesting that God continues to demonstrate His power here by controlling just how much harm the locusts can inflict? It reminds me a bit of the story of Job, where God allows Satan to inflict harm on Job and his family, but always within limits.

He also controls how long the torment lasts—we are told they were to be tortured for five months. Why five months? The only other place in Scripture where I've found reference to this time period is in Luke 1:24 where we are told that Elizabeth, when she was pregnant with John, remained in seclusion for five months. Perhaps there's a correlation here with that, but I'm having trouble seeing it. It may be that what we are to take from this reference to five months is simply that it is a somewhat manageable amount of time.

"They Will Long To Die" (v.6)

Why aren't they allowed to die? Why are they forced to suffer and then, presumably recover? In one way I see it as God proving His power, not only over the things around us such as the locusts, but on us, and on Death itself. I also believe He is acting as what might be considered a hopeful God, keeping the people alive so they can have an opportunity to repent. Giving them a second chance perhaps?

Describing the Locusts (v.7–10)

> *⁷ The locusts looked like horses prepared for battle. On their heads they wore something like crowns of gold, and their faces resembled human faces.*

Why, I wonder, are we given such an elaborate description of these locusts? Did John simply want to stimulate our imaginations, to draw us into the action, or are we to learn more from the description? He certainly has succeeded in getting my imagination running overtime.

The description here echoes the description in Joel 2:4–5, "They have the appearance of horses; they gallop along like cavalry. With a noise like that of chariots they leap over the mountaintops, like a crackling fire consuming stubble, like a might army drawn up for battle." Here, in John's description, notice that he continually uses the word 'like'— whatever he has seen, and recognized to be locusts, he is having some trouble coming up with a clear and simple description.

And then we are once again told that this torment lasted for five months. Usually, in Scripture, well actually anywhere, when we repeat something we do so because the point is important. Here we are told for a second time within a span of five verses that the torment lasts for five months. This point may be important because it indicates that it is a short period of time, or it may be important because it confirms that the time was limited— that God decided how long it would last.

"They Had As King Over Them" (v.11)

I am quite curious about the significance of this final piece of the fifth trumpet judgment. Why do we need to know that there was a king over the locusts, and why do we need to know his name? Taking it at face value, it seems that we are being told that these locusts, even with a king over them, are still subject to God's bidding. In Proverbs 30:27 it says, "locusts have no king, yet they advance together in ranks." Is the fact that we are now told that here they have a king, meant to suggest that they are even more organized then they are naturally?

And why do we need to know his name in two languages no less? In the NIV this is the only place I found the name *Abaddon* used. In several other translations it is used in Job, Psalms and Proverbs instead of the name *Destruction*. So the name seems to equate to both destroyer and destruction. It seems to me that the reason we are being told this, is to confirm that the purpose of the locusts in this judgment was one of destruction, and just as he did in the story of Job, God controls who, what, and how much destruction takes place.

"The First Woe Is Past" (v.12)

Verse 12 seems to be a transition verse. I wonder if what it means is that the events described as the fifth judgment have already taken place, historically speaking, and that the remaining two are in the future. But I'm not aware of any event in history that would correlate to what has been described. So I've gone to the commentaries for some insight. In doing so, the first thing I've noticed is that the wording in some of the other translations such as the NASB is slightly different here, "The first woe is past: behold, two woes are still coming after these things." One commentator builds on the word *behold* in conjunction with "after these things," which apparently when used in apocalyptic literature "refers not to the order of historical events but to the order of visions"[23].

"The Sixth Angel Sounded His Trumpet" (v.13–21)

> [13] *The sixth angel sounded his trumpet, and I heard a voice coming from the four horns of the golden altar that is before God.*

In Exodus 30:1-3 we read the beginnings of God's instructions to Moses regarding the construction of the Altar of Incense, which I mentioned earlier. It says, "Make an altar of acacia wood for burning incense. It is to be square, a cubit long and a cubit wide, and two cubits high - its horns of one piece with it. Overlay the top and all the sides and the horns with pure gold" In Revelation 8:3, at the beginning of the trumpet judgments, we read "Another angel, who had a golden censer, came and stood at the altar. He was given much incense to offer, with the prayers of all God's people, on the golden altar in front of the throne." So here, as we're told of the voice coming from the horns which were at the four corners of this altar, I believe this is the voice of God speaking in response to those prayers of God's people.

The voice tells this sixth angel to release four angels. Who are these four angels? I've wondered if they are the same four angels mentioned in 7:1 who were standing at the four corners of the earth. But here we are told that they were bound, so it doesn't make sense to me that they are the same. The fact that they were bound suggests to me that God has been holding them back. In Jude 1:6 we read "And the angels who did not keep their positions of authority but abandoned their own home—these he has kept in darkness, bound with everlasting chains for judgment on the great Day." Could there be a connection with these angels?

This is one of the many things I'm not sure about, but I think that the important point here—at least to my way of thinking—is that once again, God is in control.

"The Great River Euphrates" (v.14)

The Euphrates is first mentioned in Genesis 2:10 where, in describing the Garden of Eden, it says, "A river watering the garden flowed from

Eden; from there it was separated into four headwaters." Later in Genesis 2:14, "And the fourth river is the Euphrates." So we know that this river has been a part of God's design since creation—which makes me think that it's cool that here, in the words about end-times the river is mentioned again.

Later in Genesis 15:18, "On that day the LORD made a covenant with Abram and said, "To your descendants I give this land, from the river of Egypt to the great river, the Euphrates"." So the river served as a boundary on the Promised Land.

Throughout the Old Testament there are numerous other references to the Euphrates. They are typically references to battles with enemies of Israel. So for early readers of this text, the great river Euphrates would have a great deal of meaning. For us in current times, I think that the significance here is that these four angels have been kept bound just outside the boundaries of the Promised Land and now they are to be released.

The Angels Had Been Kept Ready (v.15)

> *15 And the four angels who had been kept ready for this very hour and day and month and year were released to kill a third of mankind.*

We are told here that these angels had been "kept ready for this very hour and day and month and year." Why? Not why have they been kept ready, although that's not a bad question, but why are we being told this. Again, for me, it serves as a reminder that things happen according to God's plan, according to His timing.

There are so many things that have caught my attention in this verse 15. There is the obvious increasing intensity with this judgment. Previously people died as a side effect of other plagues or disasters. In the previous trumpet judgment, people were tormented by the locusts but they weren't allowed to die. But here they are being killed! It's like God is trying to give the people every chance to listen up. First things have been happening to their environment. Then they were tormented and still wouldn't repent, so now for one-third of mankind, there are no more chances to repent.

And why only one-third? My sense is that the point here is once again to remind us of God's control. Even after unbinding the angels, God retains control over their activities.

The other thing that has caught my attention is that I don't see any assurances here that the people with the seal of God are protected. Is it safe to assume that they are? Because God is in control, I'm assuming that His people, those who bear His seal, are protected during this time.

"Mounted Troops" (v.16)

From where did these mounted troops in verse 16 come? They have just suddenly appeared in the narrative here, and we're not given any information to answer this question. But we are told that there are a lot of them. Because John says he heard their number, I'm assuming there were too many for John to count, and so he had to be told.

The fact that there are so many and we aren't told where they come from, suggests that they are spiritual forces rather than physical ones.

Describing The Troops (v.17)

> *[17] The horses and riders I saw in my vision looked like this: Their breastplates were fiery red, dark blue, and yellow as sulfur. The heads of the horses resembled the heads of lions, and out of their mouths came fire, smoke and sulfur.*

Regardless of whether they are spiritual or physical forces, we are still given a very robust description of the horses and riders. Without looking at the details of the description I appreciate that descriptions like this—common in apocalyptic literature—are great for stirring one's imagination. This description draws me into the story, just as the description of the locusts did in the fifth trumpet judgment. They are hard to read and ignore, so they work very well to keep me engaged. John wants us to pay attention—to not miss the message of this vision. He doesn't want us blandly reading and missing the point.

The colors used to describe the breastplates are interesting—fiery red, dark blue and yellow—primary colors—the strongest colors on the color wheel. They would be vibrant. Hard to ignore.

The connection to the color of sulfur immediately connects to my sense of smell. If you've ever smelled sulfur burning you won't likely forget it. And later in this verse we will be told that out of their mouths came fire, smoke and sulfur. So the burning sulfur smell, the sting of the smoke in my eyes and the heat of the fire on my skin, all contribute to the horror of this event.

We were told earlier that the locusts had teeth like lion's teeth and here the horses' heads resemble the heads of lions. Interesting. I'm reminded of the story of Daniel in the lions' den. In Daniel 6:22 it says, "My God sent his angel, and he shut the mouths of the lions. They have not hurt me, because I was found innocent in his sight." Is this another reminder of God's control?

"A Third Of Mankind Was Killed" (v.18)

> *18 A third of mankind was killed by the three plagues of fire, smoke and sulfur that came out of their mouths.*

In verse 16 we were told that these were mounted troops, but as we continue to learn of this judgment we are told that the destruction is at the hands—okay mouths and tails—of the horses. I find this interesting. For me it adds to the importance of understanding that this destruction is not the work of man, but of God. It seems that whatever or whomever is mounted on the horses and apparently wearing very colorful breastplates may be there just for show.

"The Power Of the Horses" (v.19)

Earlier in this chapter we were told that the locusts' tails had power to torment people. Here again, the power of the horses was in their mouths and in their tails. I'm sure there are a lot of deep meanings implied here, but what immediately comes to mind for me, is that these horses are powerful when faced head-on. To avoid them, I might be inclined to try to stay out of reach by moving off to the side or behind the horse. But they have power issuing from their tails as well and that power is like snakes, which would radiate out to the sides. I'm left with the impression that it would be virtually impossible to avoid them if I've been targeted.

It's also interesting that we are told in verse 18 that mankind was killed by the plagues that came out of the horses' mouths, but in verse 19 we're told that tails inflict injury. Does that mean that they don't kill? If so, that would suggest that although one-third of mankind is killed during this judgment, there may be many others who were only injured.

An Aside: *I find, as I think about these things that have been so brilliantly described, that I am looking for literal interpretations in my mind. It is very hard not to be drawn in and that, I believe, is why the apocalyptic genre was used to relay the message of Revelation. It draws us into the story. It causes us to imagine ourselves in the action and most importantly it causes us to consider our response to it all.*

The Rest Of Mankind Still Did Not Repent (v.20–21)

And still, through all of this the people who saw this destruction, or were injured during it, didn't repent. There seems to be a fairly strong correlation between the things the rest of mankind did not repent from as listed in verses 20 and 21, and the Ten Commandments listed in Exodus 20. Interesting.

How much will it take to convince the non-believer of God's ultimate power and authority? The fact that they didn't repent; that, in fact, they seemed to have been hardened against God is something we've seen before in Scripture. "Just as the plague of death against the firstborn of Egypt ultimately led to hardening instead of softening the remaining Egyptians, so the plagues here have the dual effect of death and continuing delusion for the remainder. Just as the death of the firstborn led to the decisive judgment at the Red Sea, so here the death of others as a warning sign does not induce repentance but prepares for the final judgment of the intractably impenitent at the seventh trumpet (11:18)".[24]

Some Things To Think About

As I've said before, I believe that the trumpet judgments are included in Revelation as an appeal to those of the tribes of Israel who did not acknowledge Jesus as Messiah. These judgments have been a way to connect with the Israelites, and everyone else who reads them, to remind us of God's power and authority.

The two judgments described here are intense. They are certainly much more intense then anything we've read before in Revelation.

Is that increase in intensity there to frighten us? I think it is. Not so much because they represent actual events that may take place, but because they should be giving us a sense of how important this is. God started this main vision with the throne scene. He showed us what is possible. He reminded us that He knows life in this current church age isn't perfect through the seal judgments. And now, through these trumpet judgments, He is crying out to us to please listen, to accept the offer of salvation by reminding us of His might and power.

And yet, we refuse to repent.

Revelation 10

The Angel and the Little Scroll (10:1–11)

> *¹ Then I saw another mighty angel coming down from heaven. He was robed in a cloud, with a rainbow above his head; his face was like the sun, and his legs were like fiery pillars. ² He was holding a little scroll, which lay open in his hand...*

I'm not sure what to make of the fact that this chapter starts with the word then. Is it a reference to a chronologically next event, or does it mean something else entirely—not sure on this one. It certainly signifies a change of pace, as the story that follows is different from what we've been seeing with the trumpet judgments.

When we looked at the opening of the seals everything seemed to flow along until the sixth seal was complete, and then John seemed to step aside from the action to answer a few questions, or to provide some additional information before moving on to the seventh seal. The same thing seems to be happening here. We have been told of the six trumpet judgments, and now John moves into another aside.

"Mighty Angel" (v.1)

We were introduced to a mighty angel with a loud voice in 5:2 when we first began the story of the seals on the scroll. It's interesting to me that we are given this same image as the opening to another story about a scroll.

It seems the angel is coming down from heaven. When this main vision started in chapter 4, John was given access to a view of heaven through a door standing open (4:1). All that has transpired since then has been described as if John were in heaven looking down on it—viewing from a distance. Here, however, he uses the phrase "coming down" rather than going down, which suggests that the perspective in this vision is different. John is now back on earth. Now to be fair, I'm not sure that this change in perspective makes much difference to the story, but it's something I'm going to pay attention to in the next chapters because I'm beginning to wonder if there is significance to it. Perhaps the stories we're told with John on earth are related to current life activities, and the stories we're told with John on a heavenly plane are intended to tell us what's going on behind the scenes or in the spiritual realm.

The description of the angel is also very interesting. He is robed in a cloud. Is this an echo once again to the Exodus when God was present in the pillar of smoke/cloud? In the throne scene of chapter 4 we were told that a rainbow surrounded the throne. In fact as I review verse 3 of that throne scene I see similarities in the description of the one who sat on the throne. Except for one key factor. In the description of that being, God, John used very concrete terms—remember the gem-like description. Here we're being told that the angel's face was *like* the sun, his legs were *like* fiery pillars. So there appears to be a connection between these beings, but this mighty angel isn't God. Perhaps he is a messenger from God, and we are given this wonderful description of him to confirm that he is acting under God's direction.

"Holding a Little Scroll" (v.2)

The angel is holding a little scroll. So, where did this scroll come from? Is it related to the scroll that started all this in chapter 5, or is it something else entirely? This scroll is open. The original Greek word for scroll in chapter 5 is *biblion* which means *book or written document*. Here in chapter 10 the Greek word is slightly different. It is *bibliaridion* which means *little book*. So if the two were related in some way, the implication would be that the scroll this angel is holding represents a subset of the information contained in the larger scroll. That's assuming they are related. There may be no connection between them at all. Referring to a scroll in the first century would be no different than referring to a book today. And we know not all books are related so why should I expect that the scrolls be?

"Right Foot On the Sea, Left Foot On the Land" (v.2–3)

As I read that the angel "planted his right foot on the sea and his left on the land," I get a sense of his authority. Isn't it a cool image! I'm sure many of us have had the opportunity to stand on a beach, and likely in doing so have one foot in the water and one on the sand. But this angel doesn't have one foot *in* the water—his foot is *on* the water. He is in control.

And then he gave a loud shout. We've heard about lots of loud voices or shouts already. Since it's unusual to shout softly, when John adds the information that the shout was loud, I assume that he does so to reinforce just how loud it really is. Through all this I get a sense of chaos. A shout like the roar of a lion would be powerful, strong, commanding. I imagine everyone turning to the angel.

There seems to be some sort of connection between this chapter and chapter 5. In 5:5 we saw that the Lion of Judah was worthy to open the seven seals on the scroll. Here we have someone holding a scroll in hand, and emitting a shout like the roar of a lion, and we are introduced to the seven thunders. Interesting, but since I don't know what to do with this connection, if in fact there is one, I'm going to leave it open for now.

"The Seven Thunders" (v.3–4)

Is this another set of judgments? Apparently if they are, we are not going to learn anything more about them.

As the seven thunders spoke, John was obviously able to hear what they said because he was about to write, but then he is told to seal up what he's heard—to not write it down. I wonder why John was able to hear it, but we're not. Is this simply a reminder that in, and throughout the story of salvation we often have things we wonder about—things we know God has answers to but still we're not given answers?

Since I am assuming that the voice from heaven was God's voice, or a messenger on His behalf, this reminds me once again, that He is in control.

Reaching Up To Heaven (v.5–6)

> *⁵ Then the angel I had seen standing on the sea and on the land raised his right hand to heaven.*

What a wonderful visual! The angel that appears to have authority over land and sea is still reaching up to heaven, and then in what appears to be a very forceful way says that there will be no more delays. Or in other words, "By the authority of God, I'm saying that enough is enough, it is time to get this show on the road!" There is an echo here to Deuteronomy 32:40–41 which says, "I lift my hand to heaven and declare: As surely as I live forever, when I sharpen my flashing sword and my hand grasps it in judgment, I will take vengeance on my adversaries and repay those who hate me."

Check out the link as well with Daniel 12:7, "The man clothed in linen, who was above the waters of the river, lifted his right hand and his left hand toward heaven, and I heard him swear by him who lives forever, saying, 'It will be for a time, times and half a time. When the power of the holy people has been finally broken, all these things will be completed.'"

"The Mystery Of God" (v.7)

It's interesting to note the wording in verse 7. It doesn't say, *when* the seventh angel sounds his trumpet, instead it says "*in the days when* the seventh angel *is about to* sound his trumpet" [italics are mine]. The implication is that there is a period of time that elapses around the sounding of the final trumpet. It is not an event that takes place in a split-second yet as we will see later in Revelation, once sounded, things appear to take place very quickly.

In Paul's writing to the Colossians 2:1–3, it says, "I want you to know how hard I am contending for you and for those at Laodicea, and for all who have not met me personally. My goal is that they may be encouraged in heart and united in love, so that they may have the full riches of complete understanding, in order that they may know the mystery of God, namely, Christ, in whom are hidden all the treasures of wisdom and knowledge."

And so here, the angel announces that with the sounding of the seventh trumpet, the mystery of God will be accomplished. Notice that it doesn't say the mystery will be revealed, but rather that it will be accomplished. One commentator suggests, "The mystery of God in Rev 10:7 ... refers to the purpose of God as revealed in the consummation of human history. In the NT this divine purpose in history is a mystery not because it is an unknown, but because it never would have been known if God had not revealed it. John is saying that with the sounding of the seventh trumpet that which God purposed in creation and made possible through the blood of the Lamb (5:9–10) will be brought to its fulfillment."[25]

More About the Angel (v.8)

For the third time in this chapter we are told that the angel is standing on the sea and on the land. Don't you find it interesting that this information is repeated so many times in such a short space? I certainly do.

In this case, it seems extremely important that we understand that this angel has great authority over things of this earth. Similarly the words on the scroll must be important and I have to believe they are from God.

That voice from heaven that told John to seal up the message of the seven thunders has new instructions for John. He is to take the scroll from the angel.

Eat the Scroll (v.9–10)

> [9] *So I went to the angel and asked him to give me the little scroll. He said to me, "Take it and eat it. It will turn your stomach sour, but 'in your mouth it will be as sweet as honey.'"*

Now the instructions seem rather odd, but they aren't exactly new. They are very similar to a story from Ezekiel chapters 2 and 3. In Ezekiel 2:9 it says, "Then I looked, and I saw a hand stretched out to me. In it was a scroll" and continuing on in 3:1, "And he said to me, 'Son of man, eat what is before you, eat this scroll; then go and speak to the house of Israel'" and in verse 3, "So I ate it, and it tasted as sweet as honey in my mouth."

Here in Revelation we're told that the scroll will taste as sweet as honey as it did in Ezekiel but then it will turn his stomach sour. So what does this mean? My first reaction to this is that John finds pleasure—the sweet taste—in being able to share the words of the scroll, but perhaps the message he shares is not readily accepted by his audience—hence turn his stomach sour. Perhaps the sweetness points us to the message of salvation, and the sourness to the fact that those who do not accept the message will suffer the consequences of judgment. But it does seem clear that with all the insight John has gained through his visions of the seals, trumpets, and thunder judgments, he is being asked to share what he has learned with others.

"Prophesy Again About" (v.11)

I'm a bit confused by the phrase "prophesy again about." Is there a connection between the many peoples, nations, languages and kings this is about that is meant to connect us back to 7:9, where we were told about the great multitude in white robes was from every nation, tribe, people, and language?

And why does it say 'again'? Could it relate back to 1:11 when John was instructed to write what he saw and send it to the seven churches?

An Aside: *There is so much to wonder about through all of this. Yet as I continue to study it, I find myself continuing to see how simple the message is, and how elaborate the apocalyptic language is that John has chosen to make this message continue to capture our attention and fascinate us throughout the generations.*

Some Things To Think About

As we wait for the sounding of the seventh trumpet, we see that John has been instructed to continue to share the message of salvation. I wonder as we read this chapter if we, as followers of the Lamb, aren't being instructed to share the message as well.

Revelation 11

The Two Witnesses (11:1–14)

As we left Chapter 10 we saw that John had been told to prophesy again about many peoples, nations, languages, and kings. This ongoing theme that we've been seeing throughout Revelation is focused on God's authority and majesty. It is a call to worship Him.

Here in chapter 11 is a story that many look at as a literal description of events to come. I wonder if it is really a summary of what John is to share with the nations. It appears to me to be a very interesting re-enactment of the story of Jesus' ministry, His crucifixion, and ultimately His resurrection, and ascension into heaven—the mystery of God.

Or is it a complex, yet simple, look back at Jesus' ministry on earth; and at the same time, a look forward to the ministry of the church throughout the current church age up to the time of Christ's second coming?

"Measure the Temple Of God" (v.1)

> *¹ I was given a reed like a measuring rod and was told, "Go and measure the temple of God and the altar, with its worshipers..."*

We aren't told specifically who is speaking here, so I assume that it is the same voice that spoke to John in chapter 10.

114

There are a few places in Scripture where we can find references to the measuring rod. One is in Ezekiel 40, where Ezekiel described a vision he had when the Israelites were in captivity. In this vision he was given a description of a temple yet to be built. He was told to use a measuring rod (or reed in some translations) to measure the walls of the temple area. Here in Revelation we see a similar use of the measuring rod, and later in 21:15 we will see an angel using a measuring rod to measure the walls of the New Jerusalem.

In Zechariah 2:1–2 there is a similar reference to measuring, "Then I looked up, and there before me was a man with a measuring line in his hand. I asked, "Where are you going?" He answered me, "To measure Jerusalem, to find out how wide and how long it is.""

My question is whether these measurements, including the one here in chapter 11, are of something physical—a real temple with walls and such—or is the temple of God, in this case, presented as an analogy for the body of believers? If we assume that it is an analogy for the body of believers, then what is actually being measured? Is it how many of us there are as a group? Or, is it a measure of our individual worthiness? If I follow my opening line of thought on this chapter—that it is a reenactment of the story of Jesus' ministry—then I find myself looking at this entire segment of measurement as something of a baseline measurement, a starting point so-to-speak. Or, as a measurement to get a sense of who, or how many, are engaged in sharing the good news as Jesus did.

As I continue to wonder about this chapter, I am drawn to Jeremiah chapter 5. In verse 1 we read, "Go up and down the streets of Jerusalem, look around and consider, search through her squares. If you can find but one person who deals honestly and seeks the truth, I will forgive this city."

"Exclude the Outer Court" (v.2)

The vision in Ezekiel 40 has several references to an outer court. It appears to be something like a waiting area, or perhaps a space for meetings. In this case we are told that it is a space for Gentiles. This reference to Gentiles could mean non-Jews or non-believers, or pagans. I'm inclined to believe that the intent here was to refer to non-believers or pagans.

John is told that those Gentiles will trample on the city. In Luke's rendition of the Olivet discourse in Luke 21:24b, it says, "Jerusalem will be trampled on by the Gentiles until the times of the Gentiles are fulfilled."

A few decades before Revelation was written, the temple in Jerusalem was totaled destroyed by the Romans—a non-Jewish, non-believing society. First century Christians would have been painfully reminded of this event when reading this passage in Revelation. In addition, the visual serves as a reminder to every generation that non-believers continually prod at the temple or the church, trying to destroy it.

And finally, there is the question of the significance of forty-two months. Theologians and academics have gone in many directions with this time period. Forty-two months is three and a half years if we assume twelve months in a year. In the verses that follow we will see reference to 1,260 days, which is three and a half years if we consider three hundred sixty days per year. We will also see reference to "times, time and half a time" which is also thought to be three and a half years. This concept of three and a half years seems pretty significant. These numbers echo back to Daniel 7:25 where reference was made to "a time, two times, and half a time" when we were told that the little horn shall have power for this three and half years. Daniel was written in a time of great persecution by Antiochus Epiphanes, of the Israelites, followed by an overwhelming victory over the Selucid king. So in using a similar period of time here in Revelation, the reader should be reminded about what that time of tribulation was like. John isn't saying it will be three and a half years. I believe he is saying, "Remember that three and a half years we talked about in Daniel and how terrible it was, well that's what this will be like as well."

But I keep finding myself pulled in a different direction with this concept of three and a half years. Isn't it also a reminder of the length of Jesus' ministry on earth? And during his approximately three and a half years of ministry, wasn't his opposition constantly trying to trample on his teachings?

And is there significance to the fact that here the time frame is given in months and in the very next verse, what is virtually the same length of time is given in days. Months seems more generic—almost remote— while days feels very personal.

"Two Witnesses" (v.3–4)

> ³ *And I will appoint my two witnesses, and they will prophesy for 1,260 days, clothed in sackcloth."*
> ⁴ *They are "the two olive trees" and the two lampstands, and "they stand before the Lord of the earth."*

In John 8:17 it says, "In your own Law it is written that the testimony of two men is valid." In the context of this story in Revelation does this refer to two specific people or is the visual of two witnesses meant to assure the reader that the words spoken were valid and true? Is it a reminder that Jesus' teachings during his years of ministry were true?

But could the mention of two witnesses mean something else entirely? What if the concept of two is intended to bring us into the picture?

Could it be that this isn't just an overview of the story of Jesus' ministry, and of the story of salvation during his lifetime, but that it is that *plus* a message to Christians to be doing the same in our lifetimes.

And what do we make of the sackcloth? Sackcloth could represent mourning, or it could represent humility. This passage may simply mean that Jesus humbly taught the truth of God's word through his time of ministry.

Zechariah 4:2b–3 speaks of lampstands and olive trees; "I see a solid gold lampstand with a bowl at the top and seven lights on it, with seven channels to the lights. Also there are two olive trees by it, one on the right of the bowl and the other on its left." and Zechariah 4:14, the angel, in response to Zechariah's question about the olive trees says, "These are the two who are anointed to serve the Lord of all the earth." Commentators suggest that these refer to the king and the royal priesthood. Moving along with this perspective and referring back to Revelation 1:6 and 5:10, where we were told that we have been made to be a kingdom and priests to serve God, it makes sense, at least to me, that there are parallel messages happening here. One is a reminder of the story of Jesus' time on earth—King of kings—but it is overlaid with a message to current day Christians to be engaging in that same ministry—royal priesthood.

An Aside: *I realize that my interpretation of this passage isn't consistent with the views of minds far greater than mine. I know I might be completely off the mark here, but I haven't lost sight of who God is. Once again, I simply challenge you to open your mind, question, and study. Look deeper into the Scriptures. If my view doesn't work for you, so be it, but take the time to think about what you believe, and why. Please don't reject the Scripture simply because you have a different view of its message, but rather consider the opinions of others with an attitude of discernment and in doing so grow in the depth and strength of your understanding, in faith, and in awe of our sovereign Lord. Don't twist the Scripture to meet your own needs. Look elsewhere in Scripture for insight, for patterns, for clarification. Test out your ideas with others. And recognize that some of the differences you may uncover, while interesting, are not critical to developing a common faith, a trust, and a belief in the teachings of our triune God.*

"If Anyone Tries To Harm Them" (v.5)

Verse 5 puzzles me and fascinates me at the same time. In the previous verse we were told that the two witnesses were the two olive trees and lampstands. A lampstand holds a lamp, which burns with fire. John says "fire comes out of their mouths." In 1:12 and 1:20 we were told that the seven lampstands are the seven churches. But the seven churches represent all believers. So as a believer, as a member of the Church, as a lampstand, is fire coming out of my mouth? Am I sharing the gospel? Am I overwhelming Satan—my enemy?

Perhaps the real message is that anyone who wants to harm them, or us, must die. In our current church age, I'm pretty certain that if this is the intended message, that the death of our enemies is not a physical one at this time but rather a spiritual death. Similarly the protection is of a spiritual nature and doesn't guarantee physical safety.

Look again at Jeremiah 5, now in verse 14, "Therefore this is what the LORD God Almighty says: 'Because the people have spoken these words, I will make my words in your mouth a fire and these people the wood it consumes.'"

But why does it say that this is "how anyone who wants to harm them must die?" In Leviticus 24:19–20 it says, "If anyone injures his neighbor, whatever he has done must be done to him: fracture for fracture, eye for eye, tooth for tooth. As he has injured the other, so he is to be injured." Seems pretty straightforward, though somewhat harsh. Perhaps this isn't as complicated as I seem to be making it.

"They Have Power" (v.6)

When we are told someone has the power to do something, must we always assume that they use it? Here we are told they can inflict suffering in three different ways: no rain, water to blood, which means that water of any kind would no longer be usable, and they can send plagues.

Traditionally, it is from this verse that many have made the assumption that the two witnesses are Moses and Elijah because Elijah had power to shut the sky, that no rain may fall (1 Kings 17:1), and Moses had power over the waters to turn them into blood, and to smite the earth with every plague in Exodus. If John wanted us to equate these two witnesses to the lives of Moses and Elijah, I don't believe his intent was for us to simply think, "Oh, that's referring to Moses and Elijah." Obviously we need to go further and consider what the references teach us about God, and about how we are to walk as believers. Both were men who were called by God to do some difficult things. They had their bad days, but when they obeyed God, He took care of them. He gave them all they needed.

"When They Have Finished Their Testimony" (v.7)

> *7 Now when they have finished their testimony, the beast that comes up from the Abyss will attack them, and overpower and kill them.*

The thing that stands out for me in this verse, in fact in all of Revelation, is the continuous reminder of God's control and authority. Notice that this next event takes place "when they have finished their testimony." In verse 3 we had been told that the duration of their witnessing was limited to 1,260 days—God's decision. Here it isn't a coincidence that the beast comes up at this precise time—God is allowing it to happen. And just as God decided when and how Jesus' ministry on earth would end, so He allows the ministry of the witnesses to end.

Continuing with my analogy that the two witnesses represent Jesus' ministry and our on-going ministry throughout the church age; then for me, this is a reminder that this church age will also come to an end. It will end when God decides. I can't help looking back to the opening of the fifth seal in 6:11 where the martyrs under the throne were told to wait a little longer "until the full number of their fellow servants, their brothers and sisters, were killed just as they had been." Once again, a reminder of God's control and authority.

The Beast Attacks Them (v.7–9)

We will learn more about the beast in the chapters that follow. For now it is enough to understand that the beast is Satan. Here we are being told that for a time, Satan will attack and destroy. He will appear to win. Their bodies will be left lying in the street.

The bodies lying in the public square—not being allowed burial—represent the ultimate slap in the face to the witnesses, to us. It is a huge sign of disrespect and of dishonor. Can you picture the people lined up, moving through the square gazing down on the slowly decomposing bodies lying in the square? It reminds me of images of bodies left to hang on a cross for all to see. They lie there for three and a half days.

And what's all this about the great city? We are told that it was where their Lord was crucified, which suggests that the city in question is

Jerusalem. Some commentators suggest that it actually means Rome, because it was the authorities in Rome that pursued Christ's death. Others suggest that it is Babylon, since Babylon is called the "great city" elsewhere in Revelation (16:19, 18:10, 18:21).

In Jeremiah 22:8b when speaking of Jerusalem, it says "Why has the LORD done such a thing to this great city?" and then further in Jeremiah 23:14, "And among the prophets of Jerusalem I have seen something horrible: They commit adultery and live a lie. They strengthen the hands of evildoers, so that no one turns from his wickedness. They are all like Sodom to me; the people of Jerusalem are like Gomorrah." In Joel 3:19 we find a reference to Egypt that may apply here as well, "But Egypt will be desolate, ... because of violence done to the people of Judah, in whose land they shed innocent blood."

Sodom and Egypt represented dark and difficult times.

"Three and a Half Days" (v.9)

Just as Jesus was in the tomb until the third day, they are dead for three and a half days. In Jesus' life, the time in the tomb marked the beginning of a transition from His active ministry on earth to passing the torch to those He calls His disciples, who were called to continue His work. If the concept of the two witnesses includes us, as followers of the Lamb, then this event marks a transition time for us as well. When our time of ministry is complete, we will lie in wait for Christ's return. And when He does, then we will transition to life everlasting.

"Inhabitants Of the Earth" (v.10)

So far in Revelation we have seen the phrase 'inhabitants of the earth' used three times. In 3:10, the people of the church in Philadelphia were told "I will also keep you from the hour of trial that is going to come on the whole world to test the inhabitants of the earth." (Note: in some translations of the NIV this phrase is "those who live on the earth") In 6:10, "How long, Sovereign Lord, holy and true, until you judge the inhabitants of the earth." And in 8:13, "Woe! Woe! Woe to the inhabitants of the earth," It will be used again in 13:8, 13:14, 17:2 and 17:8. The phrase seems to imply a distinction between believers and non-believers; particularly in the later chapters of Revelation where for example in 13:8 it says, "All inhabitants of the earth will worship the beast—all whose names have not been written in the book of life belonging to the Lamb." Here in 11:10 we are told that the inhabitants of the earth gloat over the death of the prophets.

They are celebrating because the two prophets who had tormented those who live on the earth are now lying dead in the square. I don't understand how the two prophets torment them? Does this mean they used the powers mentioned in verse 6, or that their prophesying was a form of torment? If the torment wasn't physical, was it spiritual? Perhaps they were tormented because their comfortable life-styles were being challenged by the truths of the prophets' preaching.

They celebrated by sending each other gifts. I wonder why we are given this piece of information? John could simply have said that they were celebrating. Why did he include the bit about sending each other gifts? It seems to add a sense of almost childishness, and celebration to the gloating. It adds an extra degree of celebration that seems to make it more personal. It's one thing to say, "Let's have a party to celebrate our victory!"—somewhat spur of the moment. By adding in the exchange of gifts there is an element of planning—now I have to decide what gift to choose to give someone. Exchanging gifts also suggests, at least to me, that this could become an annual event. These guys didn't have a clue as to just how short-lived the celebration would be.

123

"They Stood On Their Feet" (v.11)

They are raised from the dead. God continues to demonstrate His power; His control; His authority. Whether this represents an actual future event or not, I find it difficult not to imagine being in the square as this event takes place.

Can you picture the looks on the faces of the revelers? What an amazing image to hold in our minds of God's authority. Partiers are exchanging gifts. They are probably dancing in the square. They're gloating over the deaths of the witnesses—can you hear them? Suddenly the witnesses stand up. This is one of those moments that would have everyone pulling out their cell phones to grab a selfie with the now standing dead bodies. They'd bring down social media in seconds with all the texts and tweets going out.

"A Loud Voice From Heaven" (v.12)

Another loud voice—they all appear to be loud voices, loud shouts and so on don't they. As John experiences his visions, they must have been terrifying and chaotic at times with all these loud voices. It's just struck me that John must have had a very special personality to be able to cope with the images that he has been pounded with in these visions.

And so the witnesses ascend from earth into heaven just as Jesus did. For me, this serves as a reminder of the entire message of Revelation— for those of us who choose to worship the Lamb, ours will be the victory.

"At That Very Hour" (v.13)

> [13] *At that very hour there was a severe earthquake and a tenth of the city collapsed. Seven thousand people were killed in the earthquake, and the survivors were terrified and gave glory to the God of heaven.*

This verse seems to mark a transition in the story. So far in this chapter, we have been reminded of Christ's ministry, of God's authority in the timing of events, and of the ultimate result—He wins!

And as we move forward through the chapter the message is a reminder that non-believers will be judged. Isaiah 29:6 says, "the LORD Almighty will come with thunder and earthquake and great noise, with windstorm and tempest and flames of a devouring fire." In Revelation 6:12, there was a great earthquake with the opening of the sixth seal. In 8:5 we saw an earthquake again as it transitioned to the story of the trumpet judgments. And here, as we finish the message of the sixth trumpet, and prepare for the seventh, once again we are told of a severe, damaging earthquake.

And now I wonder why it is only one-tenth of the city? Why not the entire city? And why are we given a relatively low number of people who are killed? Is it meant to simply tell us that a noticeable, but not overwhelming, portion of the city is harmed? It seems to be having some affect because the message is that terrified survivors gave glory to God.

An Aside: *As I ponder this passage, I am reminded of how often through Scripture we read stories of how the Israelites sin, are punished, and then repent, and then forget, and then sin again, and then are punished, and then repent and so on and so on. The story repeats throughout Biblical history, and often throughout our lives as Christians.*

"The Second Woe Has Passed" (v.14)

> *[14] The second woe has passed; the third woe is coming soon.*

During the first woe people were tormented by the locusts. During the second woe they were tormented by the two witnesses. Non-believers have been given two significant chances to redeem themselves. It sounds like there may be only one more chance—the third woe is coming.

In 8:13, where we were first introduced to the woes, I suggested that it felt like a transition point to things much worse. Here the transition is within the woes. The first two were bad. Could the third and final woe be worse?

The Seventh Trumpet (11:15–19)

"The Seventh Angel Sounded His Trumpet" (v.15)

> [15] *The seventh angel sounded his trumpet, and there were loud voices in heaven, which said: "The kingdom of the world has become the kingdom of our Lord and of his Messiah, and he will reign for ever and ever."*

In 10:7, we read "But in the days when the seventh angel is about to sound his trumpet, the mystery of God will be accomplished, just as he announced to his servants the prophets." In Colossians 2:2, "My purpose is that they may be encouraged in heart and united in love, so that they may have the full riches of complete understanding, in order that they may know the mystery of God, namely, Christ." Now we read that the angel has sounded his trumpet. Does this mean that the story told in the first part of this chapter involved the revealing of who Christ is? I think it may. However, I also think that the chapter that follows further describes this mystery.

These five verses at the end of chapter 11 feel to me like a voice-over or second image of what's been happening in Heaven as things have taken place on earth. It is obvious that we are moving on in the story that is Revelation to actual end-times—the time when Christ does in fact return.

"The Kingdom Of The World" (v.15)

There are some potentially confusing terms here. I'm assuming that "the kingdom of the world" refers to things of this earth, and that "the kingdom of our Lord and of his Messiah" means that Christ has returned to be Lord of it all.

But I'm not sure what the difference is between "our Lord" and "his Messiah", and what that may mean. It's usually *the* Messiah so why refer to Him as *his*? Acts 3:18 says, "But this is how God fulfilled what he had foretold through all the prophets, saying that his Messiah would suffer." Several other translations replace *his Messiah* with *Christ* or in some cases, *his Christ*, in this passage in Acts and in the passage here in Revelation. I decided to take a look at the Greek terms used here. (By the way, I don't read or understand Greek so I could be getting this wrong. I simply have a tool that allows me to touch on a word in Scripture and see what the original term was. It includes a short definition that helps tremendously.) What I've learned is that the Greek term for *lord* here is *kyrios* which means *master*—the guy in charge. The Greek term for *messiah* is *Christos*— *anointed one*. So we're being told that the kingdom of the world has become the kingdom of our master—God—and of His anointed one, Jesus Christ.

I love how it doesn't say that *they* will reign, but rather that "*he* will reign"—one triune God.

A Change In Perspective

With the blowing of the seventh trumpet, it seems like the end has come. But at the same time, it seems like we're in a holding pattern here in the days when the seventh angel is about to sound his trumpet. Again, it's like our perspective is changing to take a higher look from a vantage point that allows us to see the end while it is still happening.

Wow, if this is confusing for us, can you imagine how John must have felt when he received the visions!

Back To the Throne Scene (v.16)

> ¹⁶ *And the twenty-four elders, who were seated on their thrones before God, fell on their faces and worshiped God,*

As I read this portion of chapter 11 I am drawn back to the second half of chapter 7. John had just heard the numbers of those who had been sealed, and had seen the great multitude, and then we were transported to the throne scene to witness the celebration and worship taking place there. Once again we are back with the elders before the throne worshipping God. This is the heavenly view of how this all ends.

"The One Who Is and Who Was" (v.17)

Notice the connection here in verse 17 back to 1:4 and 1:8 where God is referred to as "him who is, and who was, and who is to come." Except now He is called "the One who is and who was." No longer is He "the One who is to come" because in the timeframe suggested by these verses He has come.

"The Nations Were Angry" (v.18)

What does it mean that the nations were angry? Why were they angry? Was it because of the torment we heard about in verse 10? As I sit at my desk (actually it's a table but that's not relevant to the discussion) and ponder this phrase I feel a sense of turmoil—could it mean that the nations have been railing against God and finally He has had enough?

Notice that the game plan regarding what is to come in the next bit is laid out here. There are three layers: the dead will be judged, the servants rewarded, and those who destroy the earth will be destroyed. I'm not sure that the order in which these things happen is clear from this verse, but the pieces seem clear. Some suggest that the second layer—the servants rewarded—should be subdivided to show that the "servants the prophets" will be rewarded in one phase and the "people who revere your name" will be rewarded in another. I'm not sure that such a distinction matters much to me. Both segments will be rewarded—that's the important point.

"Then God's Temple In Heaven Was Opened" (v.19)

> *¹⁹ Then God's temple in heaven was opened, and within his temple was seen the ark of his covenant. And there came flashes of lightning, rumblings, peals of thunder, an earthquake and a severe hailstorm.*

As I read this verse I can't help but think about Matthew 27:51 (or Mark 15:38 or Luke 23:45) where it says, "At that moment the curtain of the temple was torn in two from top to bottom. The earth shook and the rocks split." The significance of that event was that God was now directly available to all. Are we to get the same message here? I don't think so. There is something else going on here.

It is significant that the "ark of his covenant" is now visible. In Old Testament times the ark was in the Holy of Holies in the tabernacle or temple. It was visible only to those priests who had been chosen to enter therein. Over the centuries there has been much mystery about what happened to the ark of the covenant. I've had the opportunity to travel to Aksum in Ethiopia where the Ethiopian Orthodox church says it resides. But unfortunately people are not allowed to see it. So do they really have it? I don't know, and I don't think the answer to that question matters here. What is more important is focusing on what the ark contains. The ark of the covenant held the stone tablets on which were written the Ten Commandments. The appearance of the ark shows us what will be used as the standard for the coming judgments that we have been told about.

And just as the earth shook and the rocks split when the curtain of the temple was torn in two, here we are told of a similar catastrophic event. The connection is too strong for me to ignore. Christ's death on the cross and subsequent resurrection was the single most important event in our spiritual story. Since that time we have been waiting for this next event—His second coming.

As I've mentioned before, what's not clear to me is whether all these earthquakes that have been described are separate events, or are in fact the same event, with us being given glimpses to all the layers of life in heaven and on earth taking place. I wonder.

Some Things To Think About

Just as the two witnesses did, if we choose to be followers of the Lamb:

- We are charged to minister to, and serve others.
- We can expect to be attacked by Satan and his minions.
- We will be raised to life everlasting according to God's timing and plan.

Revelation 12

The Woman and the Dragon (12:1–17)

In these next three chapters, we will be shown a series of different visions that seem to provide more information about the story of salvation, the story of good versus evil, and the triumph of good over evil. I wonder if this information is connected to what John has been told to prophesy about from chapter 10.

There is something about this story of the "Woman and the Dragon" that I like. From the first time I read it closely it has resonated with me. It reminds me of the phenomenon we often hear of, that when you die your life flashes before your eyes. That probably doesn't make sense to you right now but perhaps it will after you read it.

I also see it as a reminder of how the battle between good and evil may have started as a battle in the heavenlies but has ended up there and on earth.

"A Great Sign" (v.1)

> *1 A great sign appeared in heaven: a woman clothed with the sun, with the moon under her feet and a crown of twelve stars on her head.*

I am intrigued by this reference to a sign. My understanding of what a sign is doesn't seem to fit with the use of the term here. In fact, in the KJV, it is referred to as a wonder. That term is easier for me to understand, but I wonder if there is something for me to learn by the use of the word sign.

As I looked in Scripture for other references to signs, I found myself circling around these two: Isaiah 7:14, "Therefore the Lord himself will give you a sign: The virgin will be with child and will give birth to a son, and will call him Immanuel." and then in Luke 2:12, "This will be a sign to you: You will find a baby wrapped in cloths and lying in a manger." Could it be a coincidence that the story that follows about a woman who is pregnant and is about to give birth begins with a reference to it being a sign? There is also a part of me that wants to make a connection to Mark 13:4, "Tell us, when will these things happen? And what will be the sign that they are all about to be fulfilled?" (See also Matthew 24:3 and Luke 21:7) but it feels like I'm really stretching here so I've decided to let it go and get back to the story at hand.

So who is the woman mentioned here? Some commentators say it is Eve, some say it is Mary, and others suggest it is a metaphor for Israel. It feels to me like it is Mary, consistent with the signs mentioned earlier. Just as in the previous chapter we had a sort of replay of the story of Jesus' ministry, crucifixion, and resurrection, perhaps here we are about to relive the story of His birth seen from another perspective.

Or perhaps the story is about the birth of Christianity itself—hmmm.

The woman is clothed with the sun, which suggests that she is bathed in God's glory or approval. She has the moon under her feet, which suggests to me that she is elevated above others. This idea is confirmed by the fact that she is wearing a crown on her head.

And what do we make of the twelve stars in her crown? Well, if we assume that twelve represents completeness, or the number of God's people, then perhaps the twelve stars are supposed to cause us to think of the twelve tribes of Israel—which is probably why some commentators think of her as Israel—but maybe it's just intended to show her as royalty among God's people.

I also think it's cool that in this verse we see all the familiar heavenly bodies; sun, moon and stars, brought together in this one being.

"She Was Pregnant" (v.2)

John sees that she is pregnant. Typically, a pregnant woman won't experience serious pain until she is about to actually give birth so it seems the birth will set off the events of this chapter.

"Red Dragon" (v.3)

> ³ *Then another sign appeared in heaven: an enormous red dragon with seven heads and ten horns and seven crowns on its heads.*

This is the only place in Scripture where I can find reference to a red dragon. However, a dragon is mentioned several more times in Revelation.

Since the color red is typically associated with slaughter and violence I think it's safe to expect some nasty things to follow. Isaiah 27:1 says, "In that day, the LORD will punish with his sword, his fierce, great and powerful sword, Leviathan the gliding serpent, Leviathan the coiling serpent; he will slay the monster of the sea." With regard to this verse in the NIV Life Application Bible study notes it says, "In ancient Aramean [Ugaritic] literature, Leviathan was a seven-headed monster, the enemy of God's created order." So perhaps this seven-headed red dragon is also the Leviathan from Isaiah.

It's obviously a pretty important dragon because of all the crowns on its numerous heads. In Daniel 7:7, "After that, in my vision at night I looked, and there before me was a fourth beast ... it had 10 horns." Further in Daniel's vision it says that the ten horns represent ten kings. I wonder what to do with that information as it relates to the story in Revelation. Clearly here in John's vision the red dragon is in heaven—Daniel's vision seems to be more earth-based, so for now I'm not going to over analyze. Instead I'm simply going to go with the assumption that the red dragon represents Satan.

Childbirth (v.4)

We can see that this red dragon has some exceptional power since he's able to sweep stars out of the sky. But the power has some limits, because he is only able to remove one-third of them.

> *⁴ᵇ The dragon stood in front of the woman who was about to give birth, so that it might devour her child the moment he was born.*

As I recall my own experiences with childbirth, I am reminded that this was a process over which I had no control. Once the contractions began there was no stopping them. I wasn't able to simply ignore them and focus on other things—okay, maybe I could in the early stages but not when it came close to actual delivery. So this woman is full of the power of giving birth, but yet powerless against the evil one standing in front of her.

The imagery of this scene is stunning. Can you picture it? Imagine the red dragon, perhaps he's drooling or frothing at the mouth, boldly standing in front of the woman—actually I imagine him sort of bouncing from foot to foot in excited anticipation. The woman, who although obviously royal is the same as every other woman in existence who has ever given birth, and is bent over in pain. She is completely engaged in the process of childbirth. She may be filled with fear because of the dragon in front of her, but she must give herself over to delivering this child—she has no choice. Personally I can't imagine what it would be like to know that as I'm giving birth there is something waiting to take my baby and destroy it as soon as it is born. As I'm writing these words my heart goes out to any woman who has had to go through this kind of experience for whatever reason.

The good news is that the dragon didn't get the baby.

"Gave Birth To a Son" (v.5)

> [5] She gave birth to a son, a male child, who "will rule all the nations with an iron scepter." And her child was snatched up to God and to his throne.

But who is this baby? We've seen reference to ruling with an iron scepter in the letter to Thyatira in 2:27. In Psalms 2:9 this mention of ruling with an iron scepter was a reference to "the coronation of Christ, the eternal King."[26]

I wonder if in these two short sentences we are being reminded of the birth of Jesus and of his crucifixion, resurrection, and ascension into heaven? Or, as indicated earlier, is it a reminder of the birth of Christianity. I'm not sure you can separate one from the other. Cool!

"Fled Into the Wilderness" (v.6)

> [6] The woman fled into the wilderness to a place prepared for her by God, where she might be taken care of for 1,260 days.

I've been thinking that this vision was taking place in heaven, but here we are told that the woman flees to a very earth-based place—the wilderness.

This has caused me to reconsider my concept of wilderness. I've had the opportunity to stand in areas on earth that are called wildernesses. They are usually vast and somewhat empty of human life. In Scripture we often see people or groups—think the Exodus—who are cast into the wilderness to wander, often as a form of punishment. In my culture we tend to speak of wandering in the wilderness as a time of feeling lost, of waiting.

Certainly here, the woman is sent to the wilderness to wait, but it's a safe place. It's a place where God will be taking care of her just as He took care of the Israelites who fled to the wilderness to escape the Egyptians. Just as He cares for each of us as we spend time in our own wilderness areas regrouping or preparing for coming events.

Here are those 1,260 days again. In the story of the two witnesses in chapter 11, I connected that time-frame to the length of Jesus' ministry. I also suggested that perhaps we, as followers of Jesus, were expected to be ministering as well. Perhaps the time frame is intended to refer to the current church age—the time when we are to continue His work here on earth.

I wonder if the repetition of this time frame, used in chapter 11 and then again here was meant to show us that there is a link between the visions.

"War Broke Out In Heaven" (v.7)

> *[7] Then war broke out in heaven. Michael and his angels fought against the dragon, and the dragon and his angels fought back.*

We are obviously back in heaven with this phase of the vision. Is this a reminder of the ultimate battle between good and evil—a battle that continues even today unseen by us?

I find it interesting that Michael has angels helping in the battle but so does the dragon. As we continue through Revelation we will see several places where Satan seems to portray himself as having similar qualities as Jesus. Interesting.

Why are we told that it is Michael who is leading this battle? Who is this Michael? In Daniel 12:1 we are introduced to a Michael, as follows, "At that time Michael, the great prince who protects your people, will arise. There will be a time of distress such as has not happened from the beginning of nations until then. But at that time your people—everyone whose name is found written in the book—will be delivered." So the Michael of Daniel's time, true to his description as the "one who protects your people", is now shown doing exactly that as he leads a battle against the dragon.

"The Great Dragon" (v.8–9)

And so regardless of how hard the dragon and his angels fight, they lose and are cast out of heaven.

The reference in verse 9 to the "great dragon" almost seems sarcastic. Notice as well that he wasn't just thrown down to earth—he was hurled—we're told this twice! Seems pretty intense.

His identity is also made very clear. This red dragon is Satan.

I love the fact that here in Revelation we are given a link all the way back to creation. Here we see the serpent from the Garden of Eden that led Adam and Eve astray being hurled to the earth. I can almost hear the splat as he hits the ground. But I'm afraid it isn't that easy. We aren't told that he is destroyed, only that he was hurled to the earth, and that can't be a good thing for those of us living here on earth as well.

"Loud Voice In Heaven" (v.10–11)

> *[10] Then I heard a loud voice in heaven say: "Now have come the salvation and the power and the kingdom of our God, and the authority of his Messiah. For the accuser of our brothers and sisters, who accuses them before our God day and night, has been hurled down.*

In chapter 11, as we finished the story of the two witnesses we heard a pronouncement by loud voices in heaven, and here we hear another loud voice in heaven making a somewhat similar pronouncement. In case we didn't get it in the story so far, this interlude in verses 10–12 makes it very clear to us that Satan—also known as the accuser—loses.

I think that this is the last time we will see any reference to Satan existing anywhere other than on earth—no longer does he have a place in the heavenlies.

But there is so much more to this passage. I wonder who the "brothers and sisters" are. My best guess is that they are fellow believers. In verse 11 we are told that they triumphed over him by the blood of the Lamb. It serves as a reminder that Christ died for our sins, and in doing so, freed us from the grasp of the accuser.

The statement "did not love their lives so much as to shrink from death" makes me wonder if this is also a nod to the martyrs waiting under the altar that we saw when the fifth seal was opened in 6:9 where we read "I saw under the altar the souls of those who had been slain because of the word of God and the testimony they had maintained."

We are told that they triumphed by the blood of the Lamb and the word of their testimony. According to that favorite pastor of mine, the word of their testimony is "our collective declaration of reality in Jesus - Jesus is King"[27] In other words, those who have survived much in their lives were able to do so because of their unfailing faith in Jesus Christ.

"Woe To the Earth" (v.12)

In Luke 10, Jesus sent out the seventy-two to go ahead of him as he traveled teaching others. When they returned they told Jesus that "even the demons submit to us in your name" (v.17). Jesus responded to them, "I saw Satan fall like lightning from heaven" (v.18), and then in verse 20, "do not rejoice that the spirits submit to you, but rejoice that your names are written in heaven."

And just as Jesus told the seventy-two, the battle appears to be finished in heaven. He saw Satan hurled down. But we need to beware because it is just getting started on earth. The dragon obviously didn't like getting hurled down to earth because he is now out for revenge.

Interesting, up to now he obviously didn't know he was going to lose the battle but now we're told that he knows his time is short.

As I try to make sense of this entire passage I wonder if this is another reminder of life in our current church age.

"He Pursued the Woman" (v.13)

> [13] *When the dragon saw that he had been hurled to the earth, he pursued the woman who had given birth to the male child.*

This scene with the woman and the dragon that seemed to start in heaven—or is it actually someplace in between—now appears to be active on earth. Why is he so focused on her? Why not the child? Or is that what the heavenly battle was about? He couldn't have the child so he goes after the mother, perhaps with the intent of hurting the child as a side-effect. Perhaps the more important point here is that we recognize that Satan doesn't give up easily. He can be, and is persistent.

Satan Persists, God Provides (v.14)

In Exodus 19:4, it says, "You yourselves have seen what I did to Egypt, and how I carried you on eagles' wings and brought you to myself." In that passage the Israelites are reminded of God's faithfulness in bringing them out of Egypt and into the wilderness on their way to the land that He had promised them. Just as he kept the Israelites safe, in this story, the woman is being kept safe during this time of ministry on the earth—time, times and half a time.

"The Serpent Spewed Water" (v.15)

The visual of the serpent spewing water from his mouth is interesting. Is it a rush of words spewing from his mouth? Is Satan trying to convince the woman to come over to his side?

"But the Earth Helped the Woman" (v.16)

But it doesn't work. We're told the earth helped the woman. So once again we are reminded that Satan is not all-powerful.

> *[17] Then the dragon was enraged at the woman and went off to wage war against the rest of her offspring—those who keep God's commands and hold fast their testimony about Jesus.*

Look out fellow believers! The dragon couldn't get the son. He couldn't get the woman. So he is coming after us!

Some Things To Think About

So is this a story about Jesus' birth, and the battle between God, via Michael, and Satan? I think that it is in part. I think that with almost everything else we have seen so far in Revelation that it also continues to be a reminder of how God is in control of all these events:

- He saved the child.
- He protects the woman.
- He cast down the dragon.
- He provides justice to those "who did not love their lives so much as to shrink from death."

Revelation 13

The Beast Out Of the Sea (13:1–10)

The following chapters are very challenging for me to understand. We are stepping into an area of Revelation that continues to confuse, and I apologize right up front for the fact that you will see far more questions than answers as we proceed. I have, however, been inspired by a rather simplistic take on this immediate passage. Bear with me as I attempt to share it with you here.

In the RSV, the last verse of chapter 12 says "Then the dragon was angry with the woman, and went off to make war on the rest of her offspring, on those who keep the commandments of God and bear testimony to Jesus. And he stood on the sand of the sea." And then this chapter begins with, "And I saw a beast rising out of the sea." This is also the case for the ESV, the HCSB, and some other translations— interesting. It completely changes how one sees this vision. If we stick to the NIV version as shown here, this chapter could imply a new vision. Read the other way, it is a continuation of the previous one. That being said, I don't think it actually changes the message of the text.

The Dragon From the Sea (v.1)

> ¹ The dragon stood on the shore of the sea. And I saw a beast coming out of the sea. It had ten horns and seven heads, with ten crowns on its horns, and on each head a blasphemous name.

Based on the difference discussed above I think it's safe to assume that this dragon standing on the shore of the sea is the red dragon introduced to us in chapter 12.

Often in Scripture the term 'beast' is used in the context of man and beast. However, in the story of the two witnesses in 11:7 we saw a more intimidating type of beast as "the beast that comes up from the Abyss" that attacked them. In Daniel's vision described in Daniel chapter 7 the idea of a beast takes on a similar menacing meaning. Daniel 7:3 says, "Four great beasts, each different from the others, came up out of the sea." And here in Revelation we are told of a beast coming out of the sea. The connection between these visions is too strong to ignore. First century readers of Revelation would be very familiar with Daniel's vision, as are many of us today. Through Daniel's visions we saw a story very similar to the message of Revelation. Evil exists through Satan. He battles with God's angels and is present on the earth. But God is on His throne and when the time is come, Satan and his followers lose the ultimate battle—God wins!

Is there more to be learned by the link between these visions? Perhaps; but it feels too big for me to understand. I'm going to look at these connections from the perspective that by weaving them into the story here, God, through John, wants us to remember the message of Daniel's vision which I think is summed up nicely in Daniel 7:26–27, "But the court will sit, and his power will be taken away and completely destroyed forever. Then the sovereignty, power and greatness of all the kingdoms under heaven will be handed over to the holy people of the Most High. His kingdom will be an everlasting kingdom, and all rulers will worship and obey him."

Throughout Daniel 7 the four beasts are described as follows: "The first was like a lion, and it had the wings of an eagle" (v.4a), "a second beast, which looked like a bear."(v.5a), "another beast, one that looked like a leopard"(v.6a), "a fourth beast—terrifying and frightening and very powerful. It had large iron teeth ... it was different from all the former beasts, and it had ten horns." (v.7) We're seeing ten horns here as well. This one also has a blasphemous name on each head.

In Matthew 27:37 we read, "Above his head they placed the written charge against him: THIS IS JESUS, THE KING OF THE JEWS." This passage from the story of the crucifixion of Christ immediately came into mind as I read about the blasphemous names on each of the seven heads of this beast. I wonder if this beast is mocking Jesus. In fact as I progress through this chapter it seems like Satan is setting up his own version of a trinity in an effort to pretend he has God-like qualities and a God-like nature.

Describing the Beast (v.2)

As we learn more about this beast from the sea, it is interesting to see that it bears most of the key features of the beasts described in Daniel's vision. Features from the leopard, bear and lion are each part of this description as well. Only thing missing is the wings of an eagle. Cool stuff! I'm not sure what to make of that but it's impossible to ignore the connection.

The relationship between the red dragon and this beast is also very interesting. The dragon gave the beast his power and his throne which suggests to me that this beast, without the dragon, was powerless.

We haven't seen a reference to a beast and a throne before this in Scripture—is this an attempt to parody the throne scenes we've seen earlier in Revelation? Perhaps it is an attempt to warn the reader that

Satan has his minions, his sidekicks so-to-speak, and that Satan is worshipped by some.

"Fatal Wound" (v.3)

> ³ *One of the heads of the beast seemed to have had a fatal wound, but the fatal wound had been healed. The whole world was filled with wonder and followed the beast.*

Taking the analogy even further, now we see that this beast has had a fatal wound and that he recovered. My understanding of a fatal wound is that it causes death. So here we are being told that this beast dies, or should have died, and comes back to life—the wound is healed. It's an interesting attempt to parallel the crucifixion and resurrection of Jesus.

I am troubled by the statement that the "whole world was filled with wonder and followed the beast." Where are the followers of the Lamb through this? Some of this will be clarified in verse 8 but for now as I consider this statement I am forced to acknowledge how easy it is for me to be distracted by the temptations of living in a comfortable, rich society. I do not intentionally choose to follow Satan, but I confess that sometimes I find myself going down that path without even realizing what has happened.

"People Worshiped" (v.4)

So the dragon and the beast are clearly two different entities and both appear to be the recipients of worship.

Several times in the Old Testament we see the phrase 'Who is like you, O LORD?' In Psalms 35:10, "My whole being will exclaim, "Who is like you, O LORD? You rescue the poor from those too strong for them, the poor and needy from those who rob them."'" and in Psalms 89:6, "Who is like the LORD among the heavenly beings?" or in Psalms 113:5, "Who is like the LORD our God, the One who sits enthroned on high."

I believe we are being given a picture of how Satan tries to present himself to us. But even as he tries to make himself look as powerful as God, the vision is of one who has to borrow from the things we know of God and His son, Jesus Christ, in order to appear credible—a sad imitation.

And one more piece of Scripture that comes to mind here from 1 Chronicles 17:20, "There is no one like you, O LORD, and there is no God but you, as we have heard with our own ears."

"The Beast Was Given" (v.5–6)

We're not told here who has given the beast the mouth to utter proud words. Was it God? Has He allowed Satan to roam the earth during this church age time of ministry trying to win us over?

Something I find quite interesting here is how in verse 5 we are told that the beast was given a mouth to do something, and then in verse 6 we are told that he did them. This is a little different than some of the other places in Revelation where we have been told that something or someone has been given the power to do something, but we are never shown them actually doing it. It's another of those things I'm not sure what to do with but I still find interesting.

"Against God's Holy People" (v.7)

As we saw in chapter 12, the dragon lost the battle in heaven and was hurled to earth. There we were warned that he was off to wage war against those who keep God's commands. Here we are seeing the beast from the sea—the red dragon's guy on earth—attempting to bad-mouth the one who hurled the dragon to earth by blaspheming God.

Too bad for him, he can't defeat God. He can only speak against Him. But he does appear to have the power to try. Who gave him this power? Was it God, just as it was in the story of Job?

Ephesians 6:10–13 says, "Finally, be strong in the Lord and in his mighty power. Put on the full armor of God so that you can take your stand against the devil's schemes. For our struggle is not against flesh and blood, but against the rulers, against the authorities, against the powers of this dark world and against the spiritual forces of evil in the heavenly realms. Therefore put on the full armor of God, so that when the day of evil comes, you may be able to stand your ground, and after you have done everything, to stand."

This was a call to us as Christians living not in the end-times but right now in the current church age. This isn't a battle to take place some time in the future but right now—today.

"All Inhabitants Of the Earth" Clarified (v.8)

> *8 All inhabitants of the earth will worship the beast—all whose names have not been written in the Lamb's book of life, the Lamb who was slain from the creation of the world.*

There are a few things in this verse that resonate with me.

First, I am glad to see that having my name written in the Lamb's book of life saves me from worshipping the beast.

Second, I am struck by the fact that there appear to be only two options: if your name is written in the book of life you don't worship the beast because you've chosen to worship God; if your name isn't there, you worship the beast; there is no middle ground.

Third, I'm puzzled by the phrase "slain from the creation of the world". In the ESV verse 8 reads as follows, "and all who dwell on earth will worship it, everyone whose name has not been written before the foundation of the world in the book of life of the Lamb who was slain." This slightly different phrasing sits more comfortably for me. As I read the NIV version it feels like the message is that the Lamb was slain from the creation, whereas in the other translations (there are others besides the ESV that go with the alternate phrasing), the message is that my name was written in the book of life since creation. It's at times like this that I do wish I could read Greek so I could more clearly understand differences in the text such as this. Since I don't, I'm very glad that in today's world we have many difference translations available at our fingertips to help with our understanding.

"Whoever Has Ears" (v.9)

> *⁹ Whoever has ears, let them hear.*

We have seen a version of this phrase several times already in Revelation. It appears in each of the letters to the seven churches in chapters 2 and 3 as the refrain at the end of each letter. (See 2:7,11,17,29, 3:6,13,22.) Is the purpose of this refrain to bring us back to an understanding that this is still part of the letters to the churches and to us as believers? Is it telling us to listen-up, to pay attention to what's happening?

"Patient Endurance" (v.10)

> ^{10} *"If anyone is to go into captivity, into captivity they will go. If anyone is to be killed with the sword, with the sword they will be killed." This calls for patient endurance and faithfulness on the part of God's people.*

There seems to be a connection between verse 7 and this verse. In verse 7 we were told that the beast was given power to wage war against God's holy people and to conquer them. Here we are given some indication of what can happen as a result of the war—being made captive or killed. Then we are told that God's people will be required to display patient endurance and faithfulness throughout.

Perhaps the message to Christians in this church age is that some will have to suffer in significant ways for their faith, and others, perhaps not as much. But for all of us, as we wonder why the suffering is happening, we will have to remain patient and faithful. We are to understand that a time will come when all will be set right. And through it all there is still the underlying message that God is in control.

The Beast out of the Earth (13:11–18)

> ^{11} *Then I saw a second beast, coming out of the earth. It had two horns like a lamb, but it spoke like a dragon.*

And now we are told of a third character in Satan's band—sure looks like an attempt to pretend to be a trinity doesn't it. By the way, this is the being that some consider to be the Antichrist. Later in Revelation 16:13 it says, "Then I saw three impure spirits that looked like frogs; they came out of the mouth of the dragon, out of the mouth of the beast and out of the mouth of the false prophet." So here, it appears we are meeting the false prophet.

From the Earth (v.11)

I wonder if there is significance to the fact that this beast comes from the earth? In Daniel 7:17 in the interpretation of his dream Daniel is told, "The four great beasts are four kingdoms that will rise from the earth." I'm not sure how that plays out here but it is interesting that in Daniel's vision the beast came up from the sea as did our first beast in verse 2 and in the interpretation we find that it rises from the earth just as this beast does.

The description of this beast that comes from the earth is interesting as well. It had horns like a lamb but spoke like a dragon—a wolf in sheep's clothing perhaps?

Perhaps I don't need to understand the implications of all this—evil is evil. I need to be aware of it. I need to be on my guard because as is implied in this verse, it could look like a lamb, but actually be a dragon. A false Christ may present himself as being Christ-like but actually be filled with evil and evil intentions.

"It Exercised All the Authority Of the First Beast" (v.12)

This is fascinating and I don't know what to do with it. The dragon gave the beast that rose out of the sea power and authority, but this second beast is actually *exercising* that authority. This second beast seems to be in place to encourage or perhaps, to force people to worship the first beast as if he couldn't do so on his own.

"Even Causing Fire" (v.13)

Why does he use the word 'even' here? Is causing fire to come down from heaven something really spectacular? Or is it because in this vision it is happening in front of an audience so there will be witnesses to the event?

"Ordered Them To Set Up an Image" (v.14)

This beast is certainly acting like an agent for the beast from the sea. In ordering the inhabitants of the earth to set up an image in honor of the beast we see them falling back to ancient pagan traditions of worshiping idols or emperors.

"Give Breath To the Image" (v.15)

Not only did the beast from the sea get an image of himself, but this other beast is even giving it breath—makes for a very powerful image. I can imagine smoke coming from the mouth of this terrible beast. The visual would be awe-inspiring and frightening to observers. Isn't apocalyptic language amazing!

The image was also given power to kill. Flashback to Daniel 3 where those who didn't worship the image of Nebuchadnezzar were to be killed.

The Mark Of the Beast (v.16–17)

> [16] *It also forced all people, great and small, rich and poor, free and slave, to receive a mark on their right hands or on their foreheads,* [17] *so that they could not buy or sell unless they had the mark, which is the name of the beast or the number of its name.*

Just as in 4:7, where the followers of the Lamb were sealed, so are the followers of the beast. However, here it isn't a free-will thing—they were forced to receive the mark. By these actions it becomes clear who is a follower of the Lamb and who is not. Either you bear the Lamb's seal or the mark of the beast. Once again, there is no middle ground.

And in the vision, if you didn't have the mark of the beast you couldn't participate in commerce. For the first-century Christians who were being persecuted, this concept would be familiar. In some places as we mentioned when looking at the seven churches, we know that if a Christian refused to worship the emperor, he or she would not be able to participate fully in the economy.

This is where I find myself getting drawn into the vision, losing my perspective. Is this really going to happen? Or is it a metaphor for something else in our Christian lives? Could it mean that as Satan gains strength in today's world, it becomes more difficult for Christians to survive spiritually or perhaps literally?

This idea of the mark of the beast has caused a lot of people to wonder and worry about how it would happen. There is technology in our current society that makes it possible to implant a device under the skin that uniquely identifies a person, and that can be used to gain entry to a building and to engage in monetary transactions. Some see this as the technology that will make the mark of the beast a reality. I say that it doesn't need sophisticated technology—all it takes is a tattoo.

But the bigger concern many people seem to have is that they will receive the mark of the beast without realizing that it has happened. So for example, they will work for a company that asks its employees to get the implant I mentioned instead of carrying a security card or some such device. They get the implant and then find out that it is actually the mark of the beast. This is another of those things that doesn't make sense to me. I think the important part of verse 16 above, is that it *forced* the people to receive the mark. It didn't *sneak* the mark on them. If this passage reflects a future event I'm pretty sure we will know what's happening and that we will have a choice.

Okay, so the results of not choosing the mark may not be ideal in the short-term, once again, we know that in light of eternity not choosing the mark will be worth it.

"This Calls for Wisdom (v.18)

> [18] *This calls for wisdom. Let the person who has insight calculate the number of the beast, for it is the number of a man. That number is 666.*

I'm not sure why we're told that this calls for wisdom. Proverbs 2:6 says, "For the Lord gives wisdom; from his mouth come knowledge and understanding." By telling us that "this calls for wisdom" are we being reminded to stay rooted in God's word; to retain some perspective in all of this?

The practice of Gemetria is a form of Hebrew numerology common in early church times, and has been used to figure out what the number may mean. Common understanding is that the number 666 refers to Emperor Nero who symbolized all the evils of the Roman Empire. Early church readers would have understood the significance of thinking of Nero as the beast. For those of us, reading this two thousand years later, it may be that what we are to do with this information is to simply understand just how evil the beast is.

Others have looked at this number from a completely different perspective. The numbers three and seven are considered both perfect numbers in the Hebrew tradition. Therefore, if three sevens represent complete perfection, then the number 666 falls completely short of perfection meaning that once again Satan, while trying to imitate God, has fallen short of the mark.

Some Things To Think About

The things that strike me about this chapter are:

- Satan isn't working alone—he has his sidekicks helping him along.
- Because he lost the battle in Heaven, he is really keen to do some damage here on earth.
- We are his targets.
- It is important that we do not underestimate him.
- Some of us will die fighting against him.

As I'm writing these words I am reminded of the many Christians throughout the world right now who are being forced to choose. Christians are under attack and are being killed for choosing to proclaim Jesus Christ as their Lord and Savior. This isn't a future event—this is happening now to so many who are being martyred for their faith.

Revelation 14

This chapter seems to be a significant turning point in Revelation. Up to this point, the visions John has been sharing with us have been focused, in my opinion, on life in the current church age. We have seen the story of Salvation and been introduced to all the players—God, Jesus Christ, the Holy Spirit, those who bear the seal of the Living God, the various faces of Satan, and those who bear the mark of the beast.

The three sections of Chapter 14 move us along through the transition. We open with a scene of worshipping believers ready for battle. The second scene feels like a message that God has sent as a warning. It's like He is saying, "let me make it clear here exactly what is happening. I'm giving you a chance to hear the gospel but if and when you reject it or don't act accordingly, then you need to know that things aren't going to go well for you." Then in the final section of this chapter we are given a glimpse of the outcome.

As we move on to the remaining chapters of Revelation the stories are all focused on the punishment and fall of evil, the judgment process and ultimately with a glimpse into the reward for the followers of the Lamb and life everlasting.

The Lamb and the 144,000 (14:1–5)

> [1] Then I looked, and there before me was the Lamb, standing on Mount Zion, and with him 144,000 who had his name and his Father's name written on their foreheads.

Ready For Battle (v.1)

Wow, we've just finished a chapter in which we've seen people lining up to receive the mark of the beast and consequently become part of his team—okay not really, but my imagination takes me there. Here John's next image is one of the Lamb standing on Mount Zion surrounded by the 144,000. He has his army aligned for battle.

Throughout Scripture, Mount Zion has been associated with the concept of deliverance. Hebrews 12:22–23 says, "But you have come to Mount Zion, to the heavenly Jerusalem, the city of the living God. You have come to thousands upon thousands of angels in joyful assembly, to the church of the firstborn, whose names are written in Heaven. You have come to God, the judge of all men, to the spirits of righteous men made perfect." Obadiah 1:17a, "But on Mount Zion will be deliverance." Joel 2:32, "And everyone who calls on the name of the LORD will be saved; for on Mount Zion and in Jerusalem there will be deliverance, as the LORD has said, among the survivors whom the LORD calls." Isaiah 31:4b, "so the LORD Almighty will come down to do battle on Mount Zion and on its heights." This reference to Mount Zion is significant to believers—to readers of the New and the Old Testament alike.

The Sound From Heaven (v.2)

In 1:15 we were told that Jesus' voice was like the sound of rushing waters. In 6:1 John heard one of the living creatures call out to the horse and rider in a voice like thunder. Here the sound from heaven has gathered momentum. It has a combination of sounds—rushing water and peals of thunder. We are told that it was like "harpists playing their harps." I imagine it as confusing, somewhat chaotic but strong and forceful as well.

Can you feel the scene? We have the crowd. I'm assuming they are dressed in white—a white that almost glows with purity and holiness. They are standing on a high hill and an unforgettable cacophony of sound—rushing water, thunder, harps—surrounds us. Wow!

"Before the Throne" (v.3)

And suddenly we are transitioned back to the scene around the throne. But are we actually seeing two different scenes or is it one? Is the army gathered on Mount Zion also standing before the throne? The pull on my human imagination to fully understand is huge. It is almost impossible to make sense of these shifts. It's obvious to me that I'm not supposed to figure it all out logically. I need to relax and focus on the message of the scenes presented.

Our last visit to the throne scene was in chapter 7 where we were introduced to the great multitude in white robes. In my comments there I saw a link between that great multitude and the sealing scene in chapter 6. I wonder if in being drawn back to the throne scene as we were in chapter 7, if God, through John, is reminding us that this 144,000 is in fact the great multitude mentioned there.

Here we have been given a chance once again, to see what's happening on this other plane; to be reminded that God has gathered His followers. Although they have assumed battle positions, they are still worshipping God, singing a new song that is known only to the redeemed.

I wonder if the new song is like a battle cry. Or, perhaps a reflection of the joy that only a follower of the Lamb can experience, which is why no one else could learn the song.

"They Remained Virgins" (v.4)

It gets a bit confusing for me here in verse 4. Is this reference to remaining virgins intended to be sexual or is it metaphorical? I decided to check other translations and found that where the version of the NIV that I've used for this text refers to 'virgins', older NIV translations say "they kept themselves pure." The NASB says "kept themselves chaste." I like how the Message puts it, "lived without compromise, virgin-fresh before God." I've checked a few commentaries as well. They all seem to agree that this reference is most likely meant to represent purity or fidelity.

Reference to 2 Corinthians 11:2 comes up frequently in the commentaries here, "I am jealous for you with a godly jealousy. I promised you to one husband, to Christ, so that I might present you as a pure virgin to him." So although I'm sure that a degree of sexual morality is implied here the bigger perspective is probably one focused on fidelity to Christ as followers of the Lamb.

The term 'firstfruits' appears often in Scripture particularly when talking about presenting offerings to God. Proverbs 3:9, "Honor the LORD with your wealth, with the firstfruits of all your crops." 1 Corinthians 15:20, "But Christ has indeed been raised from the dead, the firstfruits of those who have fallen asleep." The phrase carries an implication of giving, of sacrifice, and of dedication.

So my takeaway on this verse is that the redeemed mentioned in the previous verse have remained pure in that they have no other gods; they are disciples in that they follow the Lamb; and that they have dedicated themselves to God.

"No Lie Was Found In Their Mouths" (v.5)

And finally, this gathering of the redeemed who are worshiping around the throne and are singing a new song, are seen as pure disciples dedicated to God and the Lamb. They are found to be blameless—worthy to be a part of God's army in this battle between the Lamb and Satan.

The Three Angels (14:6–13)

"Another Angel Flying In Midair" (v.6)

> [6] *Then I saw another angel flying in midair, and he had the eternal gospel to proclaim to those who live on the earth—to every nation, tribe, language and people.*

I'm not sure why we're told that this is *another* angel. The last time we specifically saw an angel doing something in John's visions was back in chapter 11 when the seventh angel blew his trumpet. Perhaps all we're to take from this is that this event is separate from the trumpet judgments. Or, perhaps it is to separate it from the eagle, or as some translations put it, angel, flying in midair in 8:13.

As I mentioned in chapter 8, I like this concept of midair. I like the idea that this angel is in a position where everyone can hear what he is saying. We are told that he is proclaiming the eternal gospel to those who live on the earth. In 8:13 the angel or eagle was proclaiming "Woe! Woe! Woe to the inhabitants of the earth." So in both of these passages the angel or eagle flying in midair is addressing inhabitants of the earth or those who live on the earth. One commentator says, "The two phrases appear to be synonyms", and he goes on to suggest that it refers to unbelievers[28]. So the angel is proclaiming the gospel to the unbelievers on earth.

"The Hour Of His Judgment Has Come" (v.7)

This angel carries a sense of foreboding much like the eagle in 8:13. In his message that the hour of God's judgment has come, this angel is offering a final opportunity for those who haven't already done so, to switch to the Lamb's team.

I love the not-so-subtle reminder that God is the one responsible for all creation when John refers to, "him who made the heavens, the earth, the sea and the springs of water."

"A Second Angel" (v.8)

> [8] *A second angel followed and said, "'Fallen! Fallen is Babylon the Great,' which made all the nations drink the maddening wine of her adulteries."*

Just as the first angel finishes his warning that the hour of judgment has come, a second angel comes flying through telling the unbelievers what's about to happen.

The city of Babylon is most often portrayed in Scripture as an enemy of Israel, and as a symbol for the evil things of this world. Things aren't going to turn out well for Babylon.

Psalms 137:8 say, "O Daughter of Babylon, doomed to destruction, happy is he who repays you for what you have done to us." Isaiah 13:19, "Babylon, the jewel of kingdoms, the glory of the Babylonians' pride, will be overthrown by God like Sodom and Gomorrah." Isaiah 21:9, "Look, here comes a man in a chariot with a team of horses. And he gives back the answer: 'Babylon has fallen, has fallen!'"

Later in Revelation 18:2 we will see a repeat of the phrase "Fallen! Fallen is Babylon the Great!" It is about to become a recurring theme.

"The Wine Of Her Adulteries" (v.8)

The NASB translates this section as, "she who made all the nations drink of the wine of the passion of her immorality." Unbelievers are participating in the evilness. It's hard to tell whether they are doing so because they want to or because they are forced to—perhaps it doesn't matter. Perhaps the point is that once you have chosen to follow the beast, you will become a part of the evil that comes with it.

"A Third Angel" (v.9)

> [9] *A third angel followed them and said in a loud voice: "If anyone worships the beast and its image and receives its mark on their forehead or on their hand, ..."*

I love the imagery of this passage. First one angel flies overhead proclaiming the gospel, calling the people to worship God, and warning them that the time of judgment has arrived. Then a second angel flies through announcing that evil Babylon, perhaps representing those who oppose God, has fallen. And now a third angel follows warning people not to follow Satan. They've been given the good news of the Gospel; given insight into how evil does not win; and for those who may be slow to get the picture, are now warned that the battle between God and Satan will now include them as well.

"The Wine Of God's Fury" (v.10)

In Jeremiah 25:15 we read, "This is what the Lord, the God of Israel, said to me: "Take from my hand this cup filled with the wine of my wrath and make all the nations to whom I send you drink it." In verse 8 we were told that the unbelievers drank the wine of Babylon's adulteries. Now, here in verse 10, that analogy is taken one step further to highlight an opposing consequence.

I imagine a conversation something like, "Sorry God, I don't choose you. I'm drinking over here with Babylon." And God replying with "You want wine! I'll give you wine!"

Personally, I have no desire to become the object of God's fury.

"Burning Sulfur" (v.10)

We will see references to burning sulfur—sometimes called brimstone—three more times in Revelation. It is first mentioned in the Bible in Genesis 19:24, "Then the Lord rained down burning sulfur on Sodom and Gomorrah—from the Lord out of the heavens."

In an effort to understand more about burning sulfur I started looking around on the Internet. Did you know that sulfur is one of the most common elements on earth? It is found in almost everything, or so it seems. The part that matters most to this discussion is that it burns in solid or powder form—the name brimstone made sense because it was a stone that burned. As it burns, it takes on a molten aspect that continues to burn, is very hot, and emits a very unpleasant odor. I watched a video of sulfur burning, and was surprised to see that it wasn't a sudden flash fire but rather a slow, hot burn.

With that in mind, the idea of torment makes sense here because it would be slow and painful. If the fire didn't kill you, the fumes could.

And I don't think one should ignore that as this is happening, the Lamb and the holy angels are watching. This is the only time in Revelation that I could find reference to "holy angels." They are not mentioned in the Old Testament, but are mentioned in the New Testament in Mark (8:38) and Luke (9:26) when Jesus is predicting his death. Luke 9:26 reads, "Whoever is ashamed of me and my words, the Son of Man will be ashamed of them when he comes in his glory and in the glory of the Father and of the holy angels." And now, here, these holy angels are present when those who did not acknowledge Jesus Christ are tormented.

"The Smoke Of Their Torment" (v.11)

It's interesting how smoke often remains after a fire has been extinguished. Here we're told that this reminder will rise for ever and ever.

Now I'm curious if that means that in the new creation there will be smoke rising on the horizon as a reminder of this event. I wonder.

"Patient Endurance" (v.12)

> *12 This calls for patient endurance on the part of the people of God who keep his commands and remain faithful to Jesus.*

This is the third and final time in Revelation that we have seen, or will see, reference to "patient endurance" (see 1:9 and 13:10). So what does this mean? In 2 Corinthians 1:6 it says, "If we are distressed, it is for your comfort and salvation; if we are comforted, it is for your comfort, which produces in you patient endurance of the same sufferings we suffer." The reference to patient endurance in chapter 1 was when John was telling us about himself. He referred to "the suffering and kingdom and patient endurance that are ours in Jesus." There he assured us that this patient endurance was available to us through Jesus. In chapter 13, we were told that "This calls for patient endurance" after being told that "If anyone is to go into captivity, into captivity they will go."

For me this seems to connect to the concept of being told that the time is soon, and yet we wait. Are we being told that things are going to happen that we won't like, that may be painful and perhaps confusing, and that we need to just hang in there—it will all turn out right in the end.

"Blessed Are the Dead" (v.13)

> *¹³ Then I heard a voice from heaven say, "Write this: Blessed are the dead who die in the Lord from now on." "Yes," says the Spirit, "they will rest from their labor, for their deeds will follow them."*

This is the second of the beatitudes in Revelation. The first was right at the beginning in 1:3 and there will be 5 more as we read on. My sense is that this blessing is specially directed at the people of God mentioned in verse 12. We're being told that we need to patiently endure what is to come, remain faithful and if we do, when we die, whether it is because of our faith (as martyrs) or not, basically we can die in peace knowing that our death is temporary (resting from our labor) and that what we have done during this life will not be forgotten. And that, to me, is extremely good news!

Harvesting the Earth and Trampling the Winepress (14:14–20)

> *¹⁴ I looked, and there before me was a white cloud, and seated on the cloud was one like a son of man with a crown of gold on his head and a sharp sickle in his hand.*

With these final verses of chapter 14 we are given a different look at the final outcome.

"White Cloud" (v.14)

When I read this the first few times I immediately connected the cloud with the cloud mentioned in the Old Testament passages on the Exodus. This cloud reflected God's presence with the Israelites. What surprised me, however, is that this is the only place where we see reference to a white cloud. It may be that here we see the cloud described as white to reinforce the concept of purity.

In Daniel 7:13 it says, "In my vision at night I looked, and there before me was one like a son of man, coming with the clouds of heaven. He approached the Ancient of Days and was led into his presence." For the reader of Revelation who is familiar with Old Testament Scripture, this connection to Daniel's visions brings a special sense of awareness to the words written here. And for the reader who isn't familiar with Daniel's visions, this image is still awe-inspiring.

We saw this reference to one *like* a son of man, not only in Daniel 7 but also earlier in Revelation 1:13. It's interesting that elsewhere in the New Testament Jesus is often referred to as *the* son of man. For example, in Matthew 24:30, "They will see the Son of Man coming on the clouds of the sky, with power and great glory. And he will send his angels with a loud trumpet call, and they will gather his elect from the four winds, from one end of the heavens to the other." In Revelation he is never called the son of man. All that is somewhat interesting but what does it mean for us here? Well, I'm not sure. Perhaps it means that this isn't Jesus but rather someone acting on his behalf. An angel perhaps? It's another question I cannot answer.

He has a crown of gold on his head confirming that this being is royal. And in his hand he holds a sharp sickle. A sickle is used to harvest grain that is ripe. As I looked for other biblical references to a sickle, one stood out for me. It's from Joel 3:12–13 which says, "Let the nations be roused; let them advance into the Valley of Jehoshaphat, for there I will sit to judge all the nations on every side. Swing the sickle, for the harvest is ripe. Come, trample the grapes, for the winepress is full and the vats overflowing so great is their wickedness!" Considering this passage in Revelation 14 and the passage from Joel 3 it seems clear, at least to me that the time for judgment has arrived.

"Came Out Of the Temple" (v.15)

> [15] *Then another angel came out of the temple and called in a loud voice to him who was sitting on the cloud, "Take your sickle and reap, because the time to reap has come, for the harvest of the earth is ripe."*

This is the first time in Revelation that we are told that an angel came out of the temple. The last time we saw reference to the temple was in 11:19 when the temple in heaven was opened, and we saw the ark of His covenant inside. This was at the time of the seventh trumpet blast.

The fact that the angel has come out of the temple seems to imply a special status here. Not only that, he is giving instructions to the one who was sitting on the cloud. This seems to support the idea that the one like the son of man isn't Jesus, but rather acting on his behalf.

"Swung His Sickle" (v.16)

Whomever it is, with one swing—at least I'm assuming it was one swing—of the sickle the earth was harvested. To harvest typically means "the act or process of gathering a crop"[29]. It seems to me that once harvested, the crop is halted in its development. It can't change other than as it is affected by external forces. For example, grains, once harvested left in the rain could get moldy and rot but they would no longer be able to grow.

This verse alone suggests to me that when the end of life on this earth happens, it will be swift.

"Yet Another Angel" (v.17)

> *¹⁷ Another angel came out of the temple in heaven, and he too had a sharp sickle.*

But here comes another angel, again out of the temple, with a sickle. My first inclination is to wonder why this is necessary since it appears that the harvest is already complete. But then we're told that he will be using this sickle to remove the grapes from the vine. What is the scriptural significance of the grapes, the vine, and the fact that the grapes are ripe? When I think of grapes on the vine, I think of something bearing fruit. This reminds me of Matthew 7:16, "By their fruit you will recognize them." It seems we are being told that the fruit is being gathered so that judgment can begin.

"Angel Had Charge Of the Fire" (v.18)

> *¹⁸ Still another angel, who had charge of the fire, came from the altar and called in a loud voice to him who had the sharp sickle, "Take your sharp sickle and gather the clusters of grapes from the earth's vine, because its grapes are ripe."*

Leviticus 1 describes the steps to process a burnt offering in the temple. In that process there was a priest who was responsible to maintain the fire on the altar. I wonder if that is why we are told this angel was in charge of the fire. He came from the altar. Is it the altar from 6:9 under which the souls are waiting? Are we about to see their blood avenged?

"The Great Winepress" (v.19)

These grapes, once harvested, are being thrown into the great winepress of God's wrath. Isaiah 63:2–3, "Why are your garments red, like those of one treading the winepress? I have trodden the winepress alone; from the nations no one was with me. I trampled them in my anger and trod them down in my wrath; their blood spattered my garments, and I stained all my clothing." Feels like God is saying, "Enough, it is time to get justice for all the injustices that have been affecting God's people throughout the generations."

"Outside the City" (v.20)

Why are we told that the winepress is outside the city? We're not told which city, although some assume it is Jerusalem; perhaps even the New Jerusalem. Since John didn't name it, I assume that we don't need to know specifically which city is being referenced. The commentaries that I checked didn't say anything about the winepress being outside the city, so it seems that most don't care or don't think that this piece of information is significant. I'm not prepared to just look past it. In Hebrews 13:12 we read, "And so Jesus also suffered outside the city gate to make the people holy through his own blood." John 19:20 tells us, "for the place where Jesus was crucified was near the city." It makes sense to me then, that this act of judgment also takes place outside the city.

The trampling of the grapes results in the flowing of blood. The judgment is severe as is evidenced by the amount of blood described here in verse 20.

Why the specific reference to sixteen hundred stadia? The measurement term *stadia* is used only two times in Scripture. This is the first occurrence and the second is later in Revelation when we are given measurements of the New Jerusalem (21:16). When I investigated this further I found that this ancient unit of measure was approximately equal to one hundred eighty miles or three hundred kilometers. This distance apparently corresponds to the estimated length of Palestine from North to South. This is rather interesting, as it would then suggest that the blood flowing out of the press covered the length of Palestine. Add to that the information on the depth of the blood (as high as the horses' bridles) and I get the message that this judgment is severe and affects a large number of people.

Some Things To Think About

This has been quite a chapter. We started with a glimpse of God's army ready to do battle, and quickly moved on to see the multitude worshipping around the throne and singing a new song.

When the angels flew through midair the focus of the scene moves to unbelievers—those who are not worshipping around the throne. They are warned of the judgment to come. Then they are given a look at just how intense it could be and are shown the severity and extent of the judgment based on the amount of blood flowing out from the winepress.

As I consider it, I am struck by a few thoughts.

- The beginning and the end of this chapter show us two extremes—worshipping around the throne and blood flowing out from the winepress.
- I'm certain I want to be worshipping around the throne and not thrown into the winepress.
- Nowhere in this do we actually see the army, the followers of the Lamb doing anything other than worship. God is handling the dirty work. We simply need to keep our eyes on the prize so-to-speak and continue to worship God.
- He will avenge the blood of the martyrs—it is not ours to do.
- God is in control!

Revelation 15

Seven Angels With Seven Plagues (15:1–8)

In 11:14, we were told that the second woe had passed and that the third woe was coming soon.

The first woe associated with the fifth trumpet (9:1–11) had smoke rising from the Abyss followed by an influx of locusts. The locusts that had power like scorpions tormented the people, who did not bear the seal of God on their foreheads.

With the second woe (9:13–11:14) which seemed to start with the sounding of the sixth trumpet and end just before the seventh trumpet was sounded, we saw mankind being killed by plagues of fire, smoke, and sulfur, along with a severe earthquake. With the sounding of the seventh trumpet in 11:15–19 the story seemed to veer off into a series of smaller scenes related to the battle between good and evil—action taking place in a space that is not earth-bound.

There have been six of these small scenes so far. The first one (12:1–17) contained two great signs appearing in heaven. It was here that we read about the vision of the woman and the dragon. The first great sign in this vision was the appearance of the woman and the second was the appearance of the red dragon. The second scene (13:1–10) showed us the beast rising out of the sea. The third (13:11–18) had the beast coming out of the earth. This was followed by the scene of the Lamb and the 144,000 (14:1–5) and then of the three angels flying through midair (14:6–13). The sixth scene was the story of harvesting the earth and trampling the winepress (14:14–20)

"Another Great and Marvelous Sign" (v.1)

> ¹ *I saw in heaven another great and marvelous sign: seven angels with the seven last plagues—last, because with them God's wrath is completed.*

Another great sign in heaven precedes this final scene in the series. It's interesting that the first great sign we saw in 12:1 introduced us to the birth of the child—Jesus. The second sign, just a few verses later in 12:3 introduced us to the red dragon—Satan. And here, another great sign introducing us to that which will bring this all to an end.

With this sign we have angels appearing. No surprise, there are seven of them. I'm not sure what to do with the seven plagues mentioned here right now. In the next few verses they seem to be forgotten in the narrative. Although they show up periodically in the remainder of this chapter we don't see anything actually happening with the plagues until chapter 16. It feels like this is a preparation for the final set of judgments that are described there.

"Sea Of Glass" (v.2)

John saw something that he says looked like a sea of glass mixed with fire. The last time we saw a sea of glass was in 4:6 as part of the throne scene. There the sea of glass was before the throne and was clear as crystal. Now the sea, assuming it's the same sea, is glowing with fire. What a fascinating visual—a sea glowing with fire. As I consider this I am confused by mixed ideas and images. We're told that it is a sea of glass—cool, calm, smooth, perhaps even steadfast. Yet it is glowing with fire—not cool, not calm, not smooth, and perhaps violent. It's like the violence is coming from a place of steadfastness. Wow!

The last time we saw something standing beside the sea, it was the dragon welcoming the beast from the sea (13:1) and now, those who have been victorious over the beast and it's buddy from the earth, are now standing beside a sea. What an image of victory! God has given them harps so I can only imagine that singing is about to begin.

A Song (v.3–4)

And as they sing, John tells us that they are singing the song of Moses and the song of the Lamb. The song sung by the Israelites after their passage through the Red Sea (Exodus 15:1–21 and Deuteronomy 32:1–43) is often called the song of God's servant Moses. The song of the Lamb has links to Psalm 139. It is a song celebrating deliverance from evil, and victory over Satan. The song is a wonderful blend of celebration on two levels. It celebrates the deliverance of the Israelites out of Egypt, and the deliverance of the followers of the Lamb over Satan. There is a melding of Old Testament and New Testament, of Christians of both Jewish and Gentile birth to one victorious group.

Saw the Temple Opened (v.5)

> [5] After this I looked, and I saw in heaven the temple—that is, the tabernacle of the covenant law—and it was opened.

When the seventh trumpet sounded (11:15–19), we saw God's temple in heaven open. Within it, we saw the ark of His covenant. It's like from here we are being taken back now to that part of the story—the side scenes are finished. And here we are reminded that the tabernacle of the covenant law is opened which suggests that it would be visible to all. Many other translations refer to the "tabernacle of the covenant law" as the "tabernacle of the testimony." This same phrase is used elsewhere in Scripture (Exodus 38:21, Numbers 1:50,53, Numbers 10:11 and Acts 7:44) to refer to the tabernacle in the wilderness.

Out Came the Angels (v.6)

> ⁶ *Out of the temple came the seven angels with the seven plagues.*

The angels that John saw in verse 1 are now coming out of the temple. Is it perhaps significant that we've just seen the temple referred to as the tabernacle of the covenant law? Are these angels somehow connected with the fulfilling of the covenant? They are wearing clean linen and golden sashes that represent holiness, purity and royalty; or as one commentator suggested—glory, but it is even more than that. The linen is shining. These are very special angels.

"The Four Living Creatures" (v.7)

If I had any doubt that we were looking on the throne scene when discussing the burning sea of glass, I have no further doubts now. It's interesting that the four living creatures are the ones giving the angels golden bowls filled with the wrath of God. Usually these guys are busy worshipping; occasionally they have spoken, but here they are more active.

They are interacting with the angels who up till now were holding the seven plagues. Well actually, I guess that's an assumption—in verse 1 we were told that the angels were *with* the seven plagues, not that they were holding them. I wonder if that matters?

As I wondered about the biblical significance of golden bowls, I thought about the articles of worship used in the temple. The golden bowl was used in the Holy Place for "the pouring out of offerings" (Exodus 25:29). In Revelation 5:8 we saw the four living creatures and the twenty-four elders around the throne "holding golden bowls full of incense, which are the prayers of God's people." Are these the same bowls? I'm not sure. If they are then it would seem that the prayers are about to be answered.

"Smoke From the Glory Of God" (v.8)

During the time of the Exodus, the presence of smoke in the temple indicated that God was present. Here we see that same thing happening. It is certainly an indicator that God is present, but the part that is particularly interesting to me here is that His presence in the temple is making it impossible for anyone else to enter.

Some Things To Think About

In the past few chapters we have been given an overview, if you like, of what Revelation is about.

- We've been shown how the conflict with Satan began with the story of the red dragon and the woman.
- We have learned a great deal more about who Satan and his minions are and what they are up to.
- We have been given an overview of how it plays out with the followers of the Lamb worshipping around the throne while the inhabitants of the earth (aka: unbelievers) are shown the downside of their choice.

What could be left?

All of the information of how it comes to an end has been presented in a fairly general way so far. From here on I believe the message of Revelation takes a distinct turn towards events of the last days.

Oh, and notice how this chapter ends with the statement that "no one could enter the temple until the seven plagues … were completed." Once again, it's God's timing and only He is in control.

Revelation 16

The Seven Bowls of God's Wrath (16:1–21)

This chapter, for me, feels somewhat different when compared to others in this apocalyptic portion of Revelation. Although it is still using apocalyptic language there aren't as many unusual images. There are no locusts—although there is a brief interlude with frogs. There are no scrolls or horsemen. It all seems pretty straightforward.

One thing that is consistent is that as John tells the story of the seven bowls of God's wrath it is impossible to deny that God is in control.

"Voice From the Temple" (v.1)

> ¹ Then I heard a loud voice from the temple saying to the seven angels, "Go, pour out the seven bowls of God's wrath on the earth."

In 15:8 we learned that God was present in the temple when we were told that the temple was filled with smoke from the glory of God. Now we are hearing a loud voice coming from the temple. There is no doubt in my mind that this is the voice of God! John 3:36 says, "Whoever believes in the Son has eternal life, but whoever rejects the Son will not see life, for God's wrath remains on them." and in Romans 12:19, "Do not take revenge, my dear friends, but leave room for God's wrath, for it is written: "It is mine to avenge; I will repay," says the Lord." These words from Romans relate directly to words from the song of Moses mentioned in 15:3 and originally recorded in Deuteronomy

32:34–36a. It says, "Have I not kept this in reserve and sealed it in my vaults? It is mine to avenge; I will repay. In due time their foot will slip; their day of disaster is near and their doom rushes upon them. The LORD will judge his people and have compassion on his servants". It appears that here in Revelation chapter 16 we are going to see God avenging.

The way John has written this verse and the remainder of this chapter, it seems that these judgments happen quickly. There isn't a great deal of fanfare once we reach this point. God promised to avenge and now He is doing so.

The First Bowl (v.2)

> *² The first angel went and poured out his bowl on the land, and ugly, festering sores broke out on the people who had the mark of the beast and worshiped its image.*

This first bowl is emptied on the land and affects only the people who bear the mark of the beast. It's a direct attack on people. Based on what is written here, no one dies as a result of this plague so while it may be painful, it isn't as bad as it could be. Interesting. It's almost as if God doesn't want anyone dying right now. He's going to take the worshippers of the beast down slowly so they are absolutely aware of what is happening.

The Second Bowl (v.3)

> *³ The second angel poured out his bowl on the sea, and it turned into blood like that of a dead person, and every living thing in the sea died.*

This second plague affects the sea and the creatures within it. Now things are starting to die. However, we aren't told of any people dying but with the death of the creatures in the sea, a source of food has been removed from them.

There is a correlation here to the second trumpet judgment (8:8) but there only one-third of each thing was affected, here we are told that every living thing died. The earlier judgment was selective—this one is not.

The Third Bowl (v.4)

> ⁴ *The third angel poured out his bowl on the rivers and springs of water, and they became blood.*

And just as the third trumpet judgment affected one-third of the rivers and springs of waters, here we have them becoming blood again. Although it doesn't say so specifically, I am assuming that here it is all of them affected.

So now the people who are dealing with festering sores on their bodies, don't have any food from the seas to eat, or water to drink or to soothe their sores.

An Aside: *Here I'm forced to go into a side discussion. If the trumpet judgments were intended to describe actual end-times events, why wouldn't we be told here that the rest of the sea or the rest of the rivers or creatures in the seas were affected? Why are we told that it was all? I'm gaining confidence in my theory that the seal judgments and the trumpet judgment stories are included in Revelation to reach out to those who are familiar with teachings of God's promises, of His power—all intended to draw us to Him. Here the reminder stories are finished. We've had our chance to choose our side—now we are being shown the consequences of making the wrong choice! And although I'm still not clear in my mind whether this passage represents actual events that will take place at*

Christ's second coming, I am certain that the passage reinforces God's promise to avenge as stated in Romans 12:19.

"I Heard the Angel" (v.5)

Wow! There are a few things that stand out for me in these next few verses.

First, I'm curious about this angel in charge of the waters. In 14:18 John told us of the angel who has charge of the fire. Now we learn of one who has charge of the waters. I'm not sure what to do with that connection or if it even matters. So who is this angel? Is it the angel who has just poured out his bowl and turned all the drinkable water to blood? Could be. Makes a certain amount of sense to me that it is when we see the reference to having given them blood to drink.

Second, remember way back in Rev 1:4,8 we were introduced to "him who is, and who was, and who is to come" and then in 11:17 with the sounding of the seventh trumpet it changed to "One who is and who was." Here again He is called "'you who are and who were." He has come—He is no longer the "one who is to come."

For me, this connection to 11:17 is important as well because it suggests that the sounding of the seventh trumpet was intended to announce the actions described here.

"Blood To Drink" (v.6)

The order of the bowls is significant. God got the people's attention by striking them with festering sores, and then turned the sources of water around them to blood as a symbol of the blood that was shed by God's holy people through persecution and martyrdom.

Now blood is being given to those who persecuted them to drink, as they deserve. This is not the redemptive blood of the Lamb; this is the blood of God's avenging wrath. I'm sure something could be made of the fact that in both cases the symbol is that of blood—redemption, or vengeance. This one is too big for me to follow through on so I'm going to leave it hanging for now.

The Altar Responds (v.7)

My first reaction to this verse was "The altar? Interesting that a piece of furniture has been given a voice." And then I thought about 6:9–10 and the souls of those who had been slain because of the word of God who John saw under the altar when he opened the fifth seal. I am immediately drawn back there and realize that their waiting is almost over.

The Fourth Bowl (v.8–9)

> *8 The fourth angel poured out his bowl on the sun, and the sun was allowed to scorch people with fire.*

The fourth trumpet judgment targeted the sun, moon, and stars. There we saw that one-third of the day and one-third of the night were without light. This judgment is quite the opposite. Here the sun has become so intense that people are being scorched with fire.

Notice once again that we aren't told that they die. He's keeping them alive! And if we consider these bowls to take place sequentially, think about being out in the intense heat without water to drink while suffering with painful sores all over your body!

After reading this, if I were not a follower of the Lamb I'd be rethinking things—this is not a fate I'd wish on my worst enemy.

By cursing the name of God, the people were apparently acknowledging His existence, His power and authority. How stubborn can we get? What would cause us, in light of all this evidence, to NOT repent?

The Fifth Bowl (v.10–11)

> [10] *The fifth angel poured out his bowl on the throne of the beast, and its kingdom was plunged into darkness. People gnawed their tongues in agony* [11] *and cursed the God of heaven because of their pains and their sores, but they refused to repent of what they had done.*

I find myself drawn to some interesting, and perhaps irrelevant, connections here. With the fifth seal judgment we were told of the martyrs under the altar, and here the attack is on the throne of the beast. Both vital pieces of furniture—one in God's temple and the other in Satan's throne scene.

Then I'm connecting to the fifth trumpet judgment where locusts from the abyss attacked those who didn't bear the seal of the Lamb and were tortured but not killed. And here people are once again in agony but still they don't appear to be dying.

When I read that the kingdom of the beast is plunged into darkness, I imagine a great deal of chaos, of confusion, and perhaps of fear. Why I wonder, are they gnawing their tongues? Are they swollen from a lack of water? Can't they speak, or, are they being punished for what they have said? And still they refuse to repent. Wow!

The Sixth Bowl (v.12)

> [12] *The sixth angel poured out his bowl on the great river Euphrates, and its water was dried up to prepare the way for the kings from the East.*

So many thoughts are jumping through my mind with this verse. I've immediately connected back to the sixth trumpet judgment (9:13–21) that started at the great river Euphrates. There we had four angels who were released to kill one-third of mankind. Along with these four angels were a huge number of mounted troops to assist in the attack. So the Euphrates, which was one of the boundaries to the Promised Land, once again features strongly. With its water dried up here, it would be like opening the border to allow anyone to enter.

The drying up of the water draws me back to the story of the Exodus from Egypt. The final scene of the direct flight to escape Pharaoh's army takes place at the Red Sea where God holds back, or dries up, the waters of the sea to allow the Israelites to cross, and then closes it back up to drown the pursuing army, hence completing that part of the story.

And with that in mind, what of the kings from the East mentioned here? Do these represent Israel's enemies? There is a certain poetic justice to the idea that in Exodus when God held back the waters, it allowed the Israelites to attain freedom and subsequently ended in the destruction of the enemy. Here, drying the water would appear to allow the enemy to enter but perhaps ultimately to meet its destruction. Interesting.

Daniel 7:17 says, "The four great beasts are four kings that will rise from the earth." Are these the Kings from the East?

Frogs Came Out Of Their Mouths (v.13)

> *13 Then I saw three impure spirits that looked like frogs; they came out of the mouth of the dragon, out of the mouth of the beast and out of the mouth of the false prophet.*

"Why frogs?" I'm reminded of the sound they make—a rather unattractive croaking. I'm reminded of how they look—not the best looking of the animal world. I'm reminded of current day fairy tales where the lovely princess kisses the frog and he turns into a prince— you're right that's probably stretching it a bit. I'm also reminded that frogs were present in the plagues against Egypt. I guess what it comes down to is that the image of spirits that looked like frogs coming out of the dragon's mouth would be creepy. It would immediately alert us to the fact that this is probably not good. They are obviously Satan's servants.

In chapters 12 and 13 we first met the dragon, the beast from the sea and the beast from the earth. Now John calls them the dragon, the beast and the false prophet. This is the first time in Revelation that the term 'false prophet' appears and it obviously applies to one of the beasts. I'm not going to worry about which one although I'm inclined to believe it is probably the second beast described in chapter 13.

Gather For Battle (v.14)

And now we see that Satan and his servants are gathering an army. Remember in 9:3 when we were discussing the locusts that appeared out of the smoke of the Abyss? There I connected us to Joel 2 where we are told of the army of locusts. I think the final verse of Joel 2 connects strongly to what we are being shown here. In Joel 2:11 it says, "The Lord thunders at the head of his army; his forces are beyond number, and mighty is the army that obeys his command. The day of the Lord is great; it is dreadful. Who can endure it?" There we saw that God also amassed an army and there is no doubt in my mind that where in Joel it tells us "The day of the Lord is great", that is also what is called here in Revelation, "the great day of God Almighty." So Satan has his army and God has His. Let the battle begin!

"I Come Like a Thief" (v.15)

> *15 "Look, I come like a thief! Blessed is the one who stays awake and remains clothed, so as not to go naked and be shamefully exposed."*

I Thessalonians 5:2 says, "for you know very well that the day of the Lord will come like a thief in the night." 2 Peter 3:10, "But the day of the Lord will come like a thief." And in Revelation 3:3, in his letter to the church in Sardis we read, "Remember, therefore, what you have received and heard; hold it fast, and repent. But if you do not wake up, I will come like a thief, and you will not know at what time I will come to you." Notice that in all three passages we are told that He will come like a thief, but here there is no 'will'. Instead it says 'I come'. Things are happening!

Also in this verse we are given the third beatitude in Revelation. So what does it mean to "stay awake and remain clothed"? For me it suggests being ready, prepared for the event, and in this case it means to me that I have to have made my decision to be a follower of the Lamb.

I must remain true to that decision and be ready to do battle with Satan. And if I do so, I will be very happy that I did. He will come like a thief in the night. We will not receive a warning other than what we are reading here in Revelation.

"Armageddon" (v.16)

> *16 Then they gathered the kings together to the place that in Hebrew is called Armageddon.*

This is the only place in Scripture where the name Armageddon is used. Isn't it interesting that it has become a very familiar term in our current day society? In one of the definitions I found online for the word, it connects this battle to a biblical hill called Megiddo, which is an archaeological site south of present-day Haifa in Israel. I have had the opportunity to stand atop this hill and look out over the plains. The day I was there the surrounding valley was filled with smoke from fires that were happening across the Sea of Galilee and there was an eeriness to it that gave me a glimpse of what it could look like on the great day of God. While my experience was eerie, this final event at Armageddon will be so much worse.

The Seventh Bowl (v.17)

> *[17] The seventh angel poured out his bowl into the air, and out of the temple came a loud voice from the throne, saying, "It is done!"*

When the seventh seal was opened, there was silence in heaven and then we were introduced to the seven trumpets. When the seventh trumpet sounded, loud voices in heaven said, "The kingdom of the world has become the kingdom of our Lord and of his Messiah, and he will reign for ever and ever." (11:15). This was followed by a scene of worshipping around the throne and we were told in 11:18 "your wrath has come."

Since those words a few chapters back, John has shown us many scenes to remind us of who God is, of His power and might. He has also shown us who Satan is. He has given us glimpses of the on-going battle of God against Satan that is ever in play during the church age. Now here, with the pouring out of the seventh bowl, we are told in no uncertain terms "It is done!" The battle has ended.

"Earthquake" (v.18)

As the sixth seal was opened we were exposed to a great earthquake. At the seventh trumpet there were flashes of lightning, rumblings, peals of thunder, an earthquake and a severe hailstorm. But here we are told that this earthquake will be like no other that has ever happened. One can only imagine the destruction that this earthquake will cause.

"God Remembered Babylon The Great" (v.19)

In 14:8, we read, "A second angel followed and said, "'Fallen! Fallen is Babylon the Great,' which made all the nations drink the maddening wine of her adulteries.'" I mentioned there that we would see many more references to Babylon in the coming chapters.

I find it fascinating that in 14:8 we were told that Babylon made the nations drink the wine of her adulteries. And here, God is giving 'Babylon the Great'—sounds a bit sarcastic doesn't it—a cup filled with the wine of the fury of His wrath.

I wonder why we are told that the city split into three parts. Why not two? Or four? Or twenty?

"Every Island Fled" (v.20)

With the sixth seal (6:14) we saw that "every mountain and island was removed from its place." Here they're not just out of place—they cannot be found. Creation is coming undone.

"And they Cursed God" (v.21)

So they aren't dead yet, but still their hearts are hardened as they continue to curse God. Wow, once again, how stubborn can we be!

Some Things To Think About

When the end comes:

- I believe it will come suddenly and swiftly.
- Things will become progressively worse for those who bear the mark of the beast.
- This will happen according to God's timing.
- He will avenge the blood of the martyrs.

God is in control!

Revelation 17

In the previous chapter we saw God's punishment of those who bear the mark of the beast. It wasn't pretty. However, at the end, the people were still cursing God. They hadn't repented, but they were still alive.

Going forward we will see Satan and his servants and all those who worshipped him come to their ultimate end. No longer will they be cursing God—at least not that we'll know about—as they ultimately reach their version of eternity.

Babylon, the Prostitute on the Beast (17:1–18)

I wonder why God, through John, wanted us to hear this story? Is it a slap at existing societies based on materialism? Or is it integral to the scene playing out in Revelation?

2 Timothy 3:16 "All Scripture is God-breathed and is useful for teaching, rebuking, correcting and training in righteousness." This passage, as with all of Revelation had meaning to Christians in the time when it was written and has meaning to Christians throughout the generations since then. It was not written for a 21st century audience but rather for a multi-century audience. It was not written only for Christians residing in towns and cities across North America, but also for people living in villages in Africa and throughout the world.

I believe we have been given this text to teach us more about the character of Satan. Some of it is clear. Some is not. Consequently, there are quite a few references in the verses that follow that I cannot understand so I'll try to do the best I can with it.

"The Great Prostitute" (v.1)

> *¹ One of the seven angels who had the seven bowls came and said to me, "Come, I will show you the punishment of the great prostitute, who sits by many waters.*

It is important to note that the story here is introduced to John by one of the angels who participated in the pouring out of the bowl judgments. With that in mind I think we have to presume that this part of the vision is directly linked to the bowl judgments and likely is meant to give us more information specifically related, I believe to 16:19.

In just a few verses we will be told that this prostitute was given the title 'babylon the great'. It is natural, therefore, to associate the prostitute with the city of Babylon that played such a prominent role in Israel's history. According to online sources, "It has been estimated that Babylon was the largest city in the world from c. 1770 to 1670 BC, and again between c. 612 and 320 BC. It was perhaps the first city to reach a population above 200,000."[30] It is mentioned in the NIV more than three hundred times. The first entry is in Genesis 10:10 and the last time it is mentioned is in Revelation 19:1. It appears most often in the book of Jeremiah, a book that was written to God's people in an effort to get them to turn away from their sinful ways and return to God. It makes sense that here in Revelation, as God, through John is calling us to repentance that Babylon would be used to represent all that is evil.

Why refer to a city as a prostitute? The Merriam-Webster online dictionary defines a prostitute as, "a person (as a writer or painter) who deliberately debases his or her talents (as for money)."[31] There were variations of the definition that more specifically point to selling sexual favors for money which is the definition that most of us think of first.

For now, I find the first definition interesting to consider. If this is indeed a city, what could a city do to be called a prostitute? How can a city deliberately debase her talents, or sell herself for money? Obviously we aren't talking about a city per se, but rather about the leadership within a city. So, since I live in Canada, I can talk about the powers of our capital city Ottawa, but what I'm really referring to are the powers held by our country's leaders who meet and govern from within the city itself. So if these leaders were selling favors, or accepting bribes from others one could consider it a form of prostitution.

Another look online tells us "Babylon was a significant city in ancient Mesopotamia, in the fertile plain between the Tigris and Euphrates rivers. The city was built upon the Euphrates, and divided in equal parts along its left and right banks, with steep embankments to contain the river's seasonal floods."[32] It may be that the reference to many waters in this verse was simply a way to explicitly identify this city.

The first century reader would need no introduction to what this city represented. For the current day reader, a quick review of some of the references in Scripture to the city of Babylon makes it obvious that the city played a big role in the history of Israel. Jeremiah 51:13, in speaking about Babylon says, "You who live by many waters and are rich in treasures, your end has come, the time for you to be destroyed." We will look a bit more at this passage in Jeremiah in the next chapter.

"Kings Of the Earth Committed Adultery" (v.2)

The kings of the earth committed adultery with this prostitute. This probably means that although they had made commitments to others, they violated those commitments so they could be a part of the power-base of that time. Because we've been told that she is being punished, I'm assuming here that she has been held responsible for enticing others to go against their better judgment, to violate their covenants or commitments already made with others. (As opposed to others forcing her into the role of prostitute that would make her more of a victim than a perpetrator.)

It makes sense, at least to me, that since John is using a city as the symbol for evil that we're not talking about sexual activity but rather about commercial, political and perhaps military activity.

When I read that "the inhabitants of the earth were intoxicated with the wine of her adulteries"' although I'm left somewhat confused, my imagination leaves me with an image of a wild party of people celebrating the powers of the prostitute, celebrating the fact that she is able to hood-wink so many others to conform to her desires. I imagine money and wine flowing freely. This is bigger than just a government leader enticing a community leader or member of parliament to vote against his or her conscience in parliament. There is way more going on here.

"In the Spirit" (v.3)

> *³ Then the angel carried me away in the Spirit into a wilderness. There I saw a woman sitting on a scarlet beast that was covered with blasphemous names and had seven heads and ten horns.*

We have been told two times before this that John was "in the spirit." On both occasions we were then allowed to see things that are difficult for our human brains to comprehend. In Revelation 1:10 John told us he was in the Spirit when this entire revelation began. Again in 4:2 we were told that he was in the Spirit when we were first given a glimpse of the throne scene. It will happen once more in 21:10 when John is given a glimpse of the Holy City. Some commentators see these points as the beginning of new visions. Makes sense, but I wonder if the significance of being told that John was in the spirit is confirmation or a reminder that this comes from God directly as enabled by the presence of the Holy Spirit. With that in mind, I am expecting to learn some pretty important stuff in the verses that follow.

This scene takes place in a wilderness. I ignored this piece of information the first few times I read this verse. It didn't seem all that important. But it's been nagging at me. I'm drawn back to chapter 12 and the story of the woman and the dragon. There the woman was carried off to the wilderness where she would be taken care of. The red dragon followed her there but couldn't get at her so he went off to wage war against the rest of us. And so here we see another woman sitting on a scarlet beast in a wilderness. Seems that our dragon picked up someone else since he couldn't get the woman who was being kept safe by God.

The woman is sitting on the beast. This suggests to me that they are close—she's riding the beast or, perhaps he's taking her for a ride.

So who is this beast? Sounds a lot like the red dragon from chapter 12 doesn't it. There we were told that it had seven heads and ten horns and seven crowns on its heads. Here we are told that it had seven heads and ten horns and was covered with blasphemous names. Although I'm not sure what to make of the blasphemous names, I am sure that we are seeing that same beast here. In 12:9 we were told that the beast was Satan. Here we see that this great prostitute has aligned herself with Satan.

"Dressed In Purple and Scarlet" (v.4)

The prostitute appears royal in her attire but we are reminded, based on the contents of the golden cup that she is evil. If we were trying to identify who or what the prostitute represents we've been given some pretty good clues. The regal attire points us toward a place of authority, power and wealth. The evil she holds in her cup along with her affiliation to the beast suggests that she represents a place that doesn't worship God.

"The Name On Her Forehead" (v.5)

I wonder why we are told that the name on her forehead was a mystery and then told what it said. Is it because we aren't supposed to assume that this is a reference to an actual city but rather to the things she represents? Or maybe it's just the opposite; that by connecting her to an actual city we will be able to understand what it is that she represents? Hmmm. Regardless, it appears clear that she represents all things evil.

Her name was "Babylon the Great." The Babylonian empire was responsible for the destruction of Jerusalem and more importantly of the temple there (approximately 598 BCE). Ultimately, however, Babylon was conquered by the Persians (539 BCE). Early readers of Revelation would have been told stories of the exile in Babylon as well as of the fall of the empire so this link back into history would make sense to them.

Some commentators and historians suggest that John was more likely referring to Rome. It was a center of power that was also responsible for the persecution of many Christians at that time. He would have used the name Babylon instead of Rome to act as a cover to his message at the time—he says Babylon knowing people will know he means Rome.

But what does it mean for Christians throughout the subsequent generations? Has there always been a Rome in each generation or was this written with a future Rome-like place in mind? Some believe that this is the case. Personally I'm not sure, although I'm inclined to believe that instead of trying to figure it out we should look at this from the perspective of what does this passage teach us about God and in this case about Satan.

It seems that we are being warned that Satan can make himself look important and perhaps even deserving of worship and at the same time be evil. Satan can and will intentionally mislead us.

"Drunk With the Blood" (v.6)

> *⁶ I saw that the woman was drunk with the blood of God's holy people, the blood of those who bore testimony to Jesus. When I saw her, I was greatly astonished.*

We are told that she is responsible for the persecution and deaths of God's holy people. As mentioned earlier, for first century Christians and Jews, this would immediately link to both the ancient city of Babylon and the first-century city of Rome because of the persecution they were experiencing from the Roman Empire.

For the rest of us, by understanding that what we're really talking about here is Satan, it is easy to understand that he is responsible for the martyrdom of God's holy people.

John tells us he was astonished when he saw her. Can you imagine it? You see a woman sitting on a red beast whose body is covered with not-so-polite names and that has a bunch of heads and horns. She, the woman, is dressed like royalty and is dripping with gold, precious stones and pearls. She is holding a gold cup in her hand. The cup is filled with a lot of very unpleasant things—certainly not appropriate for polite company. She has writing on her forehead and is obviously drunk. Perhaps we can even see a few drops of blood dripping down her chin. Would you be astonished? I certainly would be. And so was John. But why? Was it by the simple fact that he could see her, or was he surprised at how she looked, or by what she caused him to think about?

I Will Explain the Mystery (v.7)

It seems that the angel is also wondering why he was astonished. And here it comes; at last we will have the mystery explained.

"The Beast" (v.8)

> [8] *The beast, which you saw, once was, now is not, and yet will come up out of the Abyss and go to its destruction. The inhabitants of the earth whose names have not been written in the book of life from the creation of the world will be astonished when they see the beast, because it once was, now is not, and yet will come.*

Oops, I spoke a bit too early. John appeared to be confused when he saw the woman. But although the angel says he will explain the mystery of the woman and of the beast, the explanation here seems fully focused on the beast. Perhaps they are so closely intertwined that they cannot be separated. And once again, if we keep in mind that the point here is to help us understand the character of Satan, it makes sense for the angel to go there with his explanation.

The explanation seems more confusing than that which is being explained. First it seems to be a parody of how we have seen God described elsewhere in Revelation—who was, who is, and who is to come. The part that puzzles me most is the phrase "now is not." Can this be a reference to the fact that although Satan is powerful, God is more powerful and is able to, and continues to, contain or restrain Satan's power during this church age? One commentator explains it this way "That the beast "is not" refers to the continuing effects of his defeat by Christ at the cross and resurrection[33]."

And where God no longer is the one who is to come because with His second coming He remains victorious, it is made clear that Satan will come up once more to meet with his destruction.

And then we are told that all those who became followers of Satan, will finally see the great mistake that they've made. I find it interesting that the angel is so specific about who will be astonished when they see the beast. We are told that it is those whose names have not been written in the book of life. Does that mean that the rest of us will not be surprised? That through our relationship with the Father, Son and Holy Spirit we have been given the ability to see whom Satan really is?

This Calls for Wisdom (v.9)

> [9] *"This calls for a mind with wisdom. The seven heads are seven hills on which the woman sits.*

In 13:18, when we were given the number of the beast we were told this calls for wisdom. Earlier I referred to Proverbs 2:6 for insight on wisdom. James 1:5 also says, "If any of you lacks wisdom, you should ask God, who gives generously to all without finding fault, and it will be given to you." It's like we've been given a puzzle to solve and that in attempting to understand what has been written we must seek insight from God. We must prayerfully reflect on what has been written.

We are told that the seven heads are seven hills but it seems that we are supposed to go further with that information. Geographically, there are many cities that are connected with seven hills. One of them is Rome which once again, may have made sense to the early reader of Revelation but what is the current day reader supposed to make of it? Rome still exists; should we therefore assume quite literally that this refers specifically and only to the city of Rome? I did a quick search online of cities associated with seven hills and came up with a list of more than fifty including Jerusalem, Mecca, Rome and many others. If we're supposed to read this as a future city then I say good luck figuring out which one. It seems more likely that we're supposed to take away an understanding of what Rome represented at that time. One commentator says, "this city also symbolized all the evil in the world - any person, religion, group, government, or structure that opposed Christ.[34]"

"Seven Kings" (v.10)

As we move into the information about the kings I am thrown back to Daniel 7:23–24. Just as I found that passage difficult to understand, I am similarly confused here. Are we to analyze this in detail to figure out actual kingdoms in history or are we to approach this information differently? I have trouble accepting the idea that if we study history we should be able to figure out exactly who is being represented here because that would probably change with each generation since Revelation was written.

Perhaps it makes more sense to think about the significance of the number seven. If there are seven kings, does it imply completeness—

perhaps all or world governments? And if I follow that logic here, shouldn't I do the same with the reference to the seven hills in the previous verse? Maybe that's why the commentator I mentioned there suggests that it symbolized all the evil. This is one of those things I cannot answer.

"The Beast" (v.11)

> *[11] The beast who once was, and now is not, is an eighth king. He belongs to the seven and is going to his destruction.*

Isn't it interesting how many times this reference to the beast "who once was, and now is not" appears! This is the third time in four verses. It seems he is being mocked—big time.

John tells us that he is an eighth king. Again, a section I find difficult to understand. However, let's go back to where we started in this chapter with the description of the beast with the seven heads. We were told that the seven heads of the beast were seven hills and seven kings and now we are told that the beast is not one of the seven kings. So we have this beast with seven heads that is somehow separate from his own heads but yet belongs to them—Wow! This is making my one-and-only head spin.

I think it is easier to simply focus on the knowledge that he is going to his destruction and that in some strange way those that he sees as close to him—his seven heads and what they represent—are never completely one with him.

"Ten Kings" (v.12)

I don't know what to do with the ten kings who have no kingdoms. We were introduced to ten kings in the visions in Daniel 7:24; "The ten horns are ten kings who will come from this kingdom. After them another king will arise, different from the earlier ones; he will subdue three kings." Interesting, but it doesn't help me much in my search for clarity here.

I do, however, find it interesting that these guys will receive authority—along with the beast—for a very short time. When I try to make sense of this information all I am left with is that God is still in control. Notice they will receive authority; they won't take it but will be given it. I'm assuming that it is God that will give it because it appears that the beast will receive it as well which suggests that he isn't in a position to do the giving.

The other piece of information in this verse that reassures me is that it will be for one hour—a very short period of time.

Give Their Power To the Beast (v.13)

But then they give their power to the beast. Why, having received authority for just a short time would they give it away? Inquiring minds want to know but the answer eludes me.

This power that will be given them is for a specific purpose. John tells us that God will release them to wage war against the Lamb, a battle that will be described more fully in the chapters that follow.

"The Lamb Will Triumph" (v.14)

Once again the power and authority of God is made clear. He will allow this battle to take place, knowing full well that He wins. Yet the battle must take place in order to get us to the final victory of life in Christ.

And just as the beast will have support from his kings, it is interesting to note that the Lamb will have with Him "his called, chosen and faithful followers".

"The Waters" (v.15)

> ^{15} *Then the angel said to me, "The waters you saw, where the prostitute sits, are peoples, multitudes, nations and languages.*

In the first verse of this chapter we were told that the prostitute sat by many waters. At the time I wondered if this information was simply to help us identify the city. Here we are being told that these waters represent "peoples, multitudes, nations and languages."

There is something interesting about that combination of terms. In 10:11 we read, "You must prophesy again about many peoples, nations, languages and kings." There I assumed that John was being told to prophesy about the multitudes mentioned in 7:9—basically the good guys in the story. Here, an almost identical phrase seems to point to the variety of people who were influenced by the prostitute—the other guys in the story.

"Hate the Prostitute" (v.16)

In Ezekiel chapter 16 there is a story of Jerusalem presented as an adulterous wife. It says, "'Therefore, you prostitute, hear the word of the Lord!"(v.35). And then in verse 37, "therefore I am going to gather all your lovers, with whom you found pleasure, those you loved as well as those you hated. I will gather them against you from all around and will strip you in front of them, and they will see you stark naked." And finally in verse 39, "Then I will deliver you into the hands of your lovers, ... leave you stark naked". So once again, this imagery isn't new to a reader of Scripture. The part that confuses me is that the story in

Ezekiel is about Jerusalem. So once again, is the prostitute Babylon, Jerusalem, or Rome?

"God Has Put It Into Their Hearts" (v.17–18)

And still God remains in control. We are shown that here both by the comment that "God put it into their hearts" and that these things take place "until God's words are fulfilled". It takes me right back to the martyrs waiting under the altar in 6:9. If you recall the response to their question of "How long" was "until the full number of their fellow servants, their brothers and sisters, were killed just as they had been." (6:11)

Some Things To Think About

When reading a chapter like this that is so full of things that leave me wondering, it is sometimes difficult to figure out what the take-away is. But there are a couple of things that come through very clearly in this chapter.

- Satan is able to camouflage his true character so well that his followers will be astonished when they see his real nature.
- As followers of the Lamb, marked with His seal, we are able, in fact, to recognize Satan.
- There are two sides and only two in this battle.
- Through it all God is in control.

I can't help but wonder as I read Revelation about why God allows evil to exist in this world. As the Creator, He could have created a world without evil right from the start but instead He created a world where evil was possible. He created man with free will. He gave us each the freedom to choose. But why? Our God is a God of relationship. He desires us to be in relationship with Him. He created us; He created me with an inherent desire to be part of a relationship. Being in relationship with someone who has no choice isn't very rewarding. The pleasure, the joy, the satisfaction in a relationship—whether it's between me and God, or between me and my husband or my friends— comes from knowing that we have each chosen to be a part of it. So, in creating us as a people capable of choosing, He had to know that some would not choose Him and instead choose a path that would or could result in evil happening.

So here we are with a world in which evil exists. But God maintains control over it. It may not always seem so but when we step into the New Jerusalem and life everlasting—an eternity without evil—I know that this brief time on earth will all make sense and the joy that we will experience there will make it all worthwhile.

An Aside: *I don't believe that most people choose to worship Satan. Rather they choose to not worship God or simply don't think about it and follow what they see as their own paths. As we've been seeing throughout Revelation, one of the key messages here is that there are only two paths. Either we chose to follow the Lamb or not. If we don't, then the only other path available places us on the side of Satan. That may seem harsh to many non-believers. Some would say that they are 'good people'. Some are well known as humanitarians. They live moral lives. Some would say that they in fact, show love to others more obviously than do some people who profess to be Christians. It seems in this story of Revelation there should be a third option for the good guy non-follower of the Lamb. But that's exactly the point of Revelation. We are being called to worship God. We're being told that good works are not enough if we want the gift of everlasting life. We're being asked to acknowledge God as the creator of all this and He wants us to know that this life is not all there is. There is more. There is life with Him eternally. But that life isn't available unless you acknowledge Him and the gift of salvation that He gave us through His Son. We have all sinned. No one is perfect. But God sent His Son to die on a cross as a stand-in for us so that we don't each have to experience the ultimate punishment for our sins. By accepting this gift, by acknowledging our sin and our need for forgiveness, we in turn have been given access to life everlasting. The only difference between followers of the Lamb and the non-believer is not that one group is more perfect than the other—rather it is that one group has acknowledged their imperfection and has accepted the gift of forgiveness.*

Revelation 18

Lament Over Fallen Babylon (18:1–3)

This is really cool! In case we didn't get what was going on in the last chapter, it appears that God, through John, wants to make it very clear just how evil the fallen Babylon really was.

A lament, according to numerous online sources is a passionate expression of grief or sorrow. I can't help but wonder who is doing the lamenting. Later in the chapter I think it will become clear.

"An Angel Coming Down From Heaven" (v.1)

> ¹ *After this I saw another angel coming down from heaven. He had great authority, and the earth was illuminated by his splendor.*

We have seen reference to an angel coming down from heaven once before in Revelation. In 10:1 the mighty angel came down from heaven with an open scroll in his hand. That action preceded the seven thunders about which we know nothing, and was then followed by instructions to John to eat the scroll and prophesy about the peoples, nations, languages and kings. We will see one other angel coming down from heaven later in Revelation and the only other thing, based on the language used here in the NIV, that we see coming down from heaven is the New Jerusalem as the message of Revelation reaches its peak.

All that to say that this angel must be special and his message important. We're told that he had great authority and was illuminated by his splendor—I imagine him glowing brightly.

"Fallen! Fallen Is Babylon the Great!" (v.2)

In 14:8, when we saw the angels flying through midair, the second angel said, "'Fallen! Fallen is Babylon the Great,' which made all the nations drink the maddening wine of her adulteries." Then in 16:19 we read, "God remembered Babylon the Great and gave her the cup filled with the wine of the fury of his wrath." These texts, along with the content of chapter 17 are all intertwined. It's like we're hearing the same story from several different perspectives. It suggests to me that Revelation cannot possibly be intended as a sequential play-by-play of the final days. This repetition regarding the fall of Babylon feels to me like something that is so important for us to understand that John is telling us about it, and telling it again in another way or from another perspective so that we cannot deny the evilness; so that we cannot fail to understand that evil will not prevail—Babylon Falls!

"All the Nations" (v.3)

I think that the most significant message in this verse is that *all* the nations have participated with Babylon in her evil doings. We cannot point to some other country, nation or peoples and suggest that they represent Babylon because all have drunk of her wine.

So in chapter 10, the angel that came down from heaven was instructing John, and us, to share the message of the good news of the gospel. Here the angel is reminding us that contrary to the good news of the gospel is the evilness of Satan.

Warning to Escape Babylon's Judgment (18:4–8)

"Come Out Of Her" (v.4)

> *⁴ Then I heard another voice from heaven say: "'Come out of her, my people,' so that you will not share in her sins, so that you will not receive any of her plagues;*

If we didn't get the message before, here is another voice from heaven warning us to flee from evil as personified by the city of Babylon. I wonder why we aren't told that this is an angel speaking? Why is it presented simply as a voice from heaven? And then the voice refers to 'my people'. Is this the voice of God? Feels like it doesn't it.

Here's another place where the concept of sequential actions falls apart. We've already been told that Babylon has fallen and that the bowls filled with plagues have been poured out, but here those who have fallen under Babylon's spell still have a chance to escape her control, and hence avoid sharing in her punishment. This feels like a very personal appeal. Before references were somewhat generic—peoples, nations, and multitudes—here the call is to *my* people.

"God Has Remembered Her Crimes" (v.5)

> *⁵ for her sins are piled up to heaven, and God has remembered her crimes.*

It's interesting that sins here are being referred to as crimes—we're moving to a more legal language. Occasionally in Revelation we have seen references to testifying and to witnesses. The concept of judgment has been strong throughout the text. These concepts all come together in a court of law. And so here, we move from testifying and witnessing about the good news of the gospel to one of crimes. We are typically judged based on our crimes and soon we will see that judgment will become a major story line.

"Give Her As Much Torment" (v.6–7)

In 17:16 we saw the beast turning on the prostitute. The passage here seems to suggest that God is encouraging this revolt, which makes some sense to me. Haven't we always been encouraged to battle against evil?

Babylon claims to be a queen rather than a widow. I wonder why John has introduced the widow analogy here. Being a widow implies that one's husband has died. We often feel sorry for widows. But Babylon insists that she isn't a widow. By saying she is not a widow, perhaps the message is that we aren't supposed to feel sorry for her. Or that she won't mourn—perhaps that she won't repent.

"In One Day" (v.8)

In 17:12 we were told that the ten kings would receive authority as kings for one hour. Here with the reference to one day, it suggests to me that this is a slightly longer time period but still very quick. I wonder if there is an intentional connection to creation where each phase of creation takes a day. Are we being told that although it took six days to create this world, it takes only one to destroy Babylon, and with it the evilness in this world? I'm not sure, but I like the idea of it being eradicated quickly. And here the summary of the plagues poured from the bowls reassures us that for Babylon, it is finished.

Threefold Woe Over Babylon's Fall (18:9–20)

Isaiah 33:1 says, "Woe to you, destroyer, you who have not been destroyed! Woe to you, betrayer, you who have not been betrayed! When you stop destroying, you will be destroyed; when you stop betraying, you will be betrayed." And so it seems that those who colluded with Babylon are now realizing that the good times are over.

The First Woe (v.9–10)

> *⁹ "When the kings of the earth who committed adultery with her and shared her luxury see the smoke of her burning, they will weep and mourn over her. ¹⁰ Terrified at her torment, they will stand far off and cry: "'Woe! Woe to you, great city, you mighty city of Babylon! In one hour your doom has come!'*

Isn't it interesting that the same kings who we're told in 17:16 brought her to ruin, are now whining because she has been completely destroyed. There's a lesson in human nature hidden in there I think. Is it possible that the kings of the earth took pleasure in turning against Babylon, a pleasure connected to their own perverse and evil ways? Then when it is taken out of their hands and Babylon is completely destroyed they lose out as well. Not only because they can't participate in the evil that she represented anymore, but they also can't get pleasure from their own bullying ways. I may be way off base on this one and if I am, then I apologize but it may be worth considering.

The Second Woe (v.11–16)

> *¹⁵ The merchants who sold these things and gained their wealth from her will stand far off, terrified at her torment. They will weep and mourn ¹⁶ and cry out: "'Woe! Woe to you, great city, dressed in fine linen, purple and scarlet and glittering with gold, precious stones and pearls!*

The merchants are mourning over her, we're told, and in the same breath we see that the reason they are mourning is because they have lost their source of income. No one is buying their cargoes anymore. It says something to me about the nature of the relationship between the merchants and Babylon. They aren't really mourning over Babylon. If Babylon were a person, they wouldn't really care. They're mourning over the fact that what she made possible is gone. It's the loss of their ability to make money that has caused them to mourn. Who cares about Babylon itself—certainly not these guys?

I wonder about the list of items included here. Is there a reason each one is listed? Do they represent most of the things that were considered precious and costly in the first century? Or, are they simply to represent to any generation how the things of this world can so easily be lost.

When they say, "The fruit you longed for is gone from you" are they mourning for more than the lost wealth? Typically I think of producing fruit as a result of actions. Throughout Scripture we are reminded to bear fruit. Are we to consider that Babylon was hoping to bear fruit as well? In this case, not the good kind of fruit.

It leaves me with a sense of finality. The future is over for Babylon. These guys are really wallowing in their misery. This second woe is focused on the loss of income and wealth and also on the loss of the magnificence of the city. A loss, perhaps, of an illusion.

The Third Woe (v.17–19)

And now with this third woe, they seem to be taking it more personally as they throw dust on their heads.

> ¹⁹ *They will throw dust on their heads, and with weeping and mourning cry out: "'Woe! Woe to you, great city, where all who had ships on the sea became rich through her wealth! In one hour she has been brought to ruin!'*

I can't ignore how the time frame of one hour is repeated with each cry. It reinforces the quickness, the suddenness with which this all happens. I am reminded of a phrase—shock and awe—from the Iraq war military campaigns. The mourning we have seen in these verses, for me, reinforces that as far as shock and awe is concerned we haven't seen anything yet. This destruction will come so quickly and be so powerful that it will leave those who survive it reeling.

"Rejoice Over Her" (v.20)

> *[20] "Rejoice over her, you heavens! Rejoice, you people of God! Rejoice, apostles and prophets! For God has judged her with the judgment she imposed on you."*

It may be that the voices here are the voices of the ten kings who gave their power to Satan and turned on Babylon or, perhaps it is the voice of the angel we heard in verses 2 and 3 of this chapter. Either way, I think it is obvious that God, through the destruction of Babylon, has avenged the evil of this world.

The Finality of Babylon's Doom (18:21–24)

"A Large Millstone" (v.21)

> *[21] Then a mighty angel picked up a boulder the size of a large millstone and threw it into the sea, and said: "With such violence the great city of Babylon will be thrown down, never to be found again..."*

As I looked for Scripture references regarding millstones being thrown into the sea, I came across the words of Jesus as he warns us about the dangers of temptation. In Mark 9:42 Jesus says, "If anyone causes one of these little ones—those who believe in me—to stumble, it would be better for them if a large millstone were hung around their neck and they were thrown into the sea." This image of the angel throwing the boulder into the sea should certainly remind us of this teaching. This action is exactly in accordance with His teaching.

And in Jeremiah 51:61–64 we read, "When you get to Babylon, see that you read all these words aloud. Then say, 'Lord, you have said you will destroy this place, so that neither people nor animals will live in it; it will be desolate forever.' When you finish reading this scroll, tie a stone to it and throw it into the Euphrates. Then say, 'So will

Babylon sink to rise no more because of the disaster I will bring on her. And her people will fall.'" When those words were written, Jeremiah was writing to the nation of Israel, prophesying about the ultimate destruction of Babylon. A prophecy that was proven to be true just a few years later with the physical destruction of the ancient city.

All That She Represents Destroyed (v.22–24)

And here in Revelation we aren't looking at the physical destruction of that same city but rather at the destruction of all that it represents.

And if we still don't get the message, we're told that means no music—Forget the parties. No trades—commercial activity ceases. "The light of a lamp will never shine in you again," suggests more than just physical darkness. It suggests a sense of inner darkness, of hopelessness. And ultimately with the destruction of Babylon there will be no marriages—a symbol of relationship that will no longer exist.

There is a part of me that wonders why we've been given this list of things. Is it a way to simply reinforce how final this is? I wonder.

Some Things To Think About

The evil represented by Babylon has been avenged.

As I am writing this, in the background there is a song playing...

> "And Lord, haste the day when the faith shall be sight,
> The clouds be rolled back as a scroll;
> The trump shall resound, and the Lord shall descend,
> Even so, it is well with my soul."
> (*It Is Well with My Soul | Horatio G. Spafford*)

I am filled with gratitude, with overwhelming thanksgiving, that I won't be the one mourning over the loss of Babylon. but can be assured that because I have chosen to be a follower of the Lamb, it is well with my soul.

Revelation 19

Threefold Hallelujah Over Babylon's Fall (19:1–10)

We've just experienced the threefold woe over Babylon's fall—a reaction from unbelievers who have spent a lifetime participating in the corruption of this world. Now we are given an opportunity to see the reaction from those gathered around the throne in heaven.

"The Roar Of a Great Multitude" (v.1)

> *¹ After this I heard what sounded like the roar of a great multitude in heaven shouting: "Hallelujah! Salvation and glory and power belong to our God,*

Can you imagine what it will sound like! Imagine the roar of a great multitude shouting!

I'm struck by the fact that the first words from this multitude are giving God the glory. They aren't first celebrating the victory and then saying "Oh, yes, and to God be the glory." It's a subtle difference I know, but I think it's important that we understand that their first thought was to acknowledge that this was the work of God.

"He Has Condemned the Great Prostitute" (v.2)

> *² for true and just are his judgments. He has condemned the great prostitute who corrupted the earth by her adulteries. He has avenged on her the blood of his servants."*

After acknowledging His glory they focus on why, and here we get a very quick recounting of chapters 17 and 18. This is resonating for me as I think of how I respond to situations, especially successes. Whether in prayer just between God and me, or in a public recounting of the event, I typically describe the success, and then end with "to God be the glory" or "Thank-you God." In doing this as I look at it now, it seems that I'm making sure that I get sufficient airtime—you know, to make sure everyone, or at least God, understands that I had a role to play. As if He didn't already know what my role was. Then almost as an afterthought, I acknowledge that it is by His grace and power that the event was successful. It's a subtle difference in a lesson in humility I'm thinking.

Once again, if we go back to Revelation 6:10, "They called out in a loud voice, "How long, Sovereign Lord, holy and true, until you judge the inhabitants of the earth and avenge our blood?"" Here it seems that we have a direct connection. The voice of the martyrs has been heard. Their blood has been avenged.

Bookends (v.3)

There seems to be a strong correlation here to the story of the three angels told in 14:6–13. When the first angel flew in midair, he was proclaiming "Fear God and give him glory." The second angel told us "Fallen! Fallen is Babylon the Great" and the third angel warned us that those who worshipped the beast would be tormented and "the smoke of their torment will rise for ever and ever." And here in these first verses of chapter 19 we see a similar pattern. In the first verse the multitude has been giving God glory. In the second verse we see that God has avenged the blood of His people on Babylon and in this third verse we are once again, given a visual of smoke going up for ever and ever. It's like we have bookends around the story that was told in the intervening chapters.

"Amen, Hallelujah!" (v.4)

The last time in Revelation that we saw the throne scene was, in fact, in chapter 14. The last time we heard anything from the throne was 16:17 after the seventh angel poured out his bowl and we heard "It is done." Here with the term "amen" we are being told it is so or so be it. Praise the Lord!

"A Voice Came From the Throne" (v.5)

> ⁵ *Then a voice came from the throne, saying: "Praise our God, all you his servants, you who fear him, both great and small!"*

I'm curious about who this voice belongs to. I know that God is on the throne but it doesn't make sense that He would be calling for this praise. It makes more sense for it to be Jesus, but it's hard to say. We have heard a voice from the throne earlier in Revelation in 16:17. It's that same voice that proclaimed 'It is done'. Is this the same voice? I wonder if it matters. Perhaps it's enough to know that it comes from the throne and as such represents the center of all that we worship. And apparently it doesn't matter where we fit in the earthly perspective of greatness; we are all called to praise Him.

"What Sounded Like a Great Multitude" (v.6)

I am struck by just how huge this celebration is. It is steadily increasing in intensity and seems to be responsive in nature. In the first verse John heard the roar of a great multitude praising God. Then from around the throne came a response. Then a voice from the throne offers up praises and a great multitude responds with hallelujah and more praises. This multitude sounds like the roar of rushing waters—imagine the sound of a waterfall. But add to that loud peals of thunder and then shouting as well. It would be chaotic. It would be loud. It goes far beyond any kind of earthly celebration we have seen.

"The Wedding Of the Lamb" (v.7)

And what fun is a celebration if it doesn't end with a meal? In this case it is the wedding of the Lamb.

We have seen the setting of a wedding or wedding feast used periodically in Scripture so we know this is significant. There is no closer bond between people than that of husband and wife, so we know that in referring to a wedding, the Lamb—Christ Jesus—is committing to a relationship that cannot be broken.

Who is the bride? In Old Testament Scripture, there are references that suggest that Israel is the bride. Isaiah 62:5, "As a young man marries a young woman, so will your Builder marry you; as a bridegroom rejoices over his bride, so will your God rejoice over you." New Testament Scripture infers that the church is the bride. Ephesians 5:23–24, "For the husband is the head of the wife as Christ is the head of the church, his body, of which he is the Savior. Now as the church submits to Christ, so also wives should submit to their husbands in everything."

"Fine Linen" (v.8)

The bride was given fine linen to wear. Throughout Scripture, when we see fine linen used, it is typically to dress someone royal, or as part of the coverings in the tabernacle built in the desert. This very expensive and special fabric now represents the righteous acts of God's holy people.

"Blessed Are Those" (v.9)

> ⁹ *Then the angel said to me, "Write this: Blessed are those who are invited to the wedding supper of the Lamb!" And he added, "These are the true words of God."*

This is the fourth beatitude in Revelation. Can there be any doubt that each one of us desires to be invited to the wedding supper of the Lamb.

The wedding of the Lamb involves a bridegroom—the Lamb—and his bride—the Church. This blessing is a personal one. Although it applies to many, it is for each one of us who have been invited to join in the celebration of the marriage. We, the followers of the Lamb have been invited to the wedding supper—we are the bride.

I'm confused by the phrase "the true words of God." Are not all the words of God true? Or is John stepping out of his story telling for a moment, to reinforce the fact that he hasn't attached any poetic license to this verse—that these are the words, exactly as he heard them from God. I wonder.

"I Fell At His Feet" (v.10)

> ¹⁰ *At this I fell at his feet to worship him. But he said to me, "Don't do that! I am a fellow servant with you and with your brothers and sisters who hold to the testimony of Jesus. Worship God! For it is the Spirit of prophecy who bears testimony to Jesus."*

How natural it would be to want to fall down in worship after hearing this blessing. But quickly John is reprimanded to not do that—to not worship inappropriately. Only one is deserving of our worship and that one is God.

As I consider this verse I wonder if we are being reminded that even within the church, within the framework of our walks of faith that we must be careful about where we focus our worship. Here John wasn't falling to worship something that we typically see as unworthy; rather he falls at the feet of an angel. It is easy to become a follower of a strong and charismatic leader in the church. I have great respect for people who have been chosen to lead the church. I am certain that these people are men and women of God, and that their intentions haven't been to entice us to worship them. But I think the message of this passage is that regardless of how much authority they may have, regardless of how charismatic they may be, or how filled with the spirit they may appear to be, they may be deserving of our love and respect, but not our worship. Only God is worthy of our worship.

The phrase 'testimony of Jesus' has appeared twice before in Revelation in 1:2 and in 1:9 Here the reference is to holding to the testimony of Jesus. My take on the meaning is that these brothers and sisters who hold to the testimony are fellow believers. They are people who have believed and are following the Lamb.

The angel tells John that the testimony of Jesus is the "Spirit of prophecy." This phrase doesn't appear anywhere else in Scripture (NIV). My take on it is quite simply that the point of the Scriptures and the prophecies within is to bring us to Jesus.

There is one other thing here that fascinates me. These final words of verse 10 say, "Worship *God*! For it is the *Spirit* of prophecy who bears testimony to *Jesus*." [italics are mine] In this single sentence we are once again reminded of the triune nature of God. We are called to worship God based on the words of prophets carried along by the Holy Spirit pointing us to the gift of salvation through Jesus Christ.

The Heavenly Warrior Defeats the Beast (19:11–21)

"Heaven Standing Open" (v.11)

> [11] I saw heaven standing open and there before me was a white horse, whose rider is called Faithful and True. With justice he judges and wages war.

In the story in Acts chapter 7 of the stoning of Stephen we read his words in verse 56, "'Look,' he said, 'I see heaven open and the Son of Man standing at the right hand of God.'" With those words he confirmed that Jesus was indeed the Messiah. And now the heavens once again stand open and John sees a white horse whose rider is called Faithful and True.

Is this white horse the same one that we saw in 6:2 when the first of the seven seals was opened? Although I'm still not convinced either way, most commentators don't think they are the same and each one that I checked had valid reasons for believing them to be different. It is interesting, however, that these two white horses with their riders act as bookends to the story of evil, it's existence in our world, and the ongoing battles of good versus evil. With this second white horse we draw an end to evil.

Similarly, in 4:1, John saw a door standing open in heaven and he was invited to go through it as a starting point to the apocalyptical portion of this vision. We saw references to the temple being open in heaven in the chapters between; however, here there is no door—here heaven is standing open. It is fully revealed to John.

And so what do we know of the rider? We are told that he is called Faithful and True. What does it mean to be faithful? When I looked online I found the following synonyms: conscientious, dependable, devoted, honest. A similar look-up on the word true bore the following:

accurate, appropriate, genuine, and honest. In 3:14, in the letter to the church in Laodicea Christ identifies himself as the faithful and true witness. Can there be any doubt that this is Jesus Christ, the Messiah?

And finally we are reassured that what he does is done with justice. We are also forewarned about what is about to happen—'he judges and wages war.'

Eyes Like Blazing Fire (v.12)

In 1:14, just as John's vision began he described the person that he saw as having eyes like blazing fire. And in 2:18, Christ described himself to the church in Thyatira as the Son of God, whose eyes are like blazing fire, another confirmation the rider is indeed Christ himself. The blazing eyes reinforce the idea that he is here to pass judgment.

And then there are the many crowns on his head—why aren't we told how many? Does it matter? Perhaps not. But then as I think about how the red dragon in chapter 12 and the beast in chapter 13 were described to us, I realize that there we were given specific counts of how many crowns they each had. Here, by being told that there are many, it's almost as if the description is intended to suggest that there are more than he could count.

And then John says He has a name that no one knows but He himself. I wonder if there is a link between this and the name Yahweh, a name so divine that no one spoke it aloud. But if the name is written on Him, shouldn't John be able to read it? I wonder.

"A Robe Dipped In Blood" (v.13)

He is wearing a robe dipped in blood. I've noticed two slightly different perspectives on the meaning of this robe. One is taken from Isaiah

63, which speaks of the day of God's vengeance and redemption. In the first 6 verses there, we read some of the following: "Who is this coming ... with his garments stained crimson? ... "It is I, proclaiming victory, mighty to save." Why are your garments red, like those of one treading the winepress? "I have trodden the winepress alone; from the nations no one was with me. I trampled them in my anger and trod them down in my wrath; their blood spattered my garments, and I stained all my clothing. ... I trampled the nations in my anger; in my wrath I made them drunk and poured their blood on the ground." So from here we could consider that the robe dipped in blood represents the blood of the trampled nations perhaps making a connection to chapter 14.

Another way to look at it is to go back to Revelation 7:14 where John saw the great multitude in white robes. There we read, "These are they who have come out of the great tribulation; they have washed their robes and made them white in the blood of the Lamb." So here the fact that the rider's robe is dipped in blood could be a reminder that while His sacrifice made it possible for our robes to be white, He had to undergo the crucifixion—His blood had to flow to make us pure.

Or perhaps it is another juxtaposition of the Lion and the Lamb— remember the Lion of Judah and the slain Lamb in chapter 5. As the Lion, He has trampled the nations. As the Lamb, He bled and died for the forgiveness of our sins.

Typically when I see the phrase "the Word of God" I go back to John 1:1, "In the beginning was the Word, and the Word was with God, and the Word was God." So here, this name confirms for me that this is Jesus. But I still have questions. In verse 12 John said He has a name no one knows and here we are told His name and then later in verse

16 we will see that He has another name written on His thigh. Why all the names? Is it perhaps, to remind us of the many aspects of God?

"The Armies Of Heaven" (v.14)

> *¹⁴ The armies of heaven were following him, riding on white horses and dressed in fine linen, white and clean.*

Can you picture it? Out comes a rider on a mighty white steed. The rider's robe is blood red, probably dripping with blood as He moves. I picture Him sitting tall in the saddle—assuming he has a saddle. He looks majestic, regal. His eyes are blazing. He is wearing many crowns on his head—okay, I'm having a bit of trouble picturing how that would work but you get the idea.

Behind the rider comes a massive army all on white horses and dressed in fine white linen—probably that same white linen we were given in verse 8 as the bride of the Lamb. It would be brilliant, impressive and if you're on the other side of this engagement probably terrifying!

"A Sharp Sword" (v.15)

> *¹⁵ Coming out of his mouth is a sharp sword with which to strike down the nations. "He will rule them with an iron scepter." He treads the winepress of the fury of the wrath of God Almighty.*

Previously in Revelation we have seen reference to the sword coming out of his mouth. It was there in 1:16 and again in 2:12 when Christ described himself for the Church in Pergamum. When we were looking at 1:16 I referred to Hebrews 4:12, "For the word of God is alive and active. Sharper than any double-edged sword, it penetrates even to dividing soul and spirit, joints and marrow; it judges the thoughts and attitudes of the heart."

So here, in verse 15, we have the one whose name is "Word of God" with a sharp sword coming out of this mouth. He will use this sword, which judges the thoughts and attitudes of the heart to strike down the nations.

In the story of the woman and the red dragon in 12:5 we were told that the child will rule with an iron scepter and here we see that promise repeated.

As I seek understanding of the final piece of this verse, I am drawn back to the words of Isaiah 63 mentioned earlier in this chapter and to 14:19–20 where we were first introduced to the winepress of God's wrath.

"King Of Kings and Lord Of Lords" (v.16)

> *[16] On his robe and on his thigh he has this name written: king of kings and lord of lords.*

I'm slightly confused about this next name. Not about the name itself but about where it is placed. Is it written twice—once on his robe and once on his thigh? Or, is it on the part of his robe that covers his thigh? The good news is that it probably doesn't matter too much whether I figure it out or not. I found it interesting when I was doing some investigation to find that typically a warrior would carry his sword on his thigh, and would touch it when proclaiming an oath. So the placement fits with our rider who is the faithful and true word of God. We saw this same phrase "king of kings and lord of lords" used in 17:14.

"The Great Supper Of God" (v.17–18)

> *¹⁷ And I saw an angel standing in the sun, who cried in a loud voice to all the birds flying in midair, "Come, gather together for the great supper of God, ¹⁸ so that you may eat the flesh of kings, generals, and the mighty, of horses and their riders, and the flesh of all people, free and slave, great and small."*

I wonder why John mentions that the angel is standing in the sun. The visual that this stirs up is once again quite spectacular. I haven't actually thought about how all these angels we've been reading about look. Do they have wings? Do they look like me—okay not exactly like me but you know, like a person who walks on the earth? I picture this angel as glowing, almost iridescent from the glow of the sun. It's what has become the stereotypical image of an angel for me.

But this glowing angel has a loud voice so he isn't passive; he speaks with authority—at least to the birds. Once again, can you picture it? The glowing angel calling out and all the birds flying to him to participate in the great supper of God.

This is the only place in Scripture where we are told of this great supper. It's interesting that the metaphor isn't used elsewhere in Scripture. It appears here, I believe, in direct contrast to the wedding supper of the Lamb mentioned earlier in this chapter.

Two meals—one I want to be a part of, the other, not so much.

As described here, this great supper will be gruesome. Although it doesn't say it here, later in verse 20 we are told that the ones who will become the meal are those who received the mark of the beast.

My friends, if you haven't already chosen which side you're on, choose now. Choose quickly. Choose to become a follower of the Lamb.

The Armies Of the Beast (v.19)

We've seen the rider on the white horse with his army behind him, and now finally we can see the other side ready to go to battle. We can see the beast, the kings of the earth, and their armies. It's a colorful group. Probably doesn't look as impressive as the shiny, radiant, white-robed side but I'm sure they will be well armed and battle-ready.

"The Beast Was Captured" (v.20)

> *²⁰ But the beast was captured, and with it the false prophet who had performed the signs on its behalf. ... The two of them were thrown alive into the fiery lake of burning sulfur.*

Unfortunately for the beast and the false prophet, they are captured and thrown alive in the lake of burning sulfur. We are given no sense of time passing. It seems like the capture was immediate. There is no chitchat taking place here, no arguing one's case. Can you imagine anything more painful then being thrown in a lake of burning sulfur?

"The Rest Were Killed" (v.21)

> *²¹ The rest were killed with the sword coming out of the mouth of the rider on the horse, and all the birds gorged themselves on their flesh.*

In chapter 16 we had been told how the people who had the mark of the beast were tormented as the angels poured out their bowls of God's wrath. At that time we noted that although they were tormented we weren't told of any deaths. But here we have the ultimate ending. There are no reprieves. They all die. It seems almost anti-climactic in a way.

I find it absolutely fascinating that the sword coming out of the mouth of the rider kills them. The army behind Him didn't lift a finger to help. Once again, God is in control. He is all-powerful. The army was there as witnesses to the event but they weren't required to fight. Cool stuff!

Some Things To Think About

God is in control and has been all along.

During the church age He has held back, letting evil tempt us, letting us choose our destinies.

But when He has determined that the time has come for this to end, it will.

Choose wisely:

- an invitation to the wedding supper of the Lamb, OR,
- food for the great supper of God!

Revelation 20

The Thousand Years (20:1–6)

And here we have the message of Revelation all tied up into one, sometimes confusing chapter. As we walk through the details that follow we will see that God controls or binds Satan during this current time. Although evil exists, it is not allowed free reign. And at the same time, followers of the Lamb will reign together with Christ. At the end, Satan is released so he can line up his forces and meet Christ in the battle described in the last few chapters and finally we will read of the fate of those who chose the mark of the beast. It all comes down to this.

"The Key" (v.1)

> *¹ And I saw an angel coming down out of heaven, having the key to the Abyss and holding in his hand a great chain.*

We have seen references to someone holding the key elsewhere in Revelation. In 1:18 we saw Jesus described as the one who holds the keys of death and Hades. In 9:1, John saw the key to the shaft of the Abyss given to the star. So the question in my mind is whether these are related to this specific passage. From the reference in chapter 1 we know that God, through Jesus Christ is in charge. In chapter 9 we are reminded of that it was God who gave the key to the star. And here, in being told that the angel is coming down out of heaven, the implication is that God has given the angel the key to the Abyss.

Later we will see that the chain in his other hand will be used to bind Satan for one thousand years.

The Thousand Years (v.2)

With this reference to a thousand years we enter into what may be a very controversial discussion.

There are three primary views of what is commonly referred to as the *millennium*. Some hold what is called a *premillennial* view. These folks believe that the thousand years mentioned here take place after the second coming of Christ. This perspective is based on a fairly literal, sequential view of what we have read so far in Revelation.

A second perspective is *postmillennialism* and is just the opposite. Here the belief is that the thousand years take place near the end of the current church age and is concluded with the second coming of Christ.

And then there is what is called *amillennialism*. Amillennialist believe that the thousand years began with Christ's resurrection and will end with His second coming. In other words that the thousand years mentioned here represent in fact, the current church age.

Most people, having chosen a perspective, remain very committed to it. This is one of the reasons I undertook my study of Revelation. I wanted to figure out who was right. And as I reach this phase of my study I realize that I still don't know—although I do find myself leaning towards the amillennialist perspective.

I looked in Scripture for other references to thousand years and millennium. I found three references to a thousand years. Psalm 90:4, "A thousand years in your sight are like a day that has just gone by, or like a watch in the night." 2 Peter 3:8, "But do not forget this one thing, dear friends: With the Lord a day is like a thousand years, and a thousand years are like a day." And Ecclesiastes 6:6, "even if he lives a thousand years twice over but fails to enjoy his prosperity. Do not all go to the same place?" All three references leave me feeling like any reference to a thousand years is intended to be symbolic and not literal.

And there are no references, at least not in the online NIV that I've been using, to the use of the word millennium.

This is one of those things that is capable of creating great divisions between believers. What I do know, based on what I've learned so far, is that it shouldn't. Having the right perspective here isn't fundamental to our faith. It doesn't affect our shared belief that Jesus is the Son of God; that He died on the cross for our sins and rose again on the third day, and subsequently ascended to heaven and that He will return at a time known only by God.

Satan Is Bound (v.2–3)

And then what does it mean that Satan is bound? I look at the evil in our world. I see what I believe to be the work of Satan, and I wonder how one can even consider the idea that Satan is bound now during our church age. But then I recall the story of Job and of how Satan could only do what God allowed him to do. Or closer to our story here, in Revelation 12:4 when we were first introduced to the red dragon where we read, "Its tail swept a third of the stars out of the sky." This seemed to be an indication that he was bound in some way, else he would have been able to sweep all the stars out of the sky and not just one third. So it seems reasonable that this could be referring to the time in which we live.

Don't you just love how the story in Revelation winds around and around? It seems to weave back and forth providing numerous perspectives on different scenes. Sometimes I do love it and sometimes, well, not so much.

There seems to be a strong parallel between these verses and the story in chapter 12:7–11 only there we were told Satan was hurled to the earth. So how do the concepts of Satan hurled to the earth and thrown into the Abyss co-exist? One commentator provides some insight that I have found useful. He says, "The abyss is one of the various metaphors representing the spiritual sphere in which the devil and his accomplices operate."[35] For me, that helps because it doesn't mean that Satan cannot continue to operate as the accuser, but only that during this time period he is not able to operate as fully as he might like. Unfortunately we are told that he will be set free for a short time. I think this ties back to the battle scene described in chapter 19 and that is foretold in chapter 17:8

"I Saw Thrones" (v.4)

> [4] *I saw thrones on which were seated those who had been given authority to judge. And I saw the souls of those who had been beheaded because of their testimony about Jesus and because of the word of God. They had not worshiped the beast or its image and had not received its mark on their foreheads or their hands. They came to life and reigned with Christ a thousand years.*

The scene immediately shifts from what we've seen taking place in that space called the Abyss to what is happening in the completely opposite realm. We're back at a variation of the throne scene that has appeared several times during our reading of Revelation.

I thought God was our judge, so now I'm confused by the fact that there are multiple thrones, and seated on them are "those who had been given authority to judge." However, Daniel 7:9 says, "As I looked, thrones were set in place and the Ancient of Days took his seat." so I can see that the concept of more than one throne was established during Daniel's vision as well.

I wonder who the "souls of those who had been beheaded" are. The easiest interpretation is probably the obvious one—they are those who have been martyred, those who have been most directly affected by the works of Satan. Are they the ones who were described as being under the altar in 6:9–11? Is this suggesting that they no longer need to wait? Or, is it simply confirmation that God knows our deeds and rewards them appropriately?

What about those of us who have been sealed in Christ but perhaps didn't die a martyr's death? Are we in this group, or are we in the group that, as we will be told in verse 5, "did not come to life until the thousand years were ended?" The answer to this question may be obvious to some but it isn't particularly clear to me. I know where I'm going—heaven. I just haven't figured out the timing. The other thing I know for sure is that I'll not be in control of the timing and once I am dead, I won't even be aware of the timing. Once I have died, my next experience whether it is immediate or centuries later according to our human sense of time will be in heaven.

And what does it mean to reign with Christ? I believe there is a strong link here with Luke 22:29–30 (or Matthew 19:28) where we read, "And I confer on you a kingdom, just as my Father conferred one on me, so that you may eat and drink at my table in my kingdom and sit on thrones, judging the twelve tribes of Israel." So are these thrones and those seated upon them are actually the twenty-four thrones with the twenty-four elders from 4:4?

Notice as well the link to 2:26–27 where in the promise to the ones who are victorious in the church in Thyatira it says they will be given authority over the nations, and 3:21, where the church in Laodicea is promised the right to sit with Christ on his throne."

So here in the heavenly realm, as Satan is bound and thrown in to the abyss, the saints are being rewarded just as Christ has promised.

"The Rest Of the Dead" (v.5)

> *⁵ (The rest of the dead did not come to life until the thousand years were ended.) This is the first resurrection.*

Who are the rest of the dead? As I mentioned earlier are they those who have been sealed in Christ but didn't die a martyr's death? Or are they those who received the mark of the beast? Or both? Or neither? This is one of those questions I still can't answer.

As with other things in this chapter I am puzzled by this concept of the first resurrection and a second death mentioned in the verse that follows. This is another one of those areas where people who have figured out what they believe it means stand very firmly on what they believe.

There are references to two resurrections elsewhere in Scripture. In Acts, where we read of Paul giving testimony to Felix in 24:15 we read, "that there will be a resurrection of both the righteous and the wicked." In John 5:28–29 we read, "Do not be amazed at this, for a time is coming when all who are in their graves will hear his voice and come out—those who have done what is good will rise to live, and those who have done what is evil will rise to be condemned." So the suggestion is that the first resurrection mentioned here is of the righteous and this makes sense based on what we read in verse 4.

We will see later in this chapter in verses 12–14 the outcome of the second resurrection.

"Blessed and Holy Are Those" (v.6)

> ⁶ *Blessed and holy are those who share in the first resurrection. The second death has no power over them, but they will be priests of God and of Christ and will reign with him for a thousand years.*

With this fifth beatitude in Revelation we receive the promise that the second death will have no power over us.

Once again, as I reflect on the message of Revelation it seems so clear by statements like this that God is in control. He has given us a choice—follow the Lamb, or not. And based on the choice to be a follower of the Lamb, He has saved me from experiencing the second death, and has promised that I will reign victorious with Christ.

One commentator says, "Therefore, there is a first death of believers that is physical and different in nature from the second death of unbelievers, which is spiritual. If there are thus two different kinds of deaths, it is plausible that the corresponding resurrections would also differ. The resurrection of believers is spiritual, whereas the resurrection of unbelievers is physical... Ironically, the first physical death of saints translates them into the first spiritual resurrection in heaven, whereas the second physical resurrection translates the ungodly into the second spiritual death."[36]

The Judgment of Satan (20:7–10)

"When the Thousand Years Are Over" (v.7)

> ⁷ *When the thousand years are over, Satan will be released from his prison ...*

It seems to me that so far in this chapter we have been given a summary of events. We were told that Satan has been bound with his power controlled. We have been told that after a time period determined by God, he will be released. We have reviewed how things play out for the martyrs, and now we review what's happening to Satan and his worshippers.

This segment, I believe, is a review of the defeat of evil, as portrayed by Babylon, and of the battle described in chapter 19:11–21 with more insight into specifically what happens to the devil.

"Gog and Magog" (v.8)

In 7:1 we saw reference to the four corners of the earth, and at that time I surmised that this phrase refers to the entire earth. It seems that same idea makes sense here.

The reference to "Gog and Magog" is confusing for me, but as I've looked at commentaries for insight they all seem to connect back to the prophecy in Ezekiel 38–39 which tells of God's victory over the nations who were enemies of Israel. So, the simplest interpretation of this verse may be that Satan has aligned the peoples of the entire world who have not chosen to become followers of the Lamb to do battle.

"The City He Loves" (v.9)

I wonder what to make of the phrase, "the city he loves." Is it the New Jerusalem? Or is it wherever God's people are gathered?

Regardless of the details, the scene is clear. In the center are the followers of the Lamb—God's people. Surrounding them are the others. I'm struck by the idea that they are not aligned for battle as we often see in movies representing battle—one army facing the other. Instead God's people are surrounded. This should be a quick win for the opponents, but no, fire comes down from heaven and they are devoured! Once again, God is in control.

"The Lake Of Burning Sulfur" (v.10)

And finally Satan joins his buddies—the beast and the false prophet from 19:11–21—in the lake of burning sulfur. Can you imagine being tormented day and night forever and ever? Who hasn't heard the phrase, "A fate worse than death"? This surely qualifies as such!

The Judgment of the Dead (20:11–15)

We've learned about the results of Satan's judgment and now it is time to see what will happen to the dead.

"A Great White Throne" (v.11)

> [11] Then I saw a great white throne and him who was seated on it. The earth and the heavens fled from his presence, and there was no place for them.

This is another of those images that speaks strongly to me. Picture it. A great white throne with someone seated on it. I am drawn back to the first time we saw the throne scene in Revelation 4:2. At the end of that scene in 4:11 we saw that those who surrounded the throne were worshipping the One on the throne, "You are worthy, our Lord and God, to receive glory and honor and power, for you created all things, and by your will they were created and have their being." I am confident that the One seated on this throne is God.

The fact that the earth and heavens fled from His presence here for me simply reinforces the magnificence of the throne. Everything else falls away. Although I've interpreted this figuratively, it is possible to assume that at this stage of the end, the earth and the heavens as we know them, as they exist in our current age, do in fact disappear to be replaced with the new heaven and new earth that we will learn about in the next chapter.

"Books Were Opened" (v.12)

> [12] *And I saw the dead, great and small, standing before the throne, and books were opened. Another book was opened, which is the book of life. The dead were judged according to what they had done as recorded in the books.*

I begin here by wondering what it means to be great or small? Great or small in relation to what? Does this mean believers and non-believers? Whatever it means, they are all about to be judged.

In John 5:24, it says "Very truly I tell you, whoever hears my word and believes him who sent me has eternal life and will not be judged but has crossed over from death to life." This passage suggests to me that believers get to skip this stage in the judgment process but then in 1 Corinthians 4:5, it says "Therefore judge nothing before the appointed time; wait until the Lord comes. He will bring to light what is hidden in darkness and will expose the motives of the heart. At that time each will receive their praise from God." and in 2 Corinthians 5:10, "For we must all appear before the judgment seat of Christ, so that each of us may receive what is due us for the things done while in the body, whether good or bad." In trying to make sense of it, it seems to me that the passage from John 5 is probably referring to the judgment based on whether my name is written in the book of life, and from the other passages that as a believer I will still be judged, not to determine whether I will be granted eternal life but rather to determine my praise from God. I'm not comfortable with my attempt to resolve this here. Once again, this is something that perhaps is too big for my head to get around but one thing is clear—What I do and how I do it during my time on earth matters. I cannot spend my short time here assuming that I can do what I want, when I want, and not consider the consequences.

I have to admit I was also caught off-guard here. I didn't expect there to be two sets of books. There are books that were opened and then another book, "which is the book of life." So based on what we read here in verse 12 it seems that our actions are recorded in the first set of books, and we will be judged based on what is written there.

For those of us who have always wondered when 'that guy who seems to get away with everything' will be found out, it seems that this will be the time.

For those of us who perhaps have been sliding through life based on an assumption that having received Christ as our Savior, we have a free pass into heaven—which may be —perhaps the words of James come into play here. In James 2:24 it says, "You see that a person is considered righteous by what they do and not by faith alone." Of course this concept has led to great division in the church over the generations as well. But I think that James' perspective, which is that if we are true followers of the Lamb, then we will be compelled to serve or contribute based on the gifts that we have been given as we strive to live our lives in a manner that Jesus would if He were in fact, living in our current age, makes sense. And it is on how we as believers demonstrate this—or attempt to do so—that we will be judged as recorded in the first set of books.

Not everyone sees this the same way. Many believe that this judgment is only for non-believers but if that is so then I'm wondering why bother? Later we will see that if your name isn't in the book of life you will be tossed into the lake of fire. What will be the outcome of this first round of judgment? If you're a non-believer, and you perhaps committed murder, will your experience in the lake of fire be different than if you're a non-believer who's worst sin, if one can judge sins, was to lie to your neighbor? Of course we can flip this the other way as well. As a believer, how will my reward in heaven differ from say, Mother Theresa who obviously lived a much more fruitful Christian life than I.

"The Sea Gave Up the Dead" (v.13)

In verse 12 we were told that John saw the dead standing before the throne. Now in verse 13 we are given an image of the dead coming up from the sea, from death, from Hades—why go there with this? Perhaps it is meant as a way to make it very clear that no one will escape this judgment. It doesn't matter how, where, or when you died. You will be judged.

About The Timing

I have more questions about the timing of all this. Is this judgment something that will happen for everyone at the same time upon Christ's second coming as one might assume based on what is written here? Or, is it something that is happening everyday? If I die tomorrow and Christ has not yet come, will I go through this judgment phase immediately upon death or will I go to some waiting stage until the second coming, and then line up with everyone else to be judged? So many questions. The answer to this question may be clear elsewhere in Scripture, but I'm not going to seek it out here primarily because I'm not sure the specific answer matters to me since I haven't been able to figure out how knowing the specifics of this process will help me.

What does matter is that I know that I will be judged, and that I must live my life accordingly while I can.

Death and Hades were thrown into the lake of fire (v.14)

In 19:20, the beast and the false prophet were thrown into the 'fiery lake of burning sulfur'. Earlier in this chapter in verse 10 the devil was thrown into the 'lake of burning sulfur'. And now, here in verse 14, death and Hades were thrown into the lake of fire. Why? What does this mean? In chapter 21:4 we are told that there will be no more death or mourning in which case death and Hades are no longer needed.

And now we are clearly told that the lake of fire is the second death that we were introduced to back in verse 6.

"The Book Of Life" (v.15)

> *15 Anyone whose name was not found written in the book of life was thrown into the lake of fire.*

And then there is the book of life. As a long-time Christian, I am very familiar with the concept of having one's name written in the book of life. So when I went to find the exact place in Scripture where we are told that based on such and such an action our names will be written in the book of life, I was surprised at how few references outside Revelation there are to it. In Psalm 69:28, "May they be blotted out of the book of life and not be listed with the righteous." This passage tells me that the righteous have their names in the book of life. In Philippians 4:3, "Yes, and I ask you, my true companion, help these women since they have contended at my side in the cause of the gospel, along with Clement and the rest of my co-workers, whose names are in the book of life." These are the only references in the online NIV that I'm using to the book of life outside of Revelation.

The promise to the victorious of the church in Sardis in 3:5 was that their names would not be removed from the book of life. Elsewhere in Revelation in 13:8 and 17:8 there is a clear distinction between those whose names have been written in the Lamb's book of life and those who worship the beast. In Malachi we see reference to *a scroll of remembrance*, which I believe, is probably the same thing as the book of life. There in chapter 3:16–18 it says, "Then those who feared the Lord talked with each other, and the Lord listened and heard. A scroll of remembrance was written in his presence concerning those who feared the Lord and honored his name. "On the day when I act," says the Lord Almighty, "they will be my treasured possession. I will spare them, just as a father has compassion and spares his son who serves him. And you will again see the distinction between the righteous and the wicked, between those who serve God and those who do not."

And so here we learn that after our actions have been judged based on entries in the first set of books, then a check will be made to determine whether our names are written in the book of life. If it is not, then that's all there is. Those who have not believed will experience the second death and be thrown into the lake of fire.

Some Things To Think About

It all comes down to one thing:

- Is your name in the book of life?

Revelation 21

A New Heaven and a New Earth (21:1–8)

In 20:11 we were told that "the earth and the heavens fled." If it wasn't clear at the time, it seems more clear now that what we were seeing was the end of the earth and the heavens as we know them to be during our current church age. As we enter into this part of John's vision we are given a glimpse of eternal life as it has been promised to us.

"A New Heaven and a New Earth" (v.1)

> [1] *Then I saw "a new heaven and a new earth," for the first heaven and the first earth had passed away, and there was no longer any sea.*

I wonder whether this new earth will be completely new; meaning it will look like nothing I've ever seen before. Or will it be a refreshed version of earth as we know it today—looking like God intended before man sinned. I think to get the answer I'll have to wait.

And I'm not sure what to make of the idea of a new heaven. I would have thought that heaven was already perfect, but maybe with Satan and his minions out of the picture the activities of heaven will change. One thing for certain, there will no longer be a need for angels to battle Satan on our behalf.

And why, you may wonder is there no longer any sea? God created the sea. God created the creatures in the sea. Why no sea? In 12:12 we read, "But woe to the earth and the sea, because the devil has gone down to you!" And in 13:1 we read of the beast coming out of the sea and in 13:11 of the second beast coming out of the earth. Here we are told that the first earth is gone and the sea is gone—perhaps as an assurance that the evil that sprang up from them is gone.

Another thought here is that waters in the form of oceans and seas divide the landmasses. Consequently we as a people are geographically divided. Perhaps another implication here is that those things that divide us will no longer exist.

"The Holy City" (v.2)

In Isaiah 52:1b Jerusalem is identified as the holy city. And then in Isaiah 62:1–2 it says, "for Jerusalem's sake I will not remain quiet, till her vindication shines out like the dawn, her salvation like a blazing torch. The nations will see your vindication, and all kings your glory; you will be called by a new name that the mouth of the Lord will bestow." and further in verse 5, "As a young man marries a young woman, so will your Builder marry you; as a bridegroom rejoices over his bride, so will your God rejoice over you." And here we see the promise of Isaiah fulfilled as the Holy City, now referred to as the 'new Jerusalem' is prepared as a bride.

The image this stirs up in my mind has always been of a great city, radiantly glowing and gently floating down from heaven. I suspect that what makes more sense, is an image of a great multitude of followers of the Lamb radiantly glowing, coming out of heaven.

"A Loud Voice" (v.3)

> [3] *And I heard a loud voice from the throne saying, "Look! God's dwelling place is now among the people, and he will dwell with them. They will be his people, and God himself will be with them and be their God.*

I have a couple of observations on this announcement. The first is likely the more important one. It doesn't say our dwelling place will be with God, but rather that He will dwell with us. Put in a literal, earthly way that means we're not going to end up wondering around in the clouds—or however you picture heaven—but rather that God will be walking with us just as He did in the garden of Eden. And so just as it says in Genesis 3:8, "Then the man and his wife heard the sound of the Lord God as he was walking in the garden in the cool of the day" we too, will hear the sound of our Lord God walking in the garden!

The part of this verse that I'm somewhat confused by is the part where we move from talking about "the people" to be told "they will be his people." Aren't we, as followers of the Lamb, already his people? In Deuteronomy 7:6 in speaking to the Israelites, it says "For you are a people holy to the Lord your God. The Lord your God has chosen you out of all the peoples on the face of the earth to be his people, his treasured possession." Is this an assurance to those of us who are not Jewish by birth that we are also his treasured possession?

No More Death, Crying Or Pain (v.4)

What a stunning promise—there will be no more death, mourning, crying or pain!

"Everything New" (v.5)

Once again we are given the promise of newness. This time the words are coming directly from the one sitting on the throne—God Himself.

Just as I was puzzled by the reference in 19:9 to the "true words of God," I am once again somewhat puzzled by why we need to be told that these words are "trustworthy and true." We will see the phrase used again in 22:6. It may mean, as I surmised back in chapter 19, that in writing these words, John has stepped out from his use of the apocalyptic genre to provide a direct quote from God. Perhaps it is intended as a reassurance. In looking elsewhere in Scripture Psalm 33:4 says, "For the word of the Lord is right and true; he is faithful in all he does." Ecclesiastes 12:10, "The Teacher searched to find just the right words, and what he wrote was upright and true." So it's not unusual to use a phrase like this. In fact at the end of Daniel 2:45 we see a similar phrase, "The great God has shown the king what will take place in the future. The dream is true and its interpretation is trustworthy." This concept of trueness is repeated elsewhere in Daniel and also in Ezekiel and in both cases, I believe, is intended to offer validity to the vision or visions.

"Alpha and the Omega" (v.6)

> *⁶ He said to me: "It is done. I am the Alpha and the Omega, the Beginning and the End. To the thirsty I will give water without cost from the spring of the water of life.*

When we began this study, in Revelation 1:8 we were told God is the Alpha and the Omega. And here we are told again. It's like a set of bookends on the story that has been Revelation. God is the beginning of all things and the end. He is the reason for all this. He is in control. He is the giver of life. If we didn't get it at the beginning of this amazing book of the Bible, we should get it now.

"Those Who Are Victorious" (v.7)

In the letters to each of the seven churches a promise was made "to the one who is victorious" (see 2:7,11,17,26 and 3:5,12,21). Through those letters, ultimately written to all of us as believers, we were given commendations for the things we are doing right, along with instructions on how to fix those things we aren't doing right, and then ultimately a promise to the ones who are victorious.

Here as we near the end of Revelation the message is clear. The content of this book written in this wonderful apocalyptic way, is intended as a message to the church. It is a reminder of God's promises to His people. It is a vision of what is to come for those of us who follow Him.

The Others (v.8)

Once again, John reminds us of the second death and the lake of burning sulfur. I wonder about the list of actions that will cause one to be consigned to this second death. I believe they can be correlated back to the initial letters to the seven churches. As I look at them, they seem to cover the gamut of sins from those who lie (who hasn't told a lie at sometime in their life), the cowardly (have we been afraid to stand up for our faith?), all the way through to the vile, the murderers, and the unbelievers. I believe we're being told that there is no sin that is worse than any other. They all qualify us for the second death.

However, as I look back to verse 7, I can hold on to the promise that those who are victorious will avoid the second death and inherit all that is new.

The New Jerusalem, the Bride of the Lamb (21:9–27)

"One Of the Seven Angels" (v.9)

> [9] *One of the seven angels who had the seven bowls full of the seven last plagues came and said to me, "Come, I will show you the bride, the wife of the Lamb."*

I wonder why John is so specific about the identity of this angel? Why does he want us to know that it is one of the seven angels who had the seven bowls full of the seven last plagues? Why didn't he just say 'an angel', or 'one of the angels'?

We saw a similar beginning to a scene in chapter 17 when one of the seven angels who had the seven bowls came over to John to show him the punishment of the great prostitute. So there we saw what happened to the non-believer. Here we are given a view into what life looks like for those who are victorious, the followers of the Lamb.

"In the Spirit" (v.10)

> [10] *And he carried me away in the Spirit to a mountain great and high, and showed me the Holy City, Jerusalem, coming down out of heaven from God.*

And just as in 17:3 where John was carried away in the Spirit, here we get those same words. Now instead of being carried into a wilderness we are taken to a mountain great and high. In Isaiah 2:2 it says, "In the last days the mountain of the Lord's temple will be established as the highest of the mountains; it will be exalted above the hills, and all nations will stream to it." These same words are repeated in Micah 4:1. It is no wonder that John has been whisked away to a mountain great and high.

In chapter 17 we were shown the prostitute representing the great city of Babylon. Here we are shown the Holy City, Jerusalem. In case we didn't get it earlier, we are told once more that the city was coming down from heaven. As I've said before, when things get repeated in Scripture it is usually because the author thinks it's pretty important—it is something God wants us to understand. And here it is so important for us to realize, to understand, that this Holy City is from God. It will be truly heaven on earth.

The Picture In My Imagination

I'm sure we can make quite a bit out of the statement that the city was coming down. It could be God's way of telling us that our eternal lives will retain many of the aspects of our current lives—only perfect in every way.

However, any time I've imagined life after death I've pictured it as a large multitude of people who now look like angels wearing robes of white floating around in some heavenly sphere and continually singing praises to God. The Holy City in my imagination surrounds the multitude. Everything sparkles and shimmers in the bright light radiating from God Himself. The thing that has always left me uncomfortable with this image is that although I've always wanted to live with God eternally, I've always wondered if the life I've pictured wouldn't be somewhat boring. Of course, after thinking that, I always feel guilty and remind myself that God wouldn't make it boring—that obviously my reaction to this kind of existence is in some way flawed. But perhaps it's my image that is flawed. The Holy City is coming down out of heaven from God! And it will be beautiful!

"It Shone With the Glory Of God" (v.11)

John 11:40 says, "Then Jesus said, "Did I not tell you that if you believe, you will see the glory of God?"" and here we are seeing that promise fulfilled as John sees the Holy City shining with the glory of God.

Elsewhere in Revelation 15:8 we saw reference to the glory of God in the form of smoke in the temple. We were told that the temple was filled with the smoke of the glory of God so that no one could enter the temple until the seven plagues were completed. Now that this has happened the glory of God is shining and brilliant.

Just as in chapter 4, when we first saw the throne in heaven, here the description of the Holy City is very tangible. We're not given colors; we're given jewels, gems, and crystal as descriptors. This city is real. It is solid. Just as God was described to us in 4:3.

"Walls and Gates" (v.12)

Why does it need walls and gates? Walls are meant to keep things out or hold things in—what is there to be kept out? So are we to see the walls and the gates as something physical or metaphorical as is often the case in this apocalyptic genre? Zechariah 2:4–5 says, "'Jerusalem will be a city without walls because of the great number of people and animals in it. And I myself will be a wall of fire around it,' declares the Lord, 'and I will be its glory within.'" In Isaiah 26:1, "We have a strong city; God makes salvation its walls and ramparts." It seems the walls and the gates are meant to remind us of what it takes to gain entry. To be a part of this Holy City one must have accepted God's promise of salvation.

But more than that, walls hold things in or together. The concept of walls whether literal, or figurative, implies that those within them belong together—they form a community if you like.

And why write the names of the twelve tribes of Israel on the gates? God made a covenant with Abraham recorded in Genesis 22:17–18. In Jeremiah 31:31–34 we read of the New Covenant God made. By including the names of the tribes on the gates is God, through John, reminding them of both the original and the new covenant?

The Gates (v.13)

I find it interesting that the gates to the city are equally divided and facing all directions. There is a link of sorts, to the tabernacle in the desert during the Exodus. The tribes were instructed to align themselves equally—three to a direction—around the tabernacle. The tabernacle itself had only one gate or door. Here the gates are on all sides making the city easily accessible for peoples of all nations from all corners of the earth.

"The Names Of the Twelve Apostles Of the Lamb" (v.14)

While verses 12 and 13 provide a link to Old Testament Scriptures, in verse 14 we have an obvious link to New Testament Scripture as well. The foundations of the church—I mean the city—are the twelve apostles of the Lamb. The apostles were first named in Matthew 10 (or Luke 6) with a replacement for Judas added in Acts 1. We first see reference to the apostles as a foundation to the church in Ephesians 2:19–22, "Consequently, you are no longer foreigners and strangers, but fellow citizens with God's people and also members of his household, built on the foundation of the apostles and prophets, with Christ Jesus himself as the chief cornerstone. In him the whole building is joined together and rises to become a holy temple in the Lord. And in him you too are being built together to become a dwelling in which God lives by his Spirit." This connection to New Testament Scripture assures me that this Holy City is not only for the twelve tribes of Israel but for those of us who have become fellow citizens with God's people.

"Measuring Rod Of Gold" (v.15)

> *15 The angel who talked with me had a measuring rod of gold to measure the city, its gates and its walls.*

In 11:1 John was given a reed and was told to measure the temple of God and the altar with its worshipers. Here we see a similar act of measuring except this time the rod isn't a reed but instead is made of gold. It will be used to measure something far more tangible and holy.

The Measurements Of the City (v.16)

Although we're told that the city was laid out like a square, we are also told that the city was twelve thousand stadia in length and that it was the same measurement in width and height. This means in fact, that it was a cube. Conceptually it was similar to the Holy of Holies in the tabernacle. By the way twelve thousand stadia would equal approximately fourteen hundred miles or twenty-two hundred kilometers.

I wonder why we're told the measurement. Why does it matter? And where else in Revelation have we seen the number twelve thousand? In chapter 7 we were told that the 144,000 who were sealed consisted of twelve thousand from each of the twelve tribes. It feels like we could go in a couple of different directions here. Twelve thousand stadia represents a distance that is approximately five and a half times the full length of current day Israel measuring from north to south. In the time it was written, this would have been seen as very large. But I don't think looking at the distance from that perspective makes sense. I think I'm taking it too literally. Rather I think the point here is that the size of the city is just right. Meaning whether we think of it literally or metaphorically, there is room in the New Jerusalem for each and every one of us.

The Measurements Of the Wall (v.17)

> *17 The angel measured the wall using human measurement, and it was 144 cubits thick.*

And now we are given a measurement of the thickness of the wall. Again the number provided is a multiple of twelve (12x12=144). If twelve as a number in Scripture represents the number of God's people, then it's probably safe to assume that the meaning of this measurement is to assure us of completeness or correctness. Perhaps one could think of this number as the result of combining the twelve tribes—God's people as we knew it from the Old Testament—and the twelve apostles—God's people from the New Testament which now includes Gentiles.

I believe that the city is a metaphor for all of God's people and in looking at the measurements we can rest assured that the number is complete.

I wonder why we are told that the measurement of the wall was done using human measurement? When Revelation was written the typical human measurement was the length of the forearm of a man. This is what was considered to be a cubit—a very human measurement indeed.

The other measurements reported as stadia were taken using the measuring rod of gold. I found a definition of stadia that says "a method of surveying in which distances are read by noting the interval on a graduated rod intercepted by two parallel cross hairs (stadia hairs or stadia wires) mounted in the telescope of a surveying instrument, the rod being placed at one end of the distance to be measured and the surveying instrument at the other."[37] I'm not certain if this applies to how the measurement would have been taken in the first century, but the definition suggests to me that this is not a measurement most people would have been able to take easily. It is far more complex than the simple use of one's forearm to determine the number of cubits of an object.

"The Wall Was Made Of Jasper" (v.18)

In 4:3 we were told that the one who sat on the throne had the appearance of jasper and here in verse 18 we find that the wall was made of jasper. That which holds the community within the Holy City together, is solid. Through the link to the throne I think we can surmise that it is God Himself.

Here we aren't told that the city was the color of gold— we are told that it was in fact, pure gold. Let's talk about a biblical significance of gold for a minute. In the Holy of Holies, the most holy place within the tabernacle and subsequently the temple, all the items contained therein were covered in gold. Gold is associated with that which is holy to God. The holiness of this New Jerusalem is confirmed here by the fact that it was made of pure gold.

I find it interesting that we are told that it is "as pure as glass." This phrase is repeated in verse 21 as a way of describing gold. Glass is such a common material in today's world that I don't automatically think of it as pure—perhaps because it isn't difficult to find examples of poorly made glass items. But one thing glass is good at is not affecting the taste of whatever it contains. A drinking glass won't change the taste of the milk it holds. I came across the following statement about glass: "Glass ... can be recycled endlessly without loss in quality or purity"[38]. Interesting.

The idea of recycling takes me off on a tangent that may or may not make sense to you but I'm going to give it a shot anyway—why stop now right. If we, the followers of the Lamb make up this Holy City which is so holy it can be said to be made of pure gold, as pure as glass; and if we know that glass can be recycled without losing its purity—I wonder if that says something about our growth as Christians. God has worked on us, refined us. Most of us have made mistakes, messed up at some point in time. Then God has to work on us, refine us, recycle us some more, and through it all, as children of God, having accepted

His offer of salvation and thus gained entry to the Holy City here we are—pure gold, as pure as glass. Cool!

The Foundations Were Decorated (v.19–20)

> ¹⁹ *The foundations of the city walls were decorated with every kind of precious stone. The first foundation was jasper, the second sapphire, the third agate, the fourth emerald,* ²⁰ *the fifth onyx, the sixth ruby, the seventh chrysolite, the eighth beryl, the ninth topaz, the tenth turquoise, the eleventh jacinth, and the twelfth amethyst.*

I wonder about the precious stones mentioned here. Some of them are familiar today; others are not. In Exodus 28 we are given a description of the priestly garments as God described them for Moses. In verses 17–21, when describing the breastplate it says, "Then mount four rows of precious stones on it. The first row shall be carnelian, chrysolite and beryl; the second row shall be turquoise, lapis lazuli and emerald; the third row shall be jacinth, agate and amethyst; the fourth row shall be topaz, onyx and jasper. Mount them in gold filigree settings. There are to be twelve stones, one for each of the names of the sons of Israel, each engraved like a seal with the name of one of the twelve tribes." These are the same stones listed here in Revelation except that instead of sapphire, in Exodus it refers to lapis lazuli, a similar blue stone, and instead of ruby, in Exodus it calls it carnelian.

So these foundations that we were told earlier bear the names of the twelve apostles, also bear the precious stones that made up the breastplate of the priestly garments. How cool is that!

An Aside: *As I continue to study this book called the Bible, I am amazed at the interconnections between Old and New Testaments. I marvel that these words, written over many years link together to tell a story of an amazing God. I have no doubt that He has inspired the texts of the*

Scriptures even though many different authors have actually penned the words.

"The Twelve Gates Were Twelve Pearls" (v.21)

In biblical times, pearls were extremely valuable, which is reason enough for them to represent the gates to the Holy City. But I think it's also interesting to think of how pearls are created. They start out as an irritant, such as a grain of sand, inside the shell of an oyster. Gradually the oyster emits a layer of something called nacre, also known as mother of pearl, to cover the irritant. This covering builds up over time and eventually we end up with something of great beauty— the pearl. It seems like another interesting analogy reflecting the maturing process of us as Christians.

"I Did Not See a Temple" (v.22)

This city that shines with the glory of God has no need for buildings dedicated to worshipping God for we will walk with the Lord God Almighty and the Lamb eternally. My human, earth-bound brain is completely incapable of imagining what that will be like.

"The City Does Not Need the Sun or the Moon" (v.23)

I wonder, does this mean that there will be no night or day? Will we sleep? All this says to me that life everlasting in this New Jerusalem is beyond my human imagination.

"The Nations Will Walk By Its Light" (v.24)

Yet, this reference to the nations suggests to me that we will retain something of our unique human identity. We will not be one homogeneous group of followers of the Lamb—we will be identifiable as nations.

The idea of the kings bringing their splendor into it leaves me a bit confused. Will there be kings? Or is the point here that the people, with our uniqueness, will contribute to the color, the splendor of the city. I can't completely resolve this image in my feeble human mind but it does make sense that since God made each of us not only in His image, but unique as well, that He wouldn't throw out the unique parts of us for what will become the eternal part of our existence.

"On No Day Will Its Gates Ever Be Shut" (v.25)

My question with this concept has always been—so why bother with gates? Perhaps the point here is not whether gates exist or not, but that their role has changed. Historically the castle owner would shut the gates of his enclave at night to protect it from predators. Here we are being told that there won't be a need to be protected from whatever may qualify as a predator in the new Jerusalem because there will be no night and there will be no predators.

This takes me back to my earlier question—will we sleep? Will we need to sleep? So many questions—so little time.

"The Glory and Honor Of the Nations" (v.26)

If the glory and honor of the nations will be brought into it, then I'm sure that we won't lose our individuality. What a marvelous place it will be.

"Nothing Impure Will Ever Enter It" (v.27)

And so to connect to 20:11–17 and 21:8, we are once again reminded that the only way in to the Holy City is to have your name written in the Book of Life.

Some Things To Think About

It doesn't seem necessary to say much more, but naturally I'll try:

- As a follower of the Lamb, one who's name is written in the Book of Life, we have been promised life everlasting, walking with God who will be present in our midst.
- Made of gold and precious stones, our new home, the Holy City is not only beautiful but also solid and dependable.

And once again, my mind turns to a song familiar from my youth— "The Holy City" by Frederick E. Weatherly.[39]

Revelation 22

Eden Restored (22:1–5)

> *¹ Then the angel showed me the river of the water of life, as clear as crystal, flowing from the throne of God and of the Lamb ² down the middle of the great street of the city. On each side of the river stood the tree of life, bearing twelve crops of fruit, yielding its fruit every month. And the leaves of the tree are for the healing of the nations.*

In 4:6 when we were first introduced to the throne scene we were told that in front of the throne was something that looked like a sea of glass, clear as crystal. Here as the description of the Holy City continues I'm noticing a few things.

"River Of the Water Of Life" (v.1)

First that it appears that the throne of God is now in the city and that no longer is there something that looks like a sea of glass. Rather it is the "river of the water of life." Still as clear as crystal, but now it is flowing. I'm not completely certain what to do with this information but somehow it makes the scene feel dynamic. The sea of glass was an interesting image, but a flowing river is moving, is active, and seems more interactive. John 7:37–39 says, "On the last and greatest day of the festival, Jesus stood and said in a loud voice, "Let anyone who is thirsty come to me and drink. Whoever believes in me, as Scripture has said, rivers of living water will flow from within them." By this he meant the Spirit, whom those who believed in him were later to receive. Up to that time the Spirit had not been given, since Jesus had not yet been glorified." So here, when we read of the river of the water of life we can be reminded of the presence of the Holy Spirit flowing through each of us.

The other piece that fascinates me is the reference to "the throne of God and of the Lamb." Are they sharing the throne? What does it mean to be the "throne of God and of the Lamb?"

Earlier in Revelation 3:21, in the letter to the church of Laodicea we were told that the Lamb sits with the Father on the throne. Later in 5:6 we were given an image of the slain Lamb standing at the center of the throne. Then in chapter 7 when we learned about the great multitude in white robes who were standing before the throne we read in verse 15, "Therefore, "they are before the throne of God and serve him day and night in his temple; and he who sits on the throne will shelter them with his presence" which once again reminds me that this is the throne of God that we're talking about. But moving on in that same chapter to verse 17, it says "For the Lamb at the center of the throne will be their shepherd; 'he will lead them to springs of living water.' 'And God will wipe away every tear from their eyes.'" This verse puts the Lamb back at the center of the throne. So it appears that throughout Revelation, God and the Lamb have been sharing the throne.

Did you see the connection in that last piece (7:17) to this first verse of chapter 22? The Lamb will shepherd His followers to the springs of living water—dare I connect this to the river of the water of life mentioned here? I may be making too big a deal about this, but I think it is very interesting that here we are specifically told that it is the throne of God and of the Lamb and flowing out from it is the water of life—aka the Holy Spirit. It's a wonderful way of viewing these three persons of the trinity. Together, but separate.

In chapter 21 we were told that the great street of the Holy City was made of gold. Here we find that the river of the water of life is flowing down the middle of it. The image this creates for me is of something like a town square. The throne of God and of the Lamb sits in the middle of the square. Can you picture it glowing in the sun? Radiating off from this square is a huge main street made of gold with a river, clear as crystal, flowing down its middle. The water would cause the gold to sparkle in the sunshine, and the gold would enhance the sparkle of the water to even greater heights.

"The Tree Of Life" (v.2)

This is one of those times when I stand amazed at the wonder of the Scriptures. Here in the final chapter of Revelation as we are learning about end-times and new beginnings in the new Jerusalem, we are taken right back to the beginning of the Bible, in fact to the beginning of life.

In Genesis 2:9 we are first introduced to the tree of life in the Garden of Eden, "The Lord God made all kinds of trees grow out of the ground—trees that were pleasing to the eye and good for food. In the middle of the garden were the tree of life and the tree of the knowledge of good and evil." Because as we read later in Genesis 3, Adam and Eve ate the forbidden fruit of the tree of the knowledge of good and evil, man is banished from the Garden of Eden. Genesis 3:22 says, "And the Lord God said, "The man has now become like one of us, knowing good and evil. He must not be allowed to reach out his hand and take also from the tree of life and eat, and live forever."" and in verse 24, "After he drove the man out, he placed on the east side of the Garden of Eden cherubim and a flaming sword flashing back and forth to guard the way to the tree of life." And now, here in the New Jerusalem we see the tree of life. Can you imagine its size? It stands on each side of the river—it must be huge!

And the tree is full of fruit that it appears we will be able to eat. Notice the reference to twelve crops of fruit. Once again we see the number that symbolizes completeness. There is a strong link here to Ezekiel 47:12, "Fruit trees of all kinds will grow on both banks of the river. Their leaves will not wither, nor will their fruit fail. Every month they will bear fruit, because the water from the sanctuary flows to them. Their fruit will serve for food and their leaves for healing."

An Aside: *Just as an aside, I find it interesting that both here in Revelation and in Ezekiel the author refers to 'every month'. In Ezekiel's vision that probably made sense, but here in Revelation it causes me to wonder. A month is a very man-made, earth-based time frame. What will time look like in eternity? Will we have any sense of the passing of time? The concept of fruit and crops implies seasons but I wonder if in both those cases John is using the only language he can to describe something that we won't be able to understand until we are there. Hmmm.*

"The Leaves Are for the Healing Of the Nations" (v.2)

We're told that its leaves are for the "healing of the nations." I find this quite puzzling. Why will we need healing? One commentator says, "When he speaks of "the healing of the nations" by the leaves of the tree, we are not to think of nations of men living on the new earth in the age to come who will need healing from pain, sickness, and dying. The contrast is between this age, inhabited by suffering and dying peoples, and the age to come. All who have access to that age will partake of the tree of life and find perfect surcease from their afflictions."[40]

"No Longer Will There Be Any Curse" (v.3)

In Genesis 3:17, "To Adam he said, "Because you listened to your wife and ate fruit from the tree about which I commanded you, 'You must not eat from it,' "Cursed is the ground because of you; through painful toil you will eat food from it all the days of your life.""" And now, in the New Jerusalem the curse will be no more.

It wasn't stated specifically before, but here we are told explicitly that the throne of God and of the Lamb will be in the city. Notice the interesting twist of grammar. It is the throne of God and of the Lamb (which implies plural) but *his* (singular) servants will serve *him* (again singular). Cool stuff!! His servants—that's us.

"See His Face" (v.4)

In Exodus 33:20, God is speaking to Moses and says, ""But," he said, "you cannot see my face, for no one may see me and live.""" and here we are told that in the new Jerusalem we will see his face!

In 7:3 we were told of the seal on the foreheads of the servants of our God. Here once again, is a reminder that life in this New Jerusalem belongs to those who bear the seal of the living God. In addition, when we think about carrying the name of God on our foreheads, besides the idea of it being visible to those around us, there is something more about it that works for me. It's like saying that He will always be forefront in my mind.

"There Will Be No" (v.5)

> ⁵ There will be no more night. They will not need the light of a lamp or the light of the sun, for the Lord God will give them light. And they will reign for ever and ever.

As we bring the description of the New Jerusalem to a close there seems to be a pattern similar to how chapter 21 ended. We are reminded that there will be no night (see 21:25), and that we won't need the light of the sun, for as it says in 21:23, "the glory of God gives it light, and the Lamb is its lamp."

In 11:15b after the sounding of the seventh trumpet we read, "The kingdom of the world has become the kingdom of our Lord and of his Messiah, and he will reign for ever and ever." Now we are being told that we, as the servants mentioned in verse 3, will reign for ever and ever as well.

It isn't clear to me what we will reign over but perhaps that isn't the point. Perhaps the point is that just as we've been told that the Lord will reign forever, now we too will reign forever. It is a promise of eternal life where the followers of the Lamb and the Lamb Himself will be together.

John and the Angel (22:6–11)

And with those words of life everlasting, we see John coming out of the vision itself.

"Trustworthy and True" (v.6)

> ⁶ *The angel said to me, "These words are trustworthy and true. The Lord, the God who inspires the prophets, sent his angel to show his servants the things that must soon take place."*

As we transition into the final words of Revelation we are once again reminded that the words are trustworthy and true. What isn't clear to me here is whether the angel is referring to the words of the text so far or to the words that follow in the next few verses. I'm not sure there is a reason to differentiate so I'm going to leave that question unanswered—they are all trustworthy and true.

Wrapping It Up

Personally I love things that are well written and cohesive. In the verses that follow we see John connecting directly back to the first chapter of Revelation where we were introduced to all of this. Verse 6, for example, connects directly back to chapter 1 and verse 1. There we were told "The revelation from Jesus Christ, which God gave him to show his servants what must soon take place. He made it known by sending his angel to his servant John." The thing that I find interesting here is that John is taken out of the line of communication. Notice now we are told the angel was sent to show his servants—we are his servants. These words weren't just for John—they were, they are for us.

"I Am Coming Soon" (v.7)

> *7 "Look, I am coming soon! Blessed is the one who keeps the words of the prophecy written in this scroll."*

And once again we are reminded that these are things that must soon take place. And once again, I say, to the concept of soon'ness, whether Jesus is returning today, tomorrow, next week or in another generation completely, for each of us, our time here is short. My life, your life, our lives can, and will end soon. We don't have generations to decide how we want to spend eternity. Each one of us has to decide now—today—because we each have no guarantee of a tomorrow. While it may be true for some under special circumstances, most of us aren't going to wake up one morning with the sure and certain knowledge that we better get our lives in order because today will be our last day. You have only the one life that you've been given to make the decision to worship God and become a follower of the Lamb. Decide today. Don't wait.

We came across the first beatitude in Revelation in 1:3. This is now the sixth one and it draws us right back to that first one. Together they are powerful. They are reminding us, dare I say, urgently reminding us of two things; one, that He is coming soon, and two, that we must take the words of this revelation seriously.

"I Fell Down To Worship" (v.8–9)

As I read this passage, which is almost a direct repetition of 19:10, I wonder if John was a bit slow in learning some things. He's already been told that he wasn't to worship the angel but to worship God, and here is doing it again. Or perhaps in both cases he has been so overwhelmed with the events of the vision, with the message he had been given, that he simply couldn't help himself. Or perhaps the interaction has been shared with us in case we're the ones who are slow to learn this key concept. It is a reminder once again, that this entire book has been a call to worship God! To focus our worship where it belongs. Not on our religious or spiritual leaders of this world, not on the things of this world, but on God.

"Do Not Seal Up the Words" (v.10)

> [10] Then he told me, "Do not seal up the words of the prophecy of this scroll, because the time is near.

When we were introduced to the scroll that had been sealed, the scroll that started all of this in chapter 5, I referred to other scrolls in Scripture. I mentioned Isaiah 29:11 where we were told that the words on the scroll that was sealed couldn't be read, which means they couldn't be shared or understood. I mentioned Daniel 8:26 and

12:4 where in both cases Daniel was told to seal up the words of the scroll until the time of the end. In Revelation 10:4, John was told to seal up what the seven thunders said. But here the message is exactly the opposite. John is told to *not* seal up the words because the time is near. The only conclusion I can draw from this is that God wants us to read them. He wants us to share them. He wants us to understand them—at least as much as we can humanly do so.

"Let the One" (v.11)

Verse 11 fascinates me and confuses me at the same time. It feels almost like a dare. A sort of 'go ahead, keep doing what you're doing. I dare you!' There is also a strong correlation here to some of the final words of Daniel. There in chapter 12:10 it says, ""Go your way, Daniel, because the words are rolled up and sealed until the time of the end. Many will be purified, made spotless and refined, but the wicked will continue to be wicked. None of the wicked will understand, but those who are wise will understand.""

Is the message that some of us can't be changed, or is it that in light of all that has been told here, some of us won't change? I wonder.

Epilogue: Invitation and Warning (22:12–21)

"Look, I Am Coming Soon" (v.12)

> [12] *"Look, I am coming soon! My reward is with me, and I will give to each person according to what they have done.*

Although there appears to be a segment divide between this verse and the previous one, I wonder if they don't make sense to be tied more closely together. We've been told, perhaps, that most of us will continue to go the way that we've chosen and now, once again we are reminded of time running out and that having made our choices, we will be judged accordingly taking us right back to 20:12, "The dead were judged according to what they had done as recorded in the books."

He is pleading with those of us who have not yet chosen to follow the Lamb to reconsider.

"The Alpha and the Omega" (v.13)

> *¹³ I am the Alpha and the Omega, the First and the Last, the Beginning and the End.*

In 1:8 we were first introduced to God as the "Alpha and the Omega." Later in verse 17 He reassured John that He was the "First and the Last." In 21:6, He told John that he was the "Alpha and the Omega, the Beginning and the End" and here we have all three versions of the same idea pulled together in one place. Can there be any doubt.

He is the reason we were created. He will determine how and when things will end and start anew. He is the reason we exist and it is through Him that we can experience life everlasting!

"Blessed Are Those" (v.14)

> *¹⁴ "Blessed are those who wash their robes, that they may have the right to the tree of life and may go through the gates into the city.*

With this final beatitude we taken back to 7:14 where we were told that the great multitude worshipping around the throne were those who "have washed their robes and made them white in the blood of the Lamb." These are the followers of the Lamb. And in these closing words we are once again reminded that our reward is the right to eternal life in the New Jerusalem.

"Outside Are the Dogs" (v.15)

In 21:8 we saw this same list describing those who will be consigned to the fiery lake of burning sulfur. And here, just to be clear, we are once again told that they will not be gaining entry to the Holy City.

"I, Jesus" (v.16)

Revelation 5:5, "Then one of the elders said to me, "Do not weep! See, the Lion of the tribe of Judah, the Root of David, has triumphed."" In 2:8, in the letter to the church in Thyatira, it says, "I will also give that one the morning star." And here Jesus is confirming his identity as the "Root and Offspring of Dave, and the bright Morning Star," and reaffirming that the words of Revelation are from Him and are for us.

"The Spirit and the Bride Say "Come!""" (v.17)

In 19:7 we identified the bride as the church. Here we are encouraged to join with the Holy Spirit to encourage others to come—to come to join us in accepting the offer of life everlasting.

A Warning (v.18–19)

> *18 I warn everyone who hears the words of the prophecy of this scroll: If anyone adds anything to them, God will add to that person the plagues described in this scroll.*
> *19 And if anyone takes words away from this scroll of prophecy, God will take away from that person any share in the tree of life and in the Holy City, which are described in this scroll.*

For me, as I've been writing these words, this verse is the most terrifying. What does it mean 'to add to them'? Very similar language is used in Deuteronomy 4:1–2, "Now, Israel, hear the decrees and laws I am about to teach you. Follow them so that you may live and may go in and take possession of the land the Lord, the God of your ancestors, is giving you. Do not add to what I command you and do not subtract from it, but keep the commands of the Lord your God that I give you." So have I added to them? Or taken away from them? As I've looked to various commentators for some insight here, the one thing they all agree on is that this is not pointing to people who are trying to better understand the text but rather to people who choose to deliberately change it. So I think I'm safe.

The take-away from these two verses I believe, is that we all clearly understand just how important the words of Revelation are. This is not a warning that shows up in numerous books of the Bible. I have found them only here, in Proverbs 30:5–6 where it says something somewhat similar, "Every word of God is flawless; he is a shield to those who take refuge in him. Do not add to his words, or he will rebuke you and prove you a liar." and in the words of Deuteronomy mentioned above.

So if I may expand a bit on this, what we are being told here is that the words of this revelation are as important as the words of the laws and decrees that God taught to Israel as outlined in Deuteronomy. They are God's words and they are not for us to change!

"He Who Testifies" (v.20)

This mention of testifying draws me back to the line of communication presented to us in the first verse of Revelation. God gave the words to Jesus, who made them known by passing them on to an angel, who then shared them with John, who in turn was giving them to us. And as we look at those who have been testifying we can work our way back. John testifies to everything he saw in that same opening verse. In 20:16 the angel gave testimony and here it seems that the one who is testifying is Jesus based on the phrase 'I' am coming soon.

We have received the testimony of all who have participated in bringing this message to us. Yes, He is coming soon.

A Blessing (v.21)

> *²¹ The grace of the Lord Jesus be with God's people. Amen.*

How wonderful that the last words not only of Revelation but of the entire canon of Scripture, are a blessing! In 1:4, in John's greeting to the churches he said, "Grace and peace to you from him who is, and who was, and who is to come, and from the seven spirits before his throne and from Jesus Christ, who is the faithful witness." and now in this benediction one has to assume that by that grace we will each understand the message, and ourselves bear witness to others.

Some Final Words

As we close the book on Revelation's message, my thoughts go to how to respond to what God through John, has written for us.

For the non-believer a typical response may be to hear the words and simply reject them; with hardened heart walk away. To you: My prayer is that you will hear the voice of God calling out to you, and respond before it is too late.

Or, you may hear the words, and be filled with terror because of the choice that you haven't made to become a follower of the Lamb. To you: I say, as Revelation reminds us over and over, you don't have much time—choose today—choose life everlasting through our Lord and Savior. We have all sinned against God. Although we might think that our sins aren't all that big a deal, or just the opposite, that they are too big a deal so that because of our sin we don't deserve the gift of eternal life, the good news is that God loves us, and because of that He sent his Son, Jesus, who lived as a man to die on a cross in our place. In doing so He took on the punishment for all our sins. What's amazing is that He then rose from the dead, and ascended into heaven where He now waits with the Father for us to respond to this gift of salvation.

For the believer, it is easy to listen to these words, and be filled with uneasiness over the terrible things that may happen during the end-times. To hope for a rapture that will take us away so we don't have to experience them. But be reminded, that if you are alive when these things take place, just as you are living through many terrible things in these last days, that we have the gift of the Holy Spirit walking with us, that we have the promise of life everlasting on the New Earth—let that promise sustain you.

Some may be concerned that somehow Satan, through the simple workings of society may somehow sneak the mark of the beast on you without your knowledge. To you I say: Nowhere in Revelation are we given any indication of such an event. If you bear the seal of the Holy Spirit which we are told in Ephesians 1 happens when you believed, then you are protected.

Or you may be overcome with joy and desire only that the end come now, that Christ return to earth today—a wonderful idea but perhaps somewhat selfish. We need to remember that with His return, many who haven't made a decision for Christ will be lost.

So much of Revelation is focused on living life today in the current church age, it seems to me to be an important message for us to consider how we are living our lives today. Are we living them as Jesus would if He were on earth today? Are we sharing the promise of eternal life with our non-believing friends and acquaintances. Are we doing our part to ensure that they have an opportunity to share in this wonderful gift of eternal life on the New Earth? Can you imagine how wonderful it will be? Can you feel the sadness that so many will not experience it, perhaps because of something we didn't say or do?

My prayer for each of us is to answer the call to worship God, to live the lives that He has for us on this earth with all the good and bad that may entail.

My prayer is that with these words, I haven't misled you. That God will forgive my feeble words in trying to share my thoughts, and that He will guide you as you further read, study and learn from this wonderful book of Revelation.

Appendix

The Beatitudes of Revelation

1:3	*Blessed is the one who reads aloud the words of this prophecy, and blessed are those who hear it and take to heart what is written in it, because the time is near.*
14:13	*Blessed are the dead who die in the Lord from now on.* *"Yes," says the Spirit, "they will rest from their labor, for their deeds will follow them."*
16:15	*Look, I come like a thief! Blessed is the one who stays awake and remains clothed, so as not to go naked and be shamefully exposed.*
19:9	*Blessed are those who are invited to the wedding supper of the Lamb!*
20:6	*Blessed and holy are those who share in the first resurrection. The second death has no power over them, but they will be priests of God and of Christ and will reign with him for a thousand years.*
22:7	*Look, I am coming soon! Blessed is the one who keeps the words of the prophecy written in this scroll.*
22:14	*Blessed are those who wash their robes, that they may have the right to the tree of life and may go through the gates into the city.*

Bibliography

Beale, G.K. *The Book of Revelation, A Commentary on the Greek Text - New International Greek Testament Commentary Series*. Grand Rapids: Wm B. Eerdmans Publishing Co., 1999.

Gaebelein, A.C. *The Olivet Discourse: An Exposition of Matthew XXIV and XXV*. Grand Rapids: Baker Book House, 1969.

Geisler, Norman L. *When Critics Ask: a Popular Handbook on Bible Difficulties*. Victor Books, 1992

Gregg, Steve. *Revelation, Four View: A Parallel Commentary*. Nashville: Thomas Nelson Publishers, 1997.

Haley, John Wesley. *An Examination of the Alleged Discrepancies of the Bible*. Baker Book House, 1951.

Hemer, Colin J. *The letters to the seven churches of Asia in their local setting*. Grand Rapids: W.B. Eerdmans Pub.,2001

Holman Christian Standard Bible (HCSB) Study Bible Notes, LifeWay Christian Resources

HCSB Strong's

Keener, Craig S. *IVP Bible Background Commentary: New Testament*, InterVarsity Press, 1993

Ladd, George Eldon. *A Commentary on The Revelation of John*. Grand Rapids: Wm B. Eerdmans Publishing Co., 1976.

MacArthur, John. *John MacArthur Study Notes*, Word Publishing, 1997.

Mounce, Robert H. *The Book of Revelation, Revised Edition.* Grand Rapids: Wm B. Eerdmans Publishing Co., 1997.

New International Version. [Colorado Springs]: Biblica, Inc., 2011. *BibleGateway.com.* 2011.

Riddlebarger, Kim. *A Case for Amillennialism: Understanding the End-times*, Baker Books, 2003

Spilsbury, Paul. *The Throne, The Lamb & the Dragon: A Reader's Guide to the Book of Revelation.* Downers Grove: InterVarsity Press, 2002.

The Life Application Study Bible, New International Version. Edited by Dr. Bruce B. Barton et al. Wheaton, Illinois: Tyndale House Publishers, Inc., 1991

Thompson, Leonard L. *Revelation - Abingdon New Testament Commentaries.* Nashville: Abingdon Press, 1998.

Walton, John H.; Matthews, Victory H.; Chavalaas, Mark W., *IVP Bible Background Commentary: Old Testament.* InterVarsity Press, 2000.

Wilson, Mark. *Charts on the Book of Revelation: Literary, Historical, and Theological Perspectives.* Grand Rapids: Kregel Publications, 2007.

Worth, Roland H. *The Seven Cities of the Apocalypse and Roman Culture.* Paulist Press, 1999

Endnotes

1. Thank you Dr. Paul Spilsbury, Vice President for Academic Affairs, Professor of New Testament (PhD, MCS, BTh) Ambrose University, Calgary, Alberta

2. http://www.olivetree.com/store/product.php?productid=17438

3. http://www.merriam-webster.com/dictionary/revelation

4. HCSB Strong's

5. MacArthur, John. *John MacArthur Study Notes*, 1:8

6. Ladd, George Eldon. *A Commentary on The Revelation of John* p.45

7. Ladd, p.56

8. http://restorationofthefamily.org/Articles/Name%20Removed.htm

9. http://www.gty.org/resources/bible-qna/BQ030713/blotted-out-of-the-book-of-life

10. Ladd, p.59

11. *The Life Application Study Bible, New International Version*, Rev 3:14

12. Mounce, Robert H. *The Book of Revelation, Revised Edition*, p.132

13. Beale, G.K. *The Book of Revelation, A Commentary on the Greek Text*, p.358

14. Wilson, Mark. *Charts on the Book of Revelation: Literary, Historical, and Theological Perspectives*. p.49

15. Wilson, p.49

16. Wilson, p.49

17. Ladd, p.106

18. Mounce, p. 156

19. Macarthur, Rev 7:3

20. Beale, p.472

21. Ladd p. 128

22. Dr. Clyde Glass at http://www.mediafusionapp.com/mediaFusion/player.php?channel=30&playerId=c4d8366&seriesId=82&lessonId=165&mediaType=video&backToArchive=#.VTvdOc4RUl8

23. Beale, p. 505

24. Beale, pp. 517-518

25. Mounce, p.207

26. *The Life Application Study Bible, New International Version*, Psalm 2: Notes on the Theme

27. Dr. Clyde Glass at http://www.mediafusionapp.com/mediaFusion/player.php?channel=30&playerId=c4d8366&seriesId=1029&lessonId=2852&mediaType=video&backToArchive=#.VT6lLM4RUl8

28. Beale p.749

29. http://www.thefreedictionary.com/harvested

30. http://en.wikipedia.org/wiki/Babylon

31. http://www.merriam-webster.com/dictionary/prostitute

32. http://en.wikipedia.org/wiki/Babylon

33. Beale, p. 864

34. *The Life Application Study Bible, New International Version*, Rev 17:9-11

[35] Beale p.987
[36] Beale p.1005
[37] http://dictionary.reference.com/browse/stadia
[38] http://www.gpi.org/recycling/glass-recycling-facts
[39] There are many versions of this song available on youtube ... I like this one because it includes the lyrics ... https://www.youtube.com/watch?v=42cKKPPmDT8
[40] Ladd, p. 288

Printed in the United States
By Bookmasters